Dr. Johnson's London

About the author—

DOROTHY MARSHALL received her B.A., M.A., and Ph.D. degrees from Cambridge University. Now retired, Dr. Marshall taught at the University of London, University of Durham, University of Wales, and at the University of Witwatersrand, Johannesburg, South Africa. In addition, she was a visiting lecturer at Vassar College and Wellesley College.

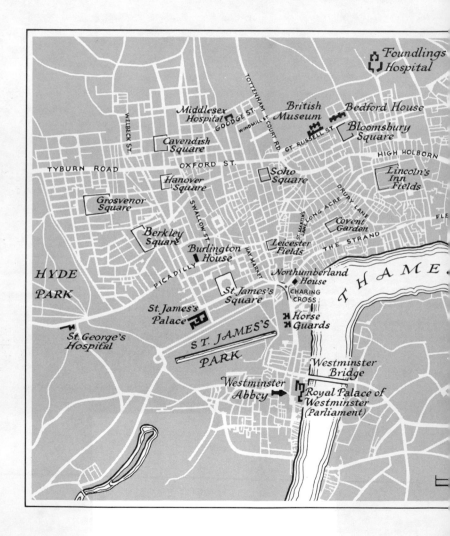

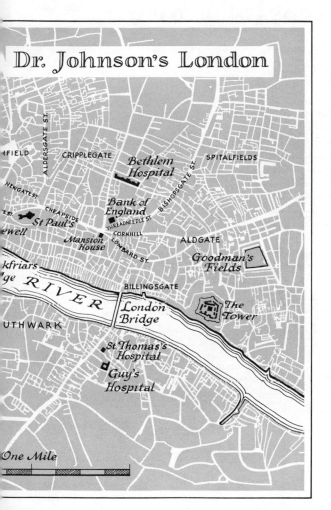

Dr. Johnson's London

ALDERSGATE ST.

HFIELD　　CRIPPLEGATE　*Bethlem Hospital*　SPITALFIELDS

NEWGATE ST.　　CHEAPSIDE　*Bank of England*　BISHOPSGATE ST.

ST.　　*St Paul's*　　THREADNEEDLE ST.

ewell　　*Mansion House*　CORNHILL　ALDGATE

LOMBARD ST.

kfriars　　*Goodman's Fields*

ge　R I V E R　　BILLINGSGATE

UTHWARK　　*London Bridge*　　*The Tower*

St Thomas's Hospital

Guy's Hospital

One Mile

NEW DIMENSIONS IN HISTORY

Historical Cities

Series Editor: Norman F. Cantor

John Wiley & Sons, Inc., New York • London • Sydney

DR. JOHNSON'S LONDON

DOROTHY MARSHALL

Library of Congress Catalog Card Number: 68-18485
GB 471 57340X
Printed in the United States of America

PREFACE

Historians are too apt to concentrate on the actors—to analyse their motives, to evaluate their difficulties, to explore their solutions—while to a greater or lesser degree ignoring the stage on which the drama is being enacted. Persons familiar with the evolution of the British Parliament, the winning of an empire, and the personalities of Chatham and George III often have no clear picture of the London that provided the setting for these activities and personalities. This is in itself a good and sufficient reason for attempting a study of London in an extremely interesting stage of its political, economic, and cultural development. It is not, however, the only reason. London made a great contribution to the life of the nation as a whole, but it was also a living entity in its own right with its own personality and rhythm. It was more than a background: it helped to shape the behaviour of the actors who played their parts on its stage. Politics, art, the conception of empire, all would have been different had London been a different place with a different pattern of life. Any study of eighteenth-century England must therefore be given a greater depth by an increased familiarity with the many-sided interests and activities of its capital. The title of this book does perhaps call for a further word of explanation. Dr. Johnson was himself a very shrewd observer of the London scene and touched its life at many angles. His most obvious interests lay in its intellectual, literary, and artistic richness: Sir Joshua Reynolds, Goldsmith, and Garrick were his close friends. But he was also familiar with the world of politics. As a political journalist he for a time covered the debates in the Commons for *The Gentleman's Magazine*; later he defended the government policy of George III in a series of pamphlets. Through Samuel Welch he had firsthand contact with the poverty and crime of the metropolis. Above all he was a great lover of the place, and through his writings we can learn how Londoners thought, worked, lived, and amused themselves. He is therefore a very fitting figure to lend his name to a study of eighteenth-century London. I have not, however, confined myself rigidly to the dates of his residence in the capital if some aspect of the subject semed to call for a wider survey, but in the main this is an attempt to recreate for modern readers a picture of the London that he knew and loved.

What I have tried to do in this short book is to examine what I consider the most important aspects of eighteenth-century London and to combine them into a composite picture. Obviously the topography and growth of London, are basic to my purpose and, therefore, are dealth with in Chapter 1. Next it seemed vital to examine the way in which Londoners earned their living and accumulated the wealth that both paid for this growth and made London the centre of a great empire of trade. This therefore comprises Chapter 2. An examination of the City as a political and administrative entity follows. Eighteenth-century politicians, as Dr. Lucy Sutherland has ably demonstrated, could never ignore the importance of the City, but earlier studies of London during this period have tended to ignore the politics of both the City and Westminster in favour of the more purely social aspects of contemporary life. Chapters 3 and 4 are intended to correct this balance; both Parliament and the Common Council were integral parts of London life. Chapter 5 is more conventional in its subject matter. The amusements, entertainments, and pleasures of London played too large a part in the lives of its inhabitants to be omitted, but this topic has already been very fully dealt with by other historians. As far as possible, therefore, I have taken my illustrations from contemporary sources, of which Count von Keilmansegge's *Diary of a Journey to England* is a delightful and less well known example. Chapter 6 is inevitably superficial, as any attempt to give even the sketchiest impression of the artistic and intellectual wealth of London must be when confined to one chapter. It is only an introductory bird's-eye view of the artist and the writer as part of a greater whole. Chapters 7 and 8 aim at creating a different kind of balance. Without some discussion of poverty and crime and the means by which Londoners attempted to deal with the widespread misery that existed, a reader might well have too favourable an impression of Dr. Johnson's London. To the nobility, the gentry, even to the middling sort it had much to offer, but for the great mass of its inhabitants life was hard, overcrowding, underemployment, and disease were the common lot, and the problems of crime, immorality, and destitution challenged the consciences of many Londoners.

Material for such a study is abundant but uncoordinated. Contemporary sources alone are overwhelming—novels, plays, periodicals, newspapers, playbills, travellers' impressions, Dr. Johnson's own writings and essays, Boswell's massive and entertaining outpourings, contemporary histories of London, such as the compilation of William Maitland which I have used freely, provide a rich treasure house. Modern sources are equally extensive and varied. They range from the many-volume *Survey of London* originally commissioned by the London County Council to specialized articles on some aspect of London's trade in such learned journals as *The Economic History Review* and are too numerous to be listed here. Even those that deal merely with Dr. Johnson and his circle, which vary in quality from the scholarly to the chatty, would make a long list. My difficulty therefore has not been lack of material, but how to select from its superabundance that which best seemed to give a fair representation of what was most characteristic of the London of the period. Inevitably much has been left out, and I can only ask for the indulgence of those readers whose selection would have been very different from my own.

DOROTHY MARSHALL

University College
Cardiff, Wales
February 1968

ACKNOWLEDGMENTS

I thank the following authors and publishers for their kind permission to quote from copyrighted material.

Edward Arnold & Co., *A History of the London Hospital*, by E. W. Morris, 1926.

Cambridge University Press, *Dr. Campbell's Diary of a Visit to England in 1775*, edited by James L. Clifford, 1947.

Clarendon Press, *Life of Samuel Johnson*, by James Boswell, edited by G. B. Hill and revised and enlarged by L. F. Powell, 1934.

The Board of Governors of Guy's Hospital for permission to quote from *Mr. Guy's Hospital*, by H. C. Cameron (Longmans) 1954.

Count Carl N. von Kielmansegge, *Diary of a Journey to England*, edited by Philippa Kielmansegge (Longmans), 1002.

Macmillan & Co. Ltd., *An Account of a Visit to England*, by P. Kalm, translated by J. Lucas, 1892.

John Murray Ltd., *A Foreign View of England in the Reigns of George I and George II*, by Cesar de Saussure, 1902.

The Board of Governors of St. Thomas's Hospital for permission to quote from *An Abstract of the Orders of St. Thomas's Hospital* in *Southwark*, 1752, now in the hospital archives.

Yale University Press, *London Journal*, by James Boswell, edited by Frederick A. Pottle (Heinemann Ltd.), 1950.

The illustrations have been reproduced from the Print Collection of the Greater London Council at County Hall (Photographers: R. B. Fleming & Co. Ltd.), and I should like to express my gratitude for the help I received in choosing them and in arranging for their reproduction.

CONTENTS

LIST OF ILLUSTRATIONS

Dr. Johnson's London

ONE

The Topography and Growth of London

Samuel Johnson loved London. When a man tires of London, he said, he must be tired of life itself. He loved it all, not only its "great streets and squares," but also its innumerable little lanes and courts. So it is only fitting that the Doctor himself should indicate the scope and plan of a book about his beloved city. "I have often," he said in 1763, "amused myself with thinking how different a place London is to different people. . . . A politician thinks of it merely as the seat of government in its different departments; a grazier as a vast market for cattle; a mercantile man, as a place where a prodigious deal of business is done upon 'Change; a dramatic enthusiast, as the grand scene of theatrical entertainments; a man of pleasure, as an assemblage of taverns, and the great emporium for ladies of easy virtue. But the intellectual man is struck with it, as comprehending the whole of human life in all its variety."[1]

This manysidedness was one of eighteenth-century London's most notable features. Westminster was the seat of government for both Britain and its empire. The City with its Lord Mayor, its Aldermen, its Common Council, and its Liverymen was the apogee of urban self-government and the heart of a great mercantile and financial community. In their fine town houses in the West End the nobility had brought elegant living to a state of near perfection. In crowded courts and alleys craftsmen worked, along

[1]J. Boswell, *Life of Samuel Johnson,* edited by G. B. Hill, revised and enlarged by L. F. Powell (Clarendon Press, 1934), Vol. 1, p. 422.

the riverside wharfs porters hauled and strained under heavy
loads. The Thames was busy with shipping, great and small, from
the ferry that carried passengers from one bank to the other to the
great East Indiaman stuffed with the treasures of the Orient. In
cramped offices clerks copied bills of lading with quill pens,
hawkers cried their wares in the congested streets, wits and literary men thronged the coffeehouses, reading the latest newssheets
and exchanging the latest rumours. Thieves, pickpockets, and
beggars plied their trades while in the prisons people cursed,
fought, starved, and died of gaol fever. Above all London was a
city of contrasts, catering to all tastes from Italian opera to the
crudest bruising matches, producing great works of art and the
coarsest of cartoons, and having in juxtaposition the greatest
luxury and the most abject and desperate poverty. Such was Dr.
Johnson's London.

When Samuel Johnson came to it in 1737, it already had a
long history behind it. Geography had destined it to be a place
of importance. The Thames Valley in its present recognizable
shape, though modified in many details by subsequent climatic
changes, dates from the retreat of the sea at the end of the Plio-
cene Age. As the water receded, it left a deep belt of clay
covering the ground on which London now stands. Subsequently
the ice sheet strewed the area with patches of chalky boulder clay
and a deposit of sand and gravel through which, in successive
stages, the Thames cut its way, leaving as it did so a series of
terraces which were cut into smaller segments by small tributaries, such as the Holborn and the Walbrook. The banks of the
Thames itself were for the most part low and marshy, but where
the first Roman settlement grew up there was a spacious site on a
gravel terrace and banks on either side firm enough for it to be
possible to build a bridge. The substratum of clay provided the
other vital necessity for an expanding community, fresh water, for
the rain falling on the North Downs and Chiltern Hills was
trapped and supplied the wells and springs that were to be an
important factor in London's growth. For the city's commercial
future it was fortunate that a bridge could be built at what was
then roughly the place where the Thames ceased to be tidal,
although since Roman times a gradual rise in the sea level has
made the river as we know it today tidal as far as Teddington.

The Thames had further advantages to offer both trader and invader in that its estuary provided a convenient approach from the Continent. It was the natural gateway to South Eastern England. In addition, its tributaries penetrated into a fertile hinterland where cattle could be raised and corn grown. As a final bonus the area was rich in building materials. For all these reasons it was the obvious place for the Romans, who were vitally concerned with the problems of communications in order to consolidate their hold on the country, to build a fortress. Even though the reason for the first Roman settlement was thus probably military, it soon became a centre of trade. By about A.D. 120 it was already so wealthy that the decision was made to protect it with a massive wall some twenty feet in height.

This wall, which enclosed the two low hills with flattish summits that had been formed by the stream of the Walbrook cutting through the gravel terrace, was important for the future plan of the city. Though Roman Londinium fell into decay and its temples, baths, and pleasant villas disappeared, the wall remained. Once the shock and disruption of the Anglo-Saxon invasions were over and ordered life began to return to South East England, the commercial advantages of the site again reasserted themselves. Traders returned and within the shelter of the walls rebuilt first the Saxon and then the medieval town. By modern standards it was still a small place, comprising an area of some 330 acres. The wall, which was nearly three miles in length, was pierced by six gates which determined the pattern of traffic in and out of the city. Nearest to the Tower of London was Aldgate through which came travellers from Colchester and the eastern counties. Those from York came via Ermine Street through Bishopsgate. Next came Cripplegate, then Aldersgate and Newgate, where in the eighteenth century the notorious prison stood. Lastly, near the foot of Ludgate Hill, dominated by the great cathedral of St. Paul, was Ludgate, which gave access to the riverbank, known as the Strand, and so to the twin city of Westminster. These were the limits of the ancient city, flanked on its river side by wharves and warehouses, and controlling the routes by which the wealth brought to them was redistributed to the rest of England. With such advantages it is understandable that London soon grew into the wealthiest community in the country.

The original settlement was, however, no longer the only place of importance on the banks of the Thames. About two miles further up the river on a patch of firmer ground among its fringing marshes a small Benedictine abbey had been founded, probably in the eighth century. Because of its position to the west of the city it became known as the West Minster. Later Edward the Confessor rebuilt the abbey and also erected a small palace for himself. Previously Winchester had been the administrative centre of the country, but Westminster offered certain special advantages. It was near enough to London to dominate its wealth without becoming a part of it. Although medieval kings were constantly on the move, asserting their authority and doing justice in every part of their dominion, they came more and more to consider Westminster as their headquarters. When it became necessary to keep government records in some permanent place, the Exchequer was located there. It was at Westminster that the kings were crowned. In this way during the Middle Ages Westminster became the centre of the government and the Court. The two communities were still separate but communication between them was easy by the river, and along the Strand great nobles like John of Gaunt built themselves palaces with gardens running down to the Thames. It was these two nuclei, Westminster and the City of London, that together formed what Dr. Johnson understood by London.

Great changes had taken place since the Middle Ages. Although Westminster and the City of London remained separate entities from the point of view of government, geographically they had become one as the empty spaces between them had filled up. Dr. Johnson was well aware of their separate identities, but for him London embraced them both, as well as much of the new building that had taken place since Tudor times and administratively belonged neither to the City proper nor to Westminster. In the Middle Ages, as the population grew, the space within the walls became too cramped to contain them, and new suburbs spread beyond. Some of these, such as Cripplegate Without, had been incorporated into the City's administration, but once their incorporation was completed, this practice ceased. As a result many parishes adjoining both Westminster and the City, though to the eye part of London, were administratively merely a part of the county to which they belonged. It will therefore be more convenient to use London as a general term to cover the whole metropolitan area.

Since the sixteenth century London had been altering and growing, under the twin pressures of increasing wealth and increasing population, at what, to contemporaries, seemed an alarming rate. Both Queen Elizabeth and James I had disliked this, had feared too great a concentration, and had tried to prevent it by prohibiting new building. The results had been more unfortunate than those they had attempted to prevent, because such prohibitions had merely led to much unplanned and surreptitious building. Medieval London had not been built thickly, and wealthy citizens had been able to surround their houses with pleasant gardens. With the prospect of profit, many gardens in the sixteenth and seventeenth centuries had been converted to a labyrinth of courts and alleys hidden behind the more substantial houses. Even when the prohibitions had been lifted, the scarcity of land within the walls had operated in the same way. By the reign of Charles II the City was too closely packed for either health or comfort, and some of the wealthier or less conservative citizens were moving out to new parishes to the east or the west. This process was enormously accelerated by the Great Fire of London in 1666. At a time when most houses were built of wood the risk of fire was ever present. As the density of building increased, so did the risk, though on previous occasions the damage had been kept within bounds. The fire that broke out on Sunday, September 2, had from the first potentialities for destruction. The house in Pudding Lane, which belonged to a baker, was full of kindling for his ovens. Many of the nearby dwellings were wooden and coated with pitch, and from them the flames spread to the neighbouring warehouses. The water supply failed, and the wind fanned the flames so disastrously that the city burned for five days. When the fire was finally brought under control, partly by blowing up houses in its path and so ringing it with empty spaces, more than four fifths of the old walled city, including St. Paul's Cathedral, had been destroyed.

The London that Johnson knew was both directly and indirectly the product of the Great Fire.[2] The City itself had to be

[2]See T. F. Reddaway, *The Rebuilding of London after the Great Fire* (Edward Arnold & Co., 1951).

rebuilt, but the effects of the Fire were even more far-reaching. It led to an exodus, which intensified the movement that had already begun to fill up the vacant ground both to the east and to the west. Dr. Johnson, first as a lodger and then as a householder, lived in the City, so that the streets and houses that he knew best were those that had been rebuilt after 1666. To him London was a comparatively modern city, only some seventy years old when he first came to live there in 1737. An act for its rebuilding, passed in 1667, understandably aimed above all at preventing the danger of fire. This meant some standardization of building practices. In the six "high and principal streets" and in the houses of "the greatest bigness" standing in their own grounds the dwellings were to be four stories high. In the lesser streets they were to be three stories, and in the by-lanes and alleys where the workers lived two stories were decreed. In all cases houses were to be built of brick or stone, and the thickness of the walls and the height of the ceilings were precisely fixed. Additional acts in 1707 and 1709 tried to eliminate the risk of fire still further by forbidding wooden eaves and cornices and by requiring that the wooden window frames be recessed into the brickwork. It was regulations such as these that were largely responsible for giving proportion and unity to the new buildings.

The Fire altered the layout of the City less than its dwellings. While the ruins were still smouldering, Sir Christopher Wren seems to have sketched out a plan for the reconstruction of the City with wide streets and open spaces, but in the circumstances this could never have been more than a pipe dream. Both time and money were against it. Because the City was the centre of a great commercial empire, its counting houses, its warehouses, its shops, and its dwellings had to be rebuilt as speedily as possible. The money to replace its churches and public buildings was raised by a tax on coal, but there was none to spare for the elaborate replanning or the rearrangement of property rights that Wren's plan would have involved. So men rebuilt as quickly as they could on the sites where their property had stood before; the main difference was that the narrow lanes that once twisted between wooden houses now twisted between brick ones. Historians of London occasionally lament that a great opportunity was thus lost. This was the view of M. Grosley, a French tourist who visited London in 1765. Having inspected the Monument, which had been built to commemorate the Great Fire, he observed that without its inscription it would be difficult to believe that "a great part of Old London was built upon a new plan. Houses scattered about at random could not form streets more narrow or irregular."[3] The condition of the streets was a further cause of criticism. "In this quarter of London," he wrote, "rebuilt after the great fire, the streets which were paved in such a manner that it is scarce possible to find a place to set one's foot, and absolutely impossible to ride in a coach, are eternally covered with dirt." Indeed, little in the City met with his approval. "Old London," he continued, "has two great streets that parallel to the Thames, the Strand, which, being joined to Fleet Street and Cheapside, etc. extends the whole length of the town; and Holborn, which is cut in a disagreeable manner by the prison of Newgate. These two streets are of a good breadth but not exactly regular. St. Paul's is the view which should naturally terminate the view of the Strand; but after walking a long time in the streets, we do not discover that fine cathedral till we are come close to the building."

Even after the Fire, therefore, the City remained a congested and bewildering place. The main streets were lined with brick houses three or four stories high, the ground floor usually being used for shops. These at least met with Grosley's approval. "The shops in the Strand, Fleet Street, Cheapside etc. are the most striking objects that London can offer to the eye of a stranger. They are all enclosed with great glass doors, all adorned with pieces of ancient architecture, the more absurd as they are liable to be spoilt by constant use; all brilliant and gay, as well on account of the things sold in them, as the exact order in which they are kept; so that they make a most splendid show, greatly superior to anything of the kind in Paris."[4] Such shops were not confined to the main streets; many equally good were to be found in the courts and narrow lanes that lay behind the thoroughfares. The City was a bustling place where both private and commercial vehicles jostled the shoppers, so that in 1737, during what seems to have been a major onslaught on the inconveniences

[3]P. J. Grosley, *A Tour of London* (1772), Vol. 1, pp. 32-33.

[4]*Ibid.*, p. 35.

of the City, the Common Council decreed that "from the great Increase of Coaches, Carts and other Carriages, and their frequent passing through the Streets, Lanes and Passages of the said City, it is become necessary for the Safety and Convenience of all Persons passing within the said City that Posts should be set up in many Streets, where now there are none, to preserve a Foot-Passage."[5] A rate was to be levied for this purpose, and the Common Council started the work. These posts must have been a boon to pedestrians, though pedestrians were still the victims of the dirt thrown up by the passing traffic. Grosley was horrified by the filthy condition of the streets where dirty puddles, three or four inches deep, splashed foot-passengers, coaches, and houses alike. As far as he could see the English were totally indifferent to the nuisance, "being defended from it by their wigs of a brownish curling hair, their black stockings, and their blue surtouts, which are made in the form of a nightgown."[6] Not everybody was as indifferent as Grosley supposed. Lord Tyrconnell, speaking in the House of Commons, declared that "The Filth, Sir, in Some Parts of the Town, and the Inequality and Ruggedness of others, cannot but in the Eyes of Foreigners disgrace our nation and incline them to imagine us a People, not only without Delicacy, but without Government, a Herd of Barbarians, or a Colony of Hotentotts,"[7] and he pressed for the setting up of a new authority to deal with the matter. Perhaps Grosley was correct and Londoners were oblivious to the filth around them, for Lord Tyrconnell's motion was defeated.

Such order and planning as there was in the City was confined to the main thoroughfares. Leading off them was a maze of courts and alleys rarely more than eight to ten feet wide. Many of these were bordered by small two-story, poorly constructed brick houses, overcrowded with artisans or city clerks. Because the population of the City was so squeezed together within its ancient walls, there was little attempt to segregate the different classes into separate areas. A court of mean houses, like Brickenton or Nun Court off Colman Street, might well have a substantial

[5]William Maitland, *The History of London* (1756), Vol. I, p. 575.

[6]Grosley, *op. cit.*, p. 34.

[7]Maitland, *op. cit.*, Vol. 1, p. 615.

merchant's house at its far end. For example, "Red-lion-court, good and large, with a Freestone Pavement, has a passage into Westharding street, in Goldsmith's rents. Johnson's Court has but a narrow Entrance, but opens into a square Court, with a Freestone Pavement and good Houses, well inhabited. Out of this Court is another, which bears the same Name, but smaller with one Row of Houses, with pretty Gardens behind them, and this runs into Gough Square, a Place lately built with very handsome Houses and well inhabited by Persons of Fashion."[8] Dr. Johnson lived there from 1748 to 1758. By good fortune his house, where he compiled his famous dictionary, survived the blitz of World War II and has now been turned into a museum dedicated to his memory. The labyrinth of houses that surrounded it has been replaced by tall modern buildings, but the interior has been restored very much to its original condition. From 1765 he occupied what Boswell described as a good house in Johnson's Court and from 1777 until his death he lived in Bolt Court.

The Great Fire altered more than the domestic architecture of the City; it was responsible also for the rebuilding of its numerous churches, including the great cathedral of St. Paul's on Ludgate Hill. Before the Fire London had been a medieval city, its houses high-gabled and timbered, St. Paul's in Gothic style with its steeple soaring above the rooftops. But by the seventeenth century the revolution in taste associated with the name of Inigo Jones had already begun. How far it would have proceeded had it not been interrupted by the Civil War is difficult to say, because already during the reign of Charles I a rather incongruous portico with Corinthian pillars was added to the west end of St. Paul's, which without the Fire might gradually have been transformed but could hardly have been rebuilt. It was this necessity that gave Sir Christopher Wren his opportunity. As surveyor general of his Majesty's Buildings he was responsible for the rebuilding of both St. Paul's and the destroyed City churches. The St. Paul's that Johnson and Boswell knew and where they frequently worshipped was a very different edifice from the previous one, for Wren in designing it had been greatly influenced by St. Peter's in Rome. Instead of a steeple there was now to be a massive dome

[8]Maitland, *op. cit.* Vol. 2, p. 961.

dominating the skyline. Boswell called it "that magnificent temple" and admitted that he could not help having a reverence for it. When he visited it on July 19, 1763, he went up to the roof of the Cupola and walked on the leads gazing on the City below, a view that he described rather disparagingly as "just a prodigious group of tiled roofs and narrow lanes opening here and there, for the streets and beauty of the buildings cannot be observed on account of the distance."[9] Peter Kalm, who visited London in 1748 on his way from Sweden to America, was more enthusiastic, writing that "there was a marvellous view on all sides if only the air had got to be clear, but the thick coal smoke, which hung on all sides, cut off the view in several places."[10] No wonder, the carping Grosley declared, "that St. Paul's being built with Portland stone seems to be built with coal,"[11] a comment that many Londoners have echoed since! In spite of the smoke, Kalm was impressed by "the very large number of churches in London, that is to say something over 60, all of which had towers and could be distinguished from the other large houses." Many of them had been built from Wren's own designs or under his general supervision. Together with St. Paul's they had given a new skyline to the City, the soaring towers setting off its magnificent dome. In Queen Anne's reign there was a fresh outburst of church building, probably due to High Church influence, but the rest of the century saw few new ecclesiastical buildings within the confines of the City, even though additional churches continued to be needed outside its boundaries as the population of London spilled further and further into the countryside.

In other respects Dr. Johnson saw many changes and improvements in the City during his lifetime. Under the growing demand for better facilities and accommodation many of its public buildings were reconstructed during these years. Before 1734 it had been the practice to allow the Lord Mayor to use one of the City Halls as his official residence during his term of office. But in that year it was decided that the City should have its own

[9] J. Boswell, *London Journal*, edited by F. Pottle (Heinemann 1950), p. 331.

[10] P. Kalm, *An Account of a Visit to England*, translated by J. Lucas (Macmillan, 1892), p. 310.

[11] Grosley, *op. cit.*, p. 26.

official residence for its leading dignitary, and a committee was appointed to which designs could be submitted. Among those asked to submit their proposals was George Dance, usually known as the Elder to distinguish him from his son. He was already being considered for the post of Clerk of the City Works, so that it is perhaps not surprising that his designs were accepted. The result was a solid and not very attractive building which, shorn of a couple of distinctly peculiar attic stories, is still the official home of the Lord Mayor. From his appointment in 1735 to his retirement in 1767 George Dance had a hand in most of the architectural activities of the City Fathers. His first major project was the building of an arcaded market over the newly covered Fleet Ditch. Between 1749 and 1750 he was occupied with the erection of a new Corn Exchange, which was intended to relieve pressure on the Royal Exchange. With its graceful Doric columns it is usually considered to have been a more pleasing piece of work than the Mansion House. The Royal Exchange, which had been burned down in the Great Fire and rebuilt on the old foundations, was further improved by the remodelling of the west side, also carried out by Dance. He was not, however, the only capable architect to play a part in the beautifying of the City: the new building of the Bank of England on the site facing Thread-needle Street was the work of Sampson. In the narrow confines of the City, Johnson must have been very conscious of these changes as he paced its streets. Perhaps even more significant of the changing times was the destruction of the old city gates in the 1760s. By then they were a complete anachronism, merely surviving to hinder the free movement of traffic, always a problem in the congested City streets, and a practically minded age decided to remove them.

Another improvement taken in the thirties was the partial removal of that most insanitary landmark, the open Fleet Ditch. Originally a stream running into the Thames near Blackfriar's, it had been canalized after the Fire for the use of small craft. Unfortunately it had proved an all too convenient receptacle for the disposal of the filth of the neighbourhood. How to get rid of every kind of refuse, both industrial and household, was a major problem for city dwellers everywhere before the feats of the sanitary engineers of the later nineteenth century. It could be carted away outside the town or thrown into the nearest river or ditch, which perforce acted as a main drain. This fate had overtaken the Fleet, which Pope in his well known vivid lines described as

> Fleet-ditch with disemboging streams
> Rolls the large tribute of dead dogs to Thames,
> The King of dykes! than whom no sluice of mud
> With deeper stable blots the silver flood.

In 1737 it was covered over as far as Holborn, and the space so made available was used for Dance's long, arcaded market. In 1754 a new campaign was started to fill the rest of this unsavoury ditch. This was done in 1755. Another anachronism was old London Bridge. During the first half of the eighteenth century this was the only bridge to span the Thames except for a rough wooden toll bridge as high up as Putney. As it was the only way of approaching London from the south without using the horseferry or making a long detour, the majority of travellers coming from this direction had to be funnelled through the squalid borough of Southwark and via the bridge into City. As a result London Bridge had to carry an overwhelming amount of traffic which the medieval bridge was ill designed to take. Earlier historians had described it as "a stately stone Bridge . . . supported by Nineteen great arches; and so furnished above with Houses and Shops of Able Tradesmen, that Passengers might rather take it for a fair Street than a Bridge."[12] But a committee of the Common Council reviewing the situation declared itself to be "Humbly of Opinion, that the Houses upon London Bridge are a public Nuisance, long felt, and universally censored and complained of, the Passage for Carriages and Foot Passengers being thereby rendered not only inconvenient but dangerous to the Citizens of London."[13] The construction of the bridge made it almost, if not more, dangerous to the people who went under it and to watermen who plied for hire: it was at once the subway and the bus service of a modern

[12]J. Stype, *A Survey of the Cities of London and Westminster Enlarged by Careful Hands* (1754), Vol. 1, p. 1.

[13]Maitland, *op. cit.*, Vol. 2, p. 711.

capital.[14] To this waterborne traffic the arches of London Bridge presented a hazard when the tide was running strongly or the wind shipping up the water, and accidents were frequent.

With the growth of the West End and the concentration of people around Westminster, the inconvenience of having only one bridge across the Thames became more and more apparent, at least to the inhabitants of that area, among whom must be included the members of both houses of Parliament. In 1734 Lord Pembroke started to campaign for another bridge to be built at Westminster. The City Fathers, ever fearful of any project that threatened to divert business, protested vigorously but in vain. In 1736 the necessary act of Parliament was passed. The next problem was to choose an architect. Englishmen had little experience of bridge building on so large a scale, and the man finally chosen was a Swiss, Charles Labelye, who had already undertaken river and harbour works. His methods were fiercely criticised by his unsuccessful rivals, possibly with some justification, as one of the piers began to sink in 1748 before the bridge was opened. When, however, it was finally opened in November 1750, it became one of the showpieces of London. Count Kielmansegge described it as "1023 feet long, consequently 200 feet longer than London Bridge. Its width of 44 feet includes a 7 foot pathway on each side for foot passengers, and a 30 foot roadway for carriages, so that three carriages and two persons on horseback can pass each other. The bridge rises a good deal from the bank towards the centre. . . . The arches under the bridge, for the shipping traffic, are nearly four times the width of London Bridge, without any water shoot, and are in consequence free from the slightest danger to boats."[15] Most people were agreed that it was a splendid achievement and a great addition, both artistically and practically, to the new London now growing so rapidly. Grosley, however, managed to insert a note of criticism both for this bridge and for the new one that followed it at Blackfriar's. One of his laments had been that, unlike the Seine with its broad quays and open

[14]See Hugh Philip, *The Thames about 1750* (Collins, 1951), for further details.

[15]Count F. von Kielmansegge, *Diary of a Journey to England,* translated by Philippa Kielmansegge (Longmans, 1902), p. 189.

London Bridge before the removal of the houses.

The new Westminster Bridge, Westminster Abbey and the old Houses of Parliament are in the background.

views, in London "All possible measures have been taken to conceal the prospect of this fine river." He found the same defect in the new bridges, complaining that they "have no prospect of the river except through a balustrade of stone, with a rail of medallions three feet high, very massy, and fastened close to each other."[16] Melancholia was regarded by foreigners as a traditional English disease, which they were inclined to attribute to the climate. In London the smoke of innumerable coal fires, both domestic and industrial, Grosley declared, "enveloped London like a mantle; a cloud which the sun pervades but rarely; a cloud which, recoiling back on itself, suffers the sun to break out only now and then, which casual appearance procures the Londoners a few of what they call 'glorious days.' "[17] No other city consumed the amount of coal that was regularly burned in London, and the pall that lay over it was a source of constant astonishment and dismay to foreigners. It was to the need to prevent suicide that Grosley therefore attributed the massive parapets of the new bridges: had they been less formidable, the temptation to eight-eenth-century Englishmen to hurl themselves into the river be-neath, he thought, might have been too great!

The success of the new bridge at Westminster inspired the City to take steps to deal with the inadequacies of London Bridge. They were, however, loath to take drastic action and for some years followed a policy of half measures. The last of the old houses were pulled down in 1757, and two years later a new centre arch was made with the hope of lessening the danger to river traffic. Such measures could only be palliatives. Since at least 1754 there had been demands for another bridge to handle traffic to and from the City, and finally it was decided to take action. A new bridge was to be built at Blackfriar's. The winning design was submitted by Robert Mylne who, in February 1760, was entrusted with the work. Mylne was an interesting man, well used to moving in good society. Boswell met him at dinner at Lord Eglington's where, it is clear, he found Mylne to be a stimulating conversationalist. The new bridge proved him to be a first-class engineer. In many ways it was an advance on Westminster

[16]Grosley, *op. cit.*, p. 20.

[17]*Ibid.*, p. 44.

Bridge, spanning the Thames in nine arches as opposed to the other's twelve, with the rise in the centre taking the form of a gentle curve rather than a hump in the middle. Horse-driven machinery was used to drive the piles. There was some discussion over the choice of a name for the new bridge. Pitt's friends in the City wanted it to be called after him as a tribute to his leadership in the Seven Years' War, but by 1770 Pitt, now Lord Chatham, as a peer in opposition had a more limited popularity, and when the bridge was opened in that year it was known merely as Black-friar's Bridge.

The alterations and improvements in the City since the Great Fire were, however, nothing when compared with the develop-ments outside the walls. Although not new in 1666, the urge to expand was greatly accelerated by the dislocation that the de-struction of the City caused. Rich merchants, and even those of modest means, when faced with the need to rebuild their houses and with the growing congestion within the walls, tended to look to new development areas to the west and to the east. Originally Westminster had been the location of the Court and of govern-ment, and only those persons who had business with either—officials, noblemen, and important church dignitaries—had need of a permanent residence there. The palaces of the wealthy had long fringed the banks of the Thames on either side of the Abbey. The old Palace at Westminster supplied headquarters for the Parliament, and after the Reformation Henry VIII took over Wolsey's palace of York House and enlarged it to make the new palace of Whitehall. This was further reconstructed by Inigo Jones under the enlightened patronage of Charles I. Between them they introduced the Italianate style of architecture to an, on the whole, unappreciative public. In so doing they laid the foun-dations for Palladian architecture, which was to be the hallmark of good taste in Georgian England and was to dominate the first great wave of building of that era. Ingio Jones's masterpiece, the new Banquetting Hall at Whitehall, still remains; it was from its windows that Charles I went to his execution. But even before his death the outbreak of Civil War had stopped the first wave of expansion around Westminster and the Strand, although not before some significant developments had taken place.

By the seventeenth century there was certainly need for an

expanded building programme. To some extent constitutional changes were making this necessary. Since Elizabeth I's reign country gentlemen rather than small town worthies had been increasingly returned by the boroughs to the House of Commons. With so many country gentlemen, often accompanied by their families, in London for at least part of the parliamentary session, there was an obvious need for additional accommodation, either to let or to sell. Both James I and Charles I had disliked the idea of an expanding London, and in 1625 a Commission for Buildings was appointed to enforce the legal restrictions, already in existence, on new buildings. So great however was the prospect of profit that enforcement proved impossible, and a new type of interest investor now appeared—the large landed proprietors of noble birth. Many of their great London houses stood in extensive grounds, occupying land the site value of which was becoming yearly more valuable. Such a one was the Earl of Bedford. He was a businessman of considerable skill, who was already interested in reclaiming much of the waterlogged Fens in Bedfordshire and anxious to turn the land behind his house in the Strand to an equally profitable use, encouraged by the fact that even before he had inherited the family property new housing developments along Drury Lane and Long Acre were bringing in some £500 a year. With some difficulty the Earl obtained the necessary permission, possibly on the understanding that his designs would be in accordance with the royal canons of taste. The result was a long rectangle composed of substantial houses, whose gardens ran back to the necessary coach houses and stables behind them on the north and east sides, the south being separated from the grounds of Bedford House by a low wall. The west side was occupied by a church, also built in the new classical style, the portico of which still stands today. Such was the new housing estate of Covent Garden.

Although Covent Garden was completed a hundred years before Johnson came to London, the story of its inception and plan is relevant to any study of eighteenth-century London because it initiated so many features that were to be characteristic of that period. Lord Bedford's business shrewdness was to be widely followed in the second half of the century. After the Restoration, Lord Southampton built himself a mansion on his

Bloomsbury estate and let off plots of land on building leases around what is now Bloomsbury Square. Building leases of this kind played a very significant part in the growth of the West End. The usual practice was to let off the land in plots for a considerable number of years at a low ground rent on condition that a house of a certain type and value was built on it. At the expiration of the lease the house as well as the land reverted to the ground landlord. In this way men or families who were lucky enough to own, or shrewd enough to acquire in advance of the market, valuable sites became eventually the owners of half the buildings in London. Acting on this plan Henry Jermyn, first Earl of St. Albans, developed the area around St. James. This was already socially eligible because from the time of Henry VIII a small former hospital dedicated to St. James had been converted into a royal hunting lodge. This, when the Palace of Whitehall was destroyed by fire in 1698, was converted into the main royal residence of the King when he was in London. St. Albans was fortunate in the timing of his scheme for just as he was prepared to go ahead, the Great Fire produced a host of prospective tenants, all eager to build new houses in the west. Because St. Albans had managed to acquire the freehold of the land, he too entered the ranks of the great London landlords. Other impressive developments are similarly associated with great families whose names are still borne by the streets and squares of the West End. Lord Scarborough was responsible for the area around Hanover Square, so named in compliment to the new king, George I, Elector of Hanover. About the same time young Lord Burlington, whose impeccable taste was to make him very much an arbiter in such matters, was building on the land to the south of his mansion in Piccadilly, where today Burlington House provides the head-quarters of the Royal Academy. The Grosvenor estate between the Oxford road and Park Lane and the area around Cavendish Square are further examples of aristocratic enterprise.

A feature that characterized Johnson's London and owed its prevalence to this controlled development was the importance of the square in urban planning. Even though it seems incongruous to apply the modern term "housing estate" to such dignified property, each landlord aimed at providing an independent social and economic unit, whose economic needs were frequently ca-

Hanover Square. Notice the typical layout and the open country, including the heights of Hampstead and Highgate, in the distance.

tered for by a market and whose spiritual needs were served by a
church, though Count Archenholtz declared that in the West End
they were "as rare as in the city they are numerous: the desire of
rearing a mansion for ourselves is infinitely stronger than that of
erecting one for the diety; there are even quarters where six
thousand houses belong to a single parish."[18] In spite of Archenholtz's comment, some very fine churches, such as St. George on
Hanover Square, were built to serve the needs of new parishes.
Leading out of the square were side streets, sometimes joining up
to a central road, such as the Strand or Piccadilly or the track that
was to become Oxford Street, but sometimes petering out in the
open country, because all these schemes were not so much a
methodical extension of the frontiers of bricks and mortar as the
speculative exploitation of estates that lay scattered and piecemeal over the fields beyond Westminster and the City. Though
many people would consider these relics of the eighteenth century among the treasures of London's architecture, Baron de Pol-
nitz, when he visited London in 1739, was more critical. He admitted that there were "several great and fine ones," but added
that "some of which in my Opinion, would be more beautiful
were it not for the Fancy of adorning them with Gardens, which
perhaps is owing to the Want of Stones for paving them. As these
are encompassed with Iron Palisades, they look very much like
churchyards."[19]

This layout of the square and subsidiary streets dictated the
familiar pattern of the London house. Frontage on the square or
street was limited. In the prototype in Covent Garden the front
doors were arranged under a dignified arcade that linked them in
a regular harmony. The same feeling for harmony was aimed at in
the streets and squares. The fronts must be uniform, with doors
and windows in a balanced relationship. To fit the maximum
number into this pattern, the front of each house had of necessity
to be narrow; multiples of twenty-four feet were common. The
usual plan was to provide one front room of good proportions
and another room behind it, sometimes divided from it only by

[18] J. W. Archenholtz, A Picture of England (1797), p. 121.

[19] C. L. Pollnitz, The Memoirs of Charles Lewis Baron de Pollnitz (1739),
p. 438.

folding doors. Access to the upper floors was by a stairway that ascended from a small hall, hardly more than a passage, which had the main door at one end and often a closet (or privy) at the other. Most substantial London houses were three or four stories in height. The kitchens, storerooms, and servants' quarters were in the basement, though the maidservants normally slept in the attics. These basements greatly intrigued foreign visitors and are still a prominent feature in many of the older parts of London. According to Grosley "this subterranean story looks into an area three feet broad, which separates the house from the street. The foot path that lies next to it stands upon vaults, which contribute greatly to ease the subterranean apartments."[20] He then goes on to describe the way in which the footpath is "separated from the area by an iron railing, more or less adorned, which forming a sort of fore-door, supports two lamps that each house is obliged to furnish towards lighting the town; and from all these circumstances united, there results a decoration by which utility and pleasure are connected." Externally the result was very pleasing, but the inside of the houses was designed with little attention to domestic convenience. This was, however, a minor consideration to the eighteenth-century householder so long as the principal rooms were commodious. Unlike their twentieth-century counterparts, they had a plentiful supply of servants whose legs did not have to be considered in the constant running up and down stairs.

One convenience that impressed both Grosley and young John Yeoman, up from Somerset for his first visit to London in 1774, was the ease with which they stocked their cellars with the ubiquitous and necessary coals. Yeoman described in his diary "the Contrivence that they have in London is a Marviell to one Who never see a City before. In the foot Road, which is all Paved with fine White Stone, Under which everyone has a colehouse. Over the Same there's a Round hole about Nine inches even with the Pavement; so they take up this iron plate, the coles are Throne down without going into People's Houses. The Water is another Curious Article, there is a F.P. 12 ft placed up in the side of the streets at every thirty yards, the meaning is that twelve feet across the Street there's a Fire plug that if you pull that up the

[20]P. Grosley, *op. cit.*, p. 20.

water flows up all over the Street in case of fire."[21] Behind each house stretched a long but equally narrow garden. Often the back of the basement opened onto the garden, for it was a peculiarity of London's houses that whereas they were below street level at the front, because of the way the streets were made when they were built up, their backs were often at ground level. The coach house and stables, as necessary an adjunct then as a garage would be today, were at the end of the garden which gave on to a back lane. Most of the aristocracy had their town houses in the more fashionable squares and streets, but few of them approached in magnificence the great mansions of the French nobility in Paris. Building land in the centre of London was too valuable and most owners were too good businessmen to waste money on large grounds or courtyards. Even at Northumberland House, which stood near Charing Cross where Northumberland Avenue now runs down to the Thames, the courtyard was clearly inadequate. Kielmansegge, who went to a reception there, declared that "the inconvenience of getting away is a very great drawback, the courtyard being too small for the quantity of carriages and sedan chairs, and everybody has to come and go out by the one gate way, which is very narrow. The quantity of sedan chairs prevented any coach from getting into the court, consequently many people had to wait until two or three o'clock before they could get away."[22] Traffic jams are not a modern invention, as some nonhistorians seem to think!

The outstanding feature of Johnson's London was its swift growth. Contemporary estimates vary. Grosley, when he visited London in 1765, thought that twenty thousand houses had been built in the previous fifteen years. Archenholtz said that "It is computed that forty-two thousand have been built in London beween the years 1762 and 1779.[23] Both figures are guesses. Accurate statistics cannot be had, but guesses of this kind illustrate the sense of almost overpowering growth that so impressed contemporaries. A common assumption was that the growth of

[21]John Yeoman, *The Diary of a Visit of John Yeoman to London in the Years 1774 & 1777*, edited by M. Yearsley (Watts & Co., 1934), p. 45.

[22]Kielmansegge, *op. cit.*, p. 145.

[23]Stype, *op. cit.*, Vol. 1., p. 4.

London was made necessary by the pressure of population. No one really knew quite how populous London was. An estimate made in 1756 declared that ". . . if we compute them an even Million we shall come pretty near the Truth, when the Town is fullest; for there is a wide Difference between the Numbers who reside here in Winter and in Summer." More sober calculations suggest that this is a considerable exaggeration. In 1700 its population may have been about 674,500 and by 1750 not more than 676,750, though by 1801, when the first official census was taken, it had risen to 900,000 in round figures. The great discrepancy between the growth of London and the increase in its inhabitants was apparently due to the fact that people were no longer prepared to live in cramped surroundings with little privacy unless forced to do so by economic necessity. Increasing productivity in agriculture and expansion of trade were bringing new wealth to Britain, and much of this came to London. More and more Londoners, even if not well-to-do, could be described as belonging to the "middling sort" or what today we should describe as the middle-class or middle-income groups. For them life was becoming less harsh. Better agricultural methods were producing better food, including fresh meat all the year round. Better knowledge of medicine and of the care of young children meant that more of their offspring were living and families were larger. These were the people who were moving out of the City or who never went back to it once their houses had been destroyed by the Fire. Archenholtz went on to say that "There has been, within the space of twenty years, truly a migration from the east end of London to the west; thousands passing from that part of the city, where new buildings are no longer carried on, and to this end, where fertile fields and the most agreeable gardens are daily metamorphosed into houses and streets."[24]

This is an aspect of eighteenth-century London that is too little realized. Those parts of it that remain today convey such an appearance of timeless stability that it requires an effort of imagination to visualize the London that Johnson knew as a place of innovation and rapid expansion. Architecturally in the districts untouched by the Fire it was a city of contrasts where the new

[24]Archenholtz, *op cit.*, p. 119.

jostled against the traditional with a fierceness that we assume to be the peculiarity of our own age. In the older parts of Westminster and along the Strand the ancient half-timbered and gabled houses predominanted for much of the first part of the century, though enterprising householders were replacing the lattice windows of the past with the newer sash ones so characteristic of the Georgian house. Sometimes a coat of stucco was applied. But such houses were increasingly unattractive to the better class of people and tended to degenerate into slums, which were finally pulled down and replaced by substantial brick houses. Even before the old buildings disappeared new ones were appearing everywhere with relentless monotony on those "fertile fields and most agreeable gardens." As early as 1739 Baron de Pollnitz could write "St. James Quarter of the Town, and all the Outparts of London in general, are very regularly built, the streets strait, broad and airy, and want nothing but to be better paved."[25] Later observers found even this defect remedied, the houses in the newer part of the town being described as "mostly new and elegant; the squares superb, the streets straight and open, nor is any city in Europe so well paved. If all London were as well built there would be nothing in the world to compare with it."[26] London was lucky in that it had good building material close at hand to make this expansion possible. London clay mixed with the refuse and rubbish from the streets provided the raw material for bricks. Maitland describes having seen "in several parts of the Suburbs (where new buildings were lately erected) Clay dug up, made into Bricks and built into the Houses, upon the spot from which they were taken."[27] Brick kilns were a common feature in the London landscape and brickmaking a flourishing local industry. The quality that they produced varied, but not the size, which was uniform, having been regulated by an act of Parliament in 1739. Good bricks were commonly employed for the outer walls, but poorer "stock," in which heavy proportion of ash and rubbish was mixed with the clay, was used for interior work,

[25]Pollnitz, *op. cit.*, p. 467.

[26]Archenholtz, *op. cit.*, p. 119.

[27]Maitland, *op. cit.*, Vol. 1, p. 17.

the cheap speculative builder being no modern phenomenon. Also the building lease tended to encourage shoddy work; a house that would revert to the ground landlord in fifty years was rarely built to last a hundred. Immediately after the Fire, for a period that extended into Queen Anne's reign, most of the brick used was red, but later this became unpopular and was replaced by a grey brick with a yellowish tinge. The majority of roofs were tiled during the first half of the century because of the high cost of slates. When the quarries in North Wales were developed, however, large quantities of slate could be economically transported by sea. Indeed, one of the most noticeable outward changes that took place in Johnson's life was the gradual substitution of slates for the old tiles, a change that must have altered the look of the houses considerably. Some glass was made locally, using the glass sands found at Stone and the Thanet Beds, but more came up the Thames from the glassworks at Newcastle. One of the great advantages of London's position was that whatever could not be produced locally could so easily and so cheaply be brought in bulk by sea.

Although the overall expansion of London was very rapid, the move toward the west, which had started even before the Fire with the developments around Covent Garden and Lincoln Inn Fields, was not one of steady progress with roughly the same number of houses built each year. It was rather a matter of waves. The first of these occurred after 1666, though in a patchy way; after the Restoration of Charles II the developments held up by the Civil War and by the uncertainty of the Protectorate were restarted. By Queen Anne's reign the first wave had spent itself. Most of her reign was a period of war, when France and Britain were contending over the fate of the crumbling empire of Spain in the struggle known as the War of the Spanish Succession and when the country's resources were devoted to other ends than the building of houses. With the Peace of Utrecht and the peaceful succession of George I to the British throne, the release of resources, and the removal of the threat of civil war some important building schemes were once again undertaken. With the South Seas Bubble, which rocked the City and for a time damped down speculative ardour, there was some slackening in the rate of expansion, though the process of modernizing and rebuilding went on constantly as the gabled houses of the seventeenth century gave way to the more uniform streets of brick. After the end of the Seven Years' War, with its triumphs and its great colonial gains, a new period of activity emerged. This was the great period of Dr. Johnson's London when all the arts seemed to burst into active life, when Reynolds and Gainsborough painted, when Garrick acted, and the Adams brothers and William Chambers put their stamp on London's architecture. In spite of the strains of the American War of Independence, London continued to grow, and it was not until after Johnson's death that the long war with first revolutionary and then Napoleonic France put on the brake. The close relationship between national prosperity and the expansion of London provides an additional proof that it was not so much the pressure of population as rising standards among the upper and middle classes that stimulated it.

In order to trace this expansion in more precise detail it is helpful to look at two factors—the general features of London's geography and the activities of the speculative landlord. A contemporary historian described London as "the most populous and opulent City and Emporium upon Earth, the Metropolis of Great Britain, and the Chamber of its Monarch, is delightfully situated upon a gentle and beautiful Eminence, on the Northern Bank of the Noble and incomparable River Thames . . . at a Place where the River in the Vale is cast into a Crescent or Half Moon; so that each Part may enjoy the Benefits thereof, and yet not be far distant from each other. . . . On the North Side it is very much sheltered from the Cold Winds by Hampstead, Highgate and the rising grounds of Islington; but it lies open to the more kindly west."[28] It is this curve of the river that provides the key to the layout of London. The early concentration of population had been on the higher northern bank, where the prevalence of gravel on top of the London clay had made building easy, and the first extensions of both the City and of Westminster had been along the riverbank, so that, as we have seen, by the beginning of the seventeenth century the two had become one continuous town. Meanwhile during the Tudor period, as might have been expected, a small settlement along the south bank began to take shape around

[28]Maitland, *op. cit.*, Vol. 2, p. 713.

the end of London Bridge and to form the borough of Southwark. Even as late as 1765 it seems to have presented a squalid appearance and was described as "a quarter of the town ill built, having but two streets in its breadth, and almost entirely occupied by tanners and weavers."[29] There was not much building opposite Westminster, where it was possible to look across to fields and gardens, but beyond Southwark the facilities that the Thames offered for shipbuilding and the construction of wharves had encouraged a ribbon of these enterprises, with poor quality houses for craftsmen and labourers stretching into the open country behind. In this sprawling growth some earlier riverside villages were absorbed. When Kielmansegge drove to Rotherhithe, he described it as "a district on the other side of the Thames, close to Deptford and nearly opposite to the end of the City; as it adjoins Southwark it is considered to belong to it and also to London, although in former times it had been a village by itself. We saw there a new East Indiaman launched which received the name of Britannia, and was built as usual to carry thirty guns."[30] By 1732 Deptford, further down the Thames, was reckoned to have 1820 houses and Greenwhich 1341. During Johnson's life, however, this commercial and industrial ribbon development had scarcely begun to eat into the rural hinterland. The main development was still on the north bank and was still residential.

The tendency was to build in depth away from the river rather than to string out new projects along its course. Here two factors were important—natural overspill from the original City and the influence of the aristocratic landowner anxious to exploit his estate. Red Lion Square and Bloomsbury Square had already taken shape by the end of the seventeenth century. A man like Lord Southampton built Bloomsbury Square because he already owned the land and argued, correctly, that it was near enough to the City to be an attractive proposition. To live a little outside the closing ring of houses was both healthier and pleasanter, and for the first part of the eighteenth century Bloomsbury remained very much on the edge of what would now be called the green belt. During this period much of the new building, as has been

[29]Grosley, *op. cit.*, p. 24.

[30]Kielmansegge, *op. cit.*, p. 210.

said earlier, was not necessarily contingent on another built-up area, and fields might surround and isolate some planned and gracious square with its small pattern of dependent streets. Nevertheless, the major developments did take place with some relation to what either were, or during the century were to become, main thoroughfares. Of these there were three that ran roughly parallel to the Thames. Nearest to the Thames and following most closely its curve were Fleet Street, the Strand, and Whitehall where by the middle of the century a good deal of replanning had already taken place. Originally the Houses of Parliament and the old palace at Whitehall had been so smothered by a mass of squalid buildings that the sovereign driving in the state coach to open Parliament had been forced into difficult detours through unsavoury streets. By the thirties this was felt to be intolerable, and Parliament, ever sensitive to its own dignity and convenience, sanctioned a massive clearance that allowed a new and broad thoroughfare, appropriately called Parliament Street, to be driven through the old chaos of alleys and lanes. This was completed by 1750 and, together with the opening of Westminister Bridge and the improvement of the approaches to it, added greatly to the amenities of Westminster.

The next main artery was less well defined. Starting from Lincoln's Inn Fields, Gt. Queen Street cut into the upper part of Drury Lane, which continued as far as St. Martin's in the Fields, and came out at the Strand near Charing Cross. Behind it lay an unsavoury slum area full of doubtful cookshops which rejoiced in the name of Porridge Island. From the juncture of Long Acre and St. Martin's Lane the way west lay through a maze of narrow streets, until the street debouched into the open space of Leicester Fields, which Leicester Square now occupies. From there Piccadilly ran westward, past the corner of Hyde Park and the new St. George's Hospital, until it merged into the Knightsbridge turnpike. This was the royal road leading to the palace at Kensington. From the top of Piccadilly the Haymarket linked up with Whitehall. The third great artery lying furthest to the north is the most important from the point of view of orientating the new urban expansion. This was made up of Holborn, High Holborn, which joined the muddy track that was to become Oxford Street, which in turn merged into Tyburn Road, notorious because at its end stood Tyburn Tree, the famous gallows and place of public execution. The only connection between Piccadilly and the Oxford Road was the long straight but narrow Swallow Street, an unprepossessing thoroughfare, cobbled and bordered with kennels for refuse and full of the humblest type of shop. Connecting Tyburn and Hyde Park Corner and running along the side of the park was Tyburn Lane, better and more pleasantly known today as Park Lane. On the south side of Hyde Park Corner the Green Park extended to Buckingham House, which then stood in the fields just beyond the end of St. James's Park. These parks marked the limits of the town and apparently game was still to be found in them, though it had long disappeared from St. James's, which had become a place for fashionable parades.

During the century the open spaces between Piccadilly and Oxford Street were filled in and the land lying to the north was similarly absorbed. Much of this, as has been said, was due to the enterprise of aristocratic landowners. Lord Scarborough's development of Hanover Square has already been mentioned, and Lord Burlington was busy with plans for new and elegant streets to replace the fields that stretched behind Burlington House, now the Royal Academy. On land owned by the Grosvenor family a more than usually large square, with two streets entering it on each side, was designed as a single unit. Little of its original architecture has survived the modern improver, but the size of the square remains as a spatial monument to the grand conception of its planners. North of Oxford Street the Harley-Cavendish family was engaged in an ambitious scheme for a square intended to house the nobility. As a speculation it was not a great success, and the square was completed only during the building wave of the second half of the century, but the family connection with the area has been preserved in the name of Cavendish Square itself and of the surrounding streets—Wimpole Street, Harley Street, Welbeck Street. Meanwhile in the thirties and forties Berkeley Square, lying to the north cf Piccadilly and to the south of Grosvenor Square, added another landmark to London's West End. The term itself is interesting. This spate of buildings, by which fields and gardens were covered with well planned streets and squares, lay outside the boundaries of both the City and of Westminster. Administratively they were merely part of

the county to which they belonged and, like any other section of
the county, were divided into parishes. Yet geographically, socially, and economically they were part of London, and by the sixties
a very wealthy and important part. Eventually these parishes got
the name of the West End, the word "town" being implied, but to
contemporaries who lived, as Johnson did, in the City itself the
new areas were merely "the other end of the town."

With the new impetus given to building after the end of the
Seven Years' War, London started a new chapter in the story of
her expansion. Its authors were largely those property owners
whose land lay just outside the fringes of the built-up areas.
Between 1761 and 1774, when the north side was started, Port-
man Square was laid out to the west of Marylebone Lane, and by
1774 Portland Place was being designed. One of the most important schemes was that sponsored by the Duke of Bedford. Lord
Southampton's Bloomsbury estate had now become part of the
Bedford property, and from 1776 the problem of their exploitation was being considered. The first fruit of this was Bedford
Square, just off the road leading out into the country to Tottenham Court, but the major developments in this area—Russell
Square and Southampton Row—did not come until after Johnson's death and are in the main the products of the early nineteenth century. The other two notable squares in this district,
Mecklenburg and Brunswick, both carved out of the estate of the
Foundling Hospital, were also of a later date. The years after
1763 have often been described as the golden age of Georgian
architecture. The inspiration derived from the Palladian school
was wearing thin; its lessons had been mastered and men were
prepared for something a little less austere. The architect who
perhaps more than anyone else met the needs of the new age was
Robert Adams with his feeling for delicate ornamentation. Together with his brother James he revolutionized both the exterior
and the interior of London's houses. If his influence is to be seen
in new extensions, such as those on the Portland estate, it was
equally to leave its mark on much of the rebuilding of areas like
the Strand, notably in his reconstruction of the Adelphi Terrace
overlooking the Thames. Though financially it proved an unfortunate speculation for the brothers, architecturally it was "news" of
the first importance. Subsequently the Adams brothers designed

some of the most elegant houses in London, houses particularly planned to be the background for the mannered and gracious pattern of aristocratic living. There was less in the way of public building in the West End than might have been expected. Apart from the construction of Westminster Bridge, already mentioned, the most spectacular was the new Horse Guards in Whitehall. This was intended to be the Headquarters of the General Staff, if anything so well organized can be attributed to the eighteenth-century army. It was started in 1750 and completed some eight years later. The architect was William Kent. Though hardly functional, for its interior plan is hardly convenient for the work to be done there, the exterior makes it one of the outstanding buildings in the Palladian style. Behind it, on the Horse Guards parade, the reigning monarch still holds the ceremony of the Trooping of the Colours. Beyond it stretches St. James's Park with its formal walks and ornamental water, where Charles II used to saunter feeding the ducks, and its tree-lined avenues. At the end stood Buckingham House, built in 1703 by the Duke of Buckingham and bought by George III in 1762. For a time the Dowager Princess of Wales, his mother, lived there, and it was only in Queen Victoria's reign that it was reconstructed and enlarged to become the chief royal residence in London. In the eighteenth century this was still St. James's, which stood on the north side of the park about halfway down. It was not very convenient, and one foreign visitor declared that "You cannot easily imagine a worse building than this, especially when seen from the outside."[31] The other important addition to London's public buildings outside the City was Somerset House. As administration grew more complex, the motley assortment of government offices in Whitehall were felt to be inadequate and it was decided to pull down the earlier palace in the Strand and replace it by a building to house the Navy Office, the Ordinance Office, and the Stamp, Salt and Tax Offices. The site was a good one, fronting on the Strand and running down to the Thames behind. On it Sir William Chambers, who was both Surveyor General and Treasurer of the Royal Academy, designed the massive structure that stands there today. It was completed in 1780, four years before John-

[31]*Ibid.* p. 198.

son's death. He must often have wandered past it while it was still being built.

Not all the new building was to the west of the City. Today there is a tendency to think of the East End as one large and monotonous area of working-class houses, shops, and pubs. Not entirely true even today, it was much less true in the eighteenth century. Even though the East End never attained the social cachet of the West, plenty of substantial merchants, shipbuilders and small industrialists, together with the shopkeepers and the professional men such as lawyers, doctors, and schoolmasters who catered to their needs, found the new suburbs to the east pleasant and convenient places in which to live. Many of these had once been small country villages, such as Deptford, Islington, Mile-End and Newington-Baths in Surrey, which had been gradually joined by ribbon development to the older urban area. Whitechapel, though once such a village, clustering around its own church of St. Mary Matfelon, had long been recognized as part of London. It was the starting point for many of the coaches that travelled to the eastern counties and was consequently a busy place, full of inns and the bustle of country folk bringing their produce into London. In the High Street, with its dignified Georgian Houses, the prosperous merchants lived, but the myriads of courts and passages and yards behind them had a less savoury reputation. Beyond Whitechapel lay the turnpike to Bethnal Green and Clapton, and in the inns information about rich travellers could be picked up. Both Jack Sheppard and Dick Turpin were familiar with them and so were lesser footpads. Between Whitechapel and Bethnal Green lay the settlement of Spitalfields, the haunt of silk weavers, and Goodman's Field, popular in its early days as a pleasant locality, full of gardens and trees and within convenient distance of the Navy Office. Wealthy Jews, who since the days of Cromwell had been allowed to settle in England, had a liking for Goodman's Fields. Along the Mile End Road was the village of Stepney. By the end of the century it was no longer a village; ribbon development had linked it to Whitechapel and made it a part of London.

The waterfront along the Thames to the east of the Tower and London Bridge was largely maritime in its character. It had some pleasant residential areas, such as Well Close, near the

Radcliffe Highway and the higher ground overlooking Wapping. Here sea captains lived and also Dr. Johnson's friend, Dr. Mayo, the pastor of a dissenting chapel in Nightingale Lane. In spite of the difference of their views, the two men were firm friends, mutual respect making up for antagonistic opinions. But except for small enclaves, most of Wapping, and Shadwell further to the east, with Limehouse beyond it, were full of small houses, chandlers' shops, brothels, cheap lodging places, and taverns and alehouses. Though small oases of better houses occupied by merchants or manufacturers who still lived by their warehouse or workplace were to be found, most of the inhabitants were rough and poor—lightermen, porters, and every kind of casual labourer. Further east still along the Thames the East India Company dominated the riverside hamlets of Poplar and Blackwall where the shipyards in which the East Indiamen were built were situated. Here, too, were brothels and drinking shops for crews coming ashore after their long voyages.

It was not only returning sailors who looked for relaxation nor debauchery the only form that it took. London was still small enough for Londoners to enjoy the pleasures of the countryside, and no account of Dr. Johnson's London would be complete without some description of its rural hinterland. In 1754 it was still described as being "incircled with an infinite Number of fine Kitchen Gardens, delightful Plains, and beautiful Elevations, covered with a perpetual Verdure, which forms an agreeable variety of pleasant beautious Objects, inriched with an incredible Number of great and stately Villages, adorned with magnificent Country-Houses of the Citizens."[32] This rich hinterland had both economic and social importance. In the days before the invention of refrigeration and modern transport it provided the metropolis with perishable foods and fresh meat. The land around Chelsea and Fulham was devoted to market gardens which supplied the London markets. There was a constant sale for vegetables, for which the nightsoil of London provided a rich manure. Flowers too were grown. Kalm, who as a botanist was particularly interested in anything to do with agriculture, described how "Men, old women and girls, walk or sit in the streets of London with baskets

[32]Stype, *op cit.*, Vol. 2, p. 718.

full of all kinds of flowers, bound in small bunches, which they offer to the passers-by, who bought them in numbers."[33] Many of the surrounding fields belonged to graziers. London's meat walked to market, often from long distances. Cattle might come from Wales, from the lush pastures of the Midlands, or from the Lowlands of Scotland. It was an exhausting journey which left the beasts jaded and thin so that a period of refreshment and good pasture was necessary before their final sale to the butcher. Dairy farmers supplied London with its milk, though there were many cow keepers even in London itself.

It is an historical truism that eighteenth-century cities were devourers of men. Many Londoners had been born elsewhere—in the small towns and villages of Britain—as had Dr. Johnson himself, and they looked with nostalgia to the countryside. London was an unhealthy place to live in, particularly in the summer when the sun and the heat brought out the stenches inseparable from bad sanitation. The smoke from coal fires, minglede with the damp from the Thames, caused constant fog and made the capital's "glorious days" all too few. Whenever they could, prosperous citizens therefore bought or built houses in the nearby villages where they could go during the summer months when the long days and more passable roads made transport safer and easier. Even if during the week they were forced to stay close to their place of business, their families could still enjoy the benefits of country air, and it was possible to join them on Sundays. Hampstead, with its airy heights, had been popular since the late seventeenth century. Between Chelsea and Fulham, Kalm describes the "Large brick houses, which belong to gentlemen and others, were scattered here and there among the gardens, to which those who lived in London, now and then, specially on Saturday afternoons, went to take the fresh air and to have the advantage of tasting the pleasures of a country life." Fulham, then about four miles southwest of London, from which it was separated by gardens and fields, he described as "a pretty town with several smooth streets. All the houses are of brick, very beautifully made." John Yeoman, describing the view from Richmond Hill, wrote that ". . . to look West was the River Thames, Vast Numbers of Villages and Gen-

[33]Kahm, *op. cit.*, p. 33.

tlemen's Seats. Looking South you could see all the County of
Surrey. It looks like a Wood, but here and there a Space where
was a Gentleman's Seat, there's Vast numbers of them there."[34]
The more substantial of these belonged to country gentlemen and
cannot be regarded as the overspill from London, but many were
elegant eighteenth-century villas belonging to politicians or men
of letters. Lord Burlington had a villa at Chiswick, Horace Walpole his extravagance at Strawberry Hill, Twickenham. Indeed,
within a radius of ten miles of the capital both the villages and
the countryside were studied with summer residence and weekend retreats. People who could not afford the expense of two
establishments often compromised by taking furnished lodgings
for the summer at outlying villages such as Kentish Town. To
people familiar with these now heavily built-up and frequently
drab parts of London, such memories are both incongruous and
sad. For those whose purses were even emptier, so that furnished
lodgings were beyond their means, a day in the country was still
possible. London's rural outskirts were still within walking distance, and the river afforded a cheap means of transport.

Such was Dr. Johnson's London, growing from year to year
as it ate up more of the countryside and devoured more and
more of the surrounding villages. At the beginning of the century Defoe had marvelled at its great size and had refused to
believe that such expansion could go on. Men called it "the Great
Wen" and said that the head was too big for the body. The Doctor himself owned that it was too large, but argued robustly that
"It is nonsense to say that the head is too big for the body. It
would be as much too big, though the body were ever so large:
that is to say, though the country were ever so extensive. It has no
similarity to a head connected with a body."[35] Even in 1784 London was not, by modern standards, very large: an active man could
know it well. But large or small, for Johnson there was "in London
all that life can afford." Its streets, its squares, its courts and alleys
were the background of his life, the infinite variety of its people
was the delight of his mind. As Boswell wrote of him in the last
year of his life, "Such was his love of London, so high a relish had

[34]Yeoman, *op. cit.*, p. 21.

[35]J. Boswell, *Life of Samuel Johnson, op. cit.*, Vol. 2, p. 356.

he of its magnificent extent, a variety of its intellectual entertainment, that he languished when absent from it, his mind having become quite luxurious from the long habit of enjoying the
metropolis."[36]

[36]*Ibid.*, Vol. 4, p. 374.

TWO

The Wealth of London: Industry, Commerce, and Banking

When Dr. Johnson first decided to try his luck in the capital, London dominated the commercial and financial life of both Britain and her empire. Its wealth was its lifeblood, and any attempt to understand its many activities must start with an examination of its economy. Rapid growth had called a host of industries into being to provide the houses and streets, the food and clothing, and the transport and amenities that it necessitated. Its geographical position, in itself a vital ingredient in this rapid urbanization, made it a natural centre for trade. The needs of trade in their turn called for an increasingly elaborate organization of commerce and financial services. This amalgam of domestic demand and overseas opportunities together produced the pattern of its economic life, a pattern ranging from the humblest craftsman to the capitalistic brewer, from the stall holder selling market produce or fish at Billingsgate to the large-scale merchant importing sugar from the Indies or tobacco from Virginia, from the pawnbroker to the director of the Bank of England. Both as a centre of conspicuous waste and as a centre of commerce and banking London afforded its inhabitants many ways of earning a living.

Much of London's industry was created by its day-to-day domestic needs. Here the scope for large-scale enterprise was limited, and small businesses employing a few craftsmen predominated. Because of its rapid expansion there was a demand for all trades connected with the building of houses, together with their equipment and furnishing. The profession of architect was only slowly becoming recognized; there were no specific qualifications that entitled a man to the title, and most so-called architects were self-taught men who claimed the more dignified status but often had little more professional skill than many a master builder. Wealthy gentlemen building a town house might employ one to draw up a design and make the necessary contract with a master builder, but most eighteenth-century houses were the work of the latter. There were fat profits to be had by any man with a good head for business who had served his time as a bricklayer or carpenter. Such men let out much of the work to subcontractors, undertaking personally only that part of the operation for which they were trained. Thus a bricklayer would build the house and put out the rest of the work—carpentering, joincring, plumbing, and glazing—to other small subcontractors. The carpenter too was employed on structural work; often his functions were combined with those of the joiner who laid the floors and made the doors and the wainscoting. Plasterers were required for the walls and ceilings and often for the stucco work that gave a fashionable finish to so many houses. Glaziers were needed for the windows, smiths to make the iron railings and banisters, locksmiths for the doors. The brisk demand for houses encouraged the enterprising craftsman to engage in building speculations. The method was to lease a promising site for sixty or ninety years and on it to errect the shell of a house in the hope that a buyer would come along, purchase it, and so provide the speculative builder with the necessary funds to build the next house. Such ventures could be very profitable; they could also be disastrous for the man who operated on too slim a margin, if the site or the house proved unattractive. Looking at the dignified architecture of the streets and squares of Georgian London, it is hard to believe that they had been erected in this haphazard, amateur, and piecemeal fashion. But although the London crafts-man might be unorganized, he was far from being untrained or unintelligent. Furthermore, he was helped by the books of plans and designs that were compiled for his use. A skilled craftsman could adapt these to the site or to the taste of the prospective owner. The result was a pleasing uniformity, a balance, and an elegance that, without this assistance, could hardly have been attained.

In addition to the buildings themselves, furnishings of every kind were required. The Quality often engaged the services of an upholder or an upholsterer. Here the eighteenth-century term implies a much wider scope of activities than its modern counterpart. He was more the equivalent of a modern interior decorator, supplying the hangings and soft furnishings but also employing cabinetmakers, chair carvers, glass grinders for the making of mirrors, and screen makers. The list could be extended almost endlessly. Seddonds in Aldersgate was one such firm, operating in a big way and employing cabinetmakers, upholsterers, in the more specialized sense of that term, carvers, gilders, mirror makers and ormolu workers. Among these craftsmen the cabinetmaker stands out as a great exponent of eighteenth-century taste. Thomas Chippendale, whose name is still a household word, had a flourishing business, first in a little court off Long Acre and then in St. Martin's Lane. Other cabinetmakers owed much to him because of his publication in 1768-1769 of his *Director*, an imposing volume containing 160 large engraved plates of designs, three editions of which were called for in the next seven years. By so doing he furnished skilled workmen who were deficient in the art of design with a series of standard patterns. In 1773 Robert Adam produced a volume containing both plans for the builder and designs for furniture and interior decoration. Hepplewaite published a similar book of designs in 1789. The cabinetmaker, therefore, like the master builder, had easily available advice. Because men of wealth and taste, who represented a considerable section of the purchasing power of the community, also subscribed to these volumes, their demand for furniture of the same high standard ensured that the cabinetmakers conformed to them also. Sir Ambrose Heal published in 1953 an extensive survey of London's furniture makers, which demonstrated how very widespread the craft was, ranging from the smallest of masters to very considerable establishments. William Linnell, whose pieces were much in demand and whose prices were correspondingly high, lived at 28 Berkeley Square. The products of such men were not confined to the London market. The aristocracy and gentry, in Town for the parliamentary season, commissioned them to supply choice pieces for their country houses. In addition to commissions of this kind, for the convenience of both London and country customers, furniture retailers, carrying a variety of goods, did a flourishing trade. During the century Tottenham Court Road first became, as it still is, a centre for this kind of business. Peter Langloi, whose establishment was on its west side, near Windmill Street, was one of the pioneers in this area, specializing in furniture after the French mode. Horace Walpole was one of his customers.

The cabinetmakers and the upholsterers were not the only craftsmen whose products were wanted to meet the rising standard of Londoners. Abovestairs beds were needed, belowstairs all the equipment of the kitchen which, though modest by modern standards, gave employment to braisers who made the copper pans and kettles and warming pans, and to the smith who made the jacks for roasting the meat, in itself a specialized trade, and the great iron pots or vats for storage. In a sizable house, therefore, there was a demand for many varied wares, most of them produced in the vicinity in small workshops scattered through the town. Nor was it only a matter of building and furnishing new houses. As we have seen, old houses were reconstructed and improved, and then as now old equipment wore out and had to be replaced. All this provided work for a great many people, whose activities are often forgotten when the economic life of a town is described. What today might well come from a distance was then far more likely to be produced near at hand. Transport also absorbed many people. In addition to the private coaches and sedan chairs of the Quality there were hackney cabs for hire and public coaches plied from point to point bringing people in from the outlying villages. Carts were used to bring coal and other heavy goods from the wharfs along the Thames. For gentlemen the horse was the normal means of transport. All this meant not only employment for drivers and coachmen, grooms, stableboys, and carters, but provided work also for the elegant coachmakers, for the manufacturers of carts, and for all the kindred crafts of harness makers, stirrup makers, buckle makers, and lorimers, as well as perpetual work for the farrier who shod the horses. Wandering in modern London, it is difficult to imagine how many smiths were busy at their forges in the eighteenth-century town.

Because London was a city of leisure as well as industry and commerce, many of its industries, whose products are collector's pieces today, were connected with the world of taste and fashion. Both Bow and Chelsea porcelain were flourishing by the mid-eighteenth century. The Bow manufactury was run by two partners, Crowther and Weatherby, with Thomas Frye, who seems to have been closely connected with the original processes, as manager. By 1758 it was at the peak of its success with a retail shop in Cornhill and a warehouse near St. Katherine's in the vicinity of the Tower. The sixties saw the beginning of its decline, and by 1776 the business, now in other hands, was unimportant. In the fifties the manufacture of Chelsea china was also well established. Between 1752 and 1757, when he moved to Piccadilly, its proprietor Nicholas Sprimont had a shop in Pall Mall, then one of the most fashionable shopping streets in London. Very fine enamelwork was produced at Battersea where the original promoter, Sir Stephen Jensen, concentrated on the production of such articles as snuffboxes, watchcases, toothpick cases, and bottle tickets with chains that are so popular with collectors today. The original designs were engraved on copper, printed on paper, and transferred to the enamel. Jensen himself went bankrupt in 1756, a fate that had also overtaken Crowther in 1763, but the manufactury seems to have continued. Some lovely specimens of this Battersea work can be seen today in the British Museum. Another skilled craft producing objects of elegance was that of the watchmaker. This trade tended to centre in Clerkenwell, but Daniel and Thomas Grignion made beautiful watches at their place in Great Russell Street. London clocks and watches were famous the world over: those that the sultans of Turkey bought are still to be seen in the Topaki Museum in Istanbul. Royalty at home bought them too. Eardly Norton, who specialized in musical and astronomical clocks, made one with four dials for George III. The making of musical instruments was another specialized craft. Harpsichords, organs and the newfangled pianoforte were also made, the latter being mostly the work of a colony of German instrument makers.

London thus supported a host of varied industries scattered throughout the metropolis. In the City it was still necessary for a man to be a freeman of one of the great livery companies to

practice a trade within its boundaries, and the records of companies such as the Stationers show that they could still be energetic
in their control of the trade. Beyond the City there was less regu-
lation and more freedom despite the formal provision that made a
seven years' apprenticeship obligatory in many trades. Both
inside the City and without, most of these industries operated on
a small scale and, according to the materials used and the tech-
niques employed, were either organized on the familiar domestic
pattern or based on the small workshop. This is obvious enough.
The smith with his forge, the sawyer with his sawpit, the rope-
maker with his walk, the dyer with his vat, all needed specialized
premises. On the other hand, the weaver himself could house his
loom and the shoemaker his bench; the seamstress required only
her needle, thread, and scissors. Within these two types much
variation was possible. Most trades still conformed to the traditional pattern of master, journeyman, and apprentice, but these
names had come to cover men of very different economic standing. The most successful were those masters who, while still
employing apprentices and journeymen of their own, put out
work to other men, taking back and arranging for the sale of the
finished product. This type of industrial organization was particularly suitable where the technique of the craft led to a considerable division of labour. There is a sentimental tendency today to
idealize the craftsman of the past as one who could find full
satisfaction for his creative urge. The historical reality is less
alluring. Even by the eighteenth century the watchmaker was
rather the watch assembler than the fashioner of its delicate parts.
Generally the work was put out to a series of craftsmen—the
movement-maker forged the wheels, the cutter cut them, a third
man made the springs, a fourth concentrated on making the caps
and studs. Successful shoemakers superintended the cutting out
of the shoes, but put them out to be made up by less successful
masters and journeymen working in their own homes. Even
where there was less division of labour, as in the silk weaving
industry, the most successful master weavers were small capital-
ists, organizing and handling the work of other men. Nevertheless,
small independent masters were still plentiful in many London
trades. Often they were helped by the labour of their families; some employed a journeyman or two and had apprentices.

Their wares when finished were sold to shops or middlemen, or they may have been "bespoke" by some customer. Economically there was often little to choose between such men and the journeyman working in his own home for an employer, because he too would be aided by his family and might in fact, though not in strict theory, take an apprentice.

The various crafts and professions of London are very fully described in *The London Tradesman*, written by Richard Campbell and first published in 1747. Campbell stated in his introduction that his intention was to help parents to choose the most appropriate career for their children with due regard to their background, education, and general aptitudes. He therefore gave detailed information on the opportunities and disadvantages of the many ways of earning a living in London. Not all of them were in industry or commerce. The lawyers, the attorneys, the sergeants-at-law, the counsellors-at-law, the solicitors in Chancery, the conveyancers and money scriveners, the physicians and surgeons, were excluded as belonging to the professions. Artists and sculptors constituted a borderline group, but the manufacture of the materials they used counted among the industries of London. The making of Prussian Blue "from Bulock's Blood by the Operation of Fire" he described as "an odious stinking Business,"[1] which was relegated to Southwark. The making of red and white lead was carried on at Whitechapel. It was a dangerous trade because the labourers contracted lead poisoning and rarely lived more than a dozen years. Red and white lead was used in house painting. Previously this craft had involved some skill, for the painters had mixed their own colours, but when Campbell wrote the colour shops were using horse mills to grind their colours, which they then sold to noblemen and gentlemen. As a result house painting had become a mere labouring job, and he described the men who were employed on it as "the dirtiest, laziest, and most debauched Set of Fellows that are of any Trade in and about London."[2] Because the trade was overstocked and very irregular, so that continuous work was usually available only from April to October and the wages were at most two to three shillings a day,

[1] R. Campbell, *The London Tradesman* (1747), p. 106.

[2] *Ibid.*, p. 104.

this is hardly surprising. Any study of the economic life of the capital makes it abundantly clear that much seasonal work and underemployment prevailed and that it was difficult for the unskilled or semiskilled man, and even more woman, to earn enough to keep him from destitution. The theme will occur again and again and serves to remind one that London was a place of great poverty, as well as of middling prosperity and, at the other extreme, of great wealth.

Among the craftsmen whose technical skill carried with it better remuneration were the printers, for whom, Campbell said, there was plenty of employment and who might earn up to a guinea a week. Engraving die and seal cutting were paid at similar rates, though "a Noted Hand" might earn up to thirty shillings a week. In engraving, etching, and metzotinting even a tolerable workman could earn thirty shillings a week and a really first-class one half a guinea a day. Such crafts were described as "very profitable and are reckoned among the genteel trades."[3] Pattern-makers too were well paid. These were the people who provided the designs for calico printers, embroiderers, laceworkers, and quilters but, as Campbell pointed out "This requires a fruitful Fancy, to invent new Whims to please the changeable Foibles of the Ladies."[4] In this trade a journeyman could earn from twenty five to thirty shillings a week, and as the London patternmakers produced designs for the whole kingdom, a good many people were employed in this way. Coachmaking was described as "a genteel, profitable Business both to the Master and the Journeyman."[5] The latter could earn five shillings a day, but to set up in the trade required adequate working capital, because it was necessary to lay out considerable sums in wages to wheelwrights and carvers, to the brass founders who specialized in coachwork, to tyre smiths and spring makers, and to the leather curriers. Eighteenth-century coaches were elaborate affairs, often embellished with gilt carvings and painted panels. They were one of the status symbols of the age, in the same way that certain

[3]*Ibid.*, p. 104.

[4]*Ibid.*, p. 115.

[5]*Ibid.*, p. 230.

makes of automobiles are so regarded today. Sir Joshua Reynolds
signified his social standing by possessing a very superior equippage; the coaches of City dignitaries were magnificent affairs. To
work for the nobility was not always an advantage. It was often
extremely difficult to get the money in! Long credit was usual;
tradesmen were often regarded as useful but inferior animals: to
pay debts to them rather than settle the so-called debts of honour
incurred in an unfortunate night's play at White's was unthink-
able. It was perhaps fortunate for the honest tradesman that in
the last resort the debtors' prison loomed ahead. Yet to employ
such measures to enforce a debt, or to put the bailiffs in, the fate
suffered by Charles Surface in *School for Scandal* and common
enough in the experience of many a London buck, might be to
lose future custom and customers. Tailors and mantua makers, for
fine ladies were equally dilatory in paying their debts, peruke
makers, and mercers were all victims. Yet to a man of fashion a
good tailor was more than a necessity; it was a burning preoccu-
pation. "There are Numbers of Beings," wrote Campbell, "in and
about this Metropolis who have no other identical Existence than
what the Taylor, Milliner, and Perriwig-Maker bestow on them."
His task was "not only to cut for the Handsome and Well-shaped,
but to bestow a good shape where Nature has not designed it."[6]
The term "milliner" was used in a much less specialized sense
than it is today and covered the provision of all kinds of wearing
apparel and personal linen. In fact, "they furnish everything to
the Ladies, that can contribute to set off their Beauty, increase
their Vanity, or render them Ridiculous."[7] The profits for a fashionable milliner were large, but once again there was the
difficulty of long credits. Supplying the same feminine market
were the staymakers, the combmakers, the capmakers, the makers
of hoops for petticoats, the fanmakers, and craftsmen in kindred
trades.

The retail trade absorbed much capital and employed a large
labour force. The distinction between retailing and manufacture
was less clearly cut than it is today when the shopkeeper gets
his supplies from the wholesaler and rarely makes the wares he

[6]*Ibid.*, p. 192.

[7]*Ibid.*, p. 207.

sells. In eighteenth-century London the practice varied. Jewellers and goldsmiths often employed journeymen on the premises to make the goods they sold, but they also put work out or bought from journeymen working in their own homes. Because of the expensive materials with which they had to work and because of the difficulty of obtaining payment, setting up in either type of business required considerable capital. A mercer, who dealt in silks, satins, and ladies' wares, required some £10,000 to run a successful business and even so was warned that he must not ape the gentry or he would soon find himself in difficulties. The Gold and Silver Laceman, whose stock in trade should include being the "Master of a handsome Bow and Cringe" and who should be able "to hand a Lady to and from her Coach politely, without being seized with the Palpitations of the Heart at the Touch of a delicate Hand, a well turned and much exposed Limb, or a handsome Face"[8] was warned that unless he were both hardworking and prudent, he might soon find himself in a debtors' prison. In the manufacture of the lace many crafts were employed—the wire-drawers, the flattening millers, the silver-thread spinners, the orris weavers, and the bone-lace makers. In addition there were gold and silver tassel makers, manufacturers of buttons made of gold and silver thread, frog makers, fringe makers, and embroiderers in gold and silver thread. Such lists are interesting because they indicate the number of trades that subsist on the demands for luxury of the fashionable world. It is easy to forget the number of persons who gained their livelihood by serving a humbler market. The Quality and the rich citizens bought gold and silver laces and rich satins and velvets and sought the services of a fashionable tailor, but the mass of the population could afford no such extravagance. Nevertheless, they too had to be clothed and shod, they too needed not only working clothes but a Sunday best. Many an apprentice scrimped and saved so that on holidays he could go fine. This market provided employment for a mass of artisans capable of producing sound, durable goods for the middling sort and shoddy wares for the poor.

Some of these trades brought in a comfortable living, a few such as those of the goldsmith, the jeweller and the mercer even

[8]*Ibid.*, p. 147.

affluence, but for the most part the reward was modest and for many actually meagre. The master craftsman who employed journeymen or the decent shopkeeper, whether a grocer, a druggist, a woollen draper, or a haberdasher, was, if he operated within the limits of the City, likely to be a master and possibly a member of the livery of his company. These men were the backbone of the City, living within its confines, usually on the premises where they worked. Again and again Campbell appeared favourably impressed with their economic position, but for the mass of journeymen and labourers the position was less good. One of the greatest drawbacks from which they suffered was the seasonal nature of much of their work, partly because of the weather and partly because of the absence from Town of many of the conspicuous spenders during the summer months. For instance, the working tailors, men who sat all day sewing seams or making buttonholes and who could never have fitted a coat or cut out a pair of breeches, were described as " . . . numerous as Locusts, are out of Business about three or four Months of the Year, and generally as poor as Rats."[9] Because of these long spells of unemployment, they were never out of debt to their House of Call. This would be a public house in the vicinity, largely patronizing by tailors. An employer wanted hands would go there and men wanting work would congregate there. When they were unemployed, the publician supplied them with food and drink and in return had the first claim on their wage. Even when they were employed, the heat and close confinement of the tailoring shops were conducive to heavy drinking, and most of them remained in a state of economic dependence on their House of Call from which they never broke free. Many trades had these recognized Houses of Call; often it was customary for wages to be paid there, and the whole system led to a considerable degree of exploitation. The house painters were another group who were usually idle for four or five months in the year, though in this instance the fashionable world liked to have the necessary painting done while they were away from London in the summer months. Their return in October, combined with the coming of bad weather, put the painters out of work. As they were paid a

[9]*Ibid.*, p. 192.

daily wage, their income over the year was plainly inadequate. Work for women was generally ill paid. Many of them were employed by milliners and mantua makers, and though the owners of such establishments were reputed to make large profits, their assistants received a mere five to six shillings a week. Similar wages were paid to the women who sewed the stays for the staymaker. Women were also hired to sew shoes made of satin or damask and to bind shoes. The majority of the spinners of gold and silver thread were girls and women. As they were reputed to be able to earn as much as twelve to fifteen shillings a week with application, they must be counted among the more fortunate. On the other hand, the women employed in making the buttons of gold and silver thread were paid only " . . . A Trifle to keep Body and Soul together."[10] Many of them seem to have been married women, addicted to gin, and prepared to accept a starvation wage, which "has reduced the Craft to a very low Ebb." The embroideresses were more fortunate; they, Campbell said, could make " . . . a very handsome Livelihood of it, if they were not initiated into the Mysteries of gin Drinking."[11] Women also found employment as washerwomen and hawkers. Some were employed as milkmaids, for London was full of cowsheds as well as stables, and on May Day they paraded the streets, wore gay garlands of flowers, and collected a tribute from the passersby. Probably the greatest number of girls and women were employed in some sort of domestic work—as cooks, housemaids, and waiting women by the better households and as household drudges by those of craftsmen and artisans. However, because these women lived with the families for which they worked, they fall into a category different from that of the trades already discussed.

No enumeration of London's craftsmen would be complete without some mention of the Spitalfields weavers. Like the potters of Chelsea and Bow and unlike most of London's industries, the silk weavers were concentrated in one district. Silk weaving had been developed in England by Huguenot refugees. Most of them were French in origin, and of the eighty-four masters who volunteered to arm their journeymen when the Young Pretender

[10]*Ibid.*, p. 152.

[11]*Ibid.*, p. 153.

seemed ready to march on the capital in 1745 most bore French names. It was in many ways a tightly knit community, held together by a common skill, common interests, and a common religion. Commercially London provided them with a good centre for their industry. The necessary raw or thrown silk could be imported via the Thames, London supplied a large market for the type of luxury goods that they produced, and, in addition, London had regular trading links with those provincial cities that were most likely to have a steady demand for their wares. The trade was, however, subject to considerable fluctuations because of the competition of French silks and the snobbery of English buyers, who were convinced that the imported silk was better, with no other justification than that it was French. When England and France were at war, a common occurrence in the eighteenth century, the weavers flourished. When peace returned, the industry was depressed. The years immediately following the Peace of Paris in particular were difficult ones in which the Spitalfields weavers, by a mixture of petitions and riots, made both the House of Commons and the people of London familiar with their sufferings.

Though a major industry, the Spitalfields weavers were organized in the traditional way—the control of the trade was in the hands of the independent master weavers and each was assisted by his own journeymen and apprentices. Georgian London had, however, other industries that were organized on a more capitalistic basis. Most of these owed their existence to the ease with which the raw materials could be imported via the Thames. Many of them needed cheap fuel for at least some of their processes, and with a regular fleet of colliers sailing between the coal fields of the Tyne and Wear and the Pool of London this too was easily procured. Moreover, what the Thames had brought, the Thames could take away. Whether the finished product was for home or foreign consumption, the river and its tributaries provided at once a waterway into the heart of London and a gateway to the North Sea and English Channel. So it is not surprising that London's industries were not confined to London's needs. From Elizabethan times there had been sugar refining around Goodman's Fields. There was some soapmaking around Cripplegate, but because land was already scarce in the City and was chiefly

The Royal Dockyard at Deptford. The vessel under construction is a typical example of shipbuilding on the Thames.

used for residential purposes in the West End, the larger industrial units tended to develop on the Surrey side of the river at Southwark and later at Lambeth. Southwark was well sited for this purpose, being linked with the City by London Bridge and having easy access to the river, so that the import and export of heavy cargoes presented no problem. Southwark also benefitted, if the word can be used in this connection, by the fact that dirty or dangerous trades were unsuitable for the already densely populated City and were accordingly discouraged by the Corporation. As a result, slaughter yards and the numerous tanneries whose raw material was provided by the hides of the cattle that fed London tended to congregate on the south bank. Bermondsey had many tanning yards; there was soapmaking at Southwark. The Quaker, Mark Beaufoy, had a malt vinegar manufactury near where Waterloo Bridge now spans the Thames. Fire was an ever present hazard, and anything that increased its likelihood, such as the making of gunpowder or the existence of large timber yards, found a home on the Surrey side. Shipbuilding was a prominent activity, and this attracted the subsidiary industries of the rope yards, anchorsmiths, manufacturers of rigging, and a host of ancillary crafts. In addition to attracting some of the more disagreeable or dangerous trades, others that needed space or the facilities of running water, such as bleaching or calico printing, spread out beyond what were strictly the boundaries of London, if indeed metropolitan London could be said to have anything so well defined as boundaries, along the banks of the tiny Wandle to Wandsworth and Mithcam. Here too were mills for grinding corn, for tobacco, and for logwood needed for dyeing. Dyers were operating in Southwark itself as well as in Wandsworth. Lambeth was another place where industry tended to thicken. The Fields family had made candles there since the seventeenth century; about 1740 they began to use spermaceti, which gave a much clearer light, for this purpose. The economic development of this district received a boost after the opening of Westminster Bridge. After 1750 Coade's Artificial Stone, so extensively used for decorations by builders in the West End, was made there. In addition various small potteries came into existence.

One of the major capitalistic industries in this period was brewing. Londoners had always been thirsty people, and the

medieval alewife had never lacked customers. Early methods of
brewing called for little outlay, and most taverns and inns either
brewed their own liquor or bought it as required from small local
brewhouses. The malt itself was not manufactured in London;
even by the sixteenth century a group of towns were specializing
in producing it for the London market. Kent provided the hops.
Though the market was extensive and the raw material at hand,
there had been little to tempt the capitalist to organize brewing in
a big way because the ale and beer brewed by the traditional
methods neither kept well nor travelled well. Early in the eighteenth century the situation was changed by a revolution both in
the technique of brewing and in the popular taste. The brewer
discovered that porter, a mixture of the malted ale and hopped
beer, the former sweet and mild and the latter bitter, could be
blended in such a way as both to economize on the more expensive raw materials and to improve its keeping qualities. The new
processes, however, required the liquor to be stored in casks for at
least a year before it was ready to drink. As a result more initial
capital was required to start a brewery, for as much as one third
of it might be tied up in the provision of casks and in the length
of time needed to mature their contents. Though a considerable
number of minor brewers continued to brew table beer and small
beer, they found themselves more and more squeezed out of the
manufacture of porter and of strong beer because of the need for
extensive and well planned premises. When Ralph Thrale bought
the Anchor Brewery in 1729, he is credited with having paid
£30,000 for it, no mean sum. One of the oldest breweries in London was the Red Lion Brewery in Lower East Smithfield, which
had a convenient wharf on the Thames and drew its supplies of
water from a very deep well on its own premises. Its owner,
Alderman Humphrey Parsons, was Lord Mayor twice, once in
1730 and again in 1740. Samuel Whitebread went into the business in 1742 and in 1750 purchased a brewery in Chiswell Street.
By 1760 his establishment had grown into the second largest in
London and by 1786 had passed into the lead. It is interesting to
notice that in the search for the latest methods one of James
Watt's steam engines had been installed. By 1778 the leading
brewers were Whitebread, Thrale, Truman, Sir William, and
Felix Calvert and Hammond. These men who represented both

wealth and power, were busily engaged in buying estates. Though only of yeoman stock, Samuel Whitebread was acquiring property in Bedfordshire from 1761 and, as his second wife, married Lady Mary Cornwallis, the second daughter of Lord Cornwallis. Brewing, therefore, must be regarded as one of the economic careers open to talent, for to be successful a man had to be a complete master of the technical aspects of the trade as well as to possess a good business head. For such a man the rewards were proportionately great. Brewers and distillers alike found it useful to sit in the House of Commons and to build up their political connections. Whitebread represented first the borough of Bedford and then Steyning; William Calvert between 1742 and 1761 represented Old Sarum. Sir Joseph Mawbrey married a Miss Pratt who owned a large distillery at Vauxhall Place in Kennington. At one time he represented Southwark and later was one of the knights of the shire for Surrey. Another famous brewer to represent Southwark was Henry Thrale, the friend of Dr. Johnson, who bent his great talents to providing him with suitable addresses with which to woo his constituents at election time. Taking in their friends and relations, the brewers and distillers of London thus were strongly represented both in the government of the City and in the affairs of the nation.

The importance of London's industry cannot be compared to that of its commerce. Industry was necessary to supply the needs of Londoners, but commerce was the reason why these needs had multiplied and grown. The Thames was the key to the capital's prosperity. A contemporary historian enumerating its advantages described it as "About sixty miles from the Sea and therefore not in Danger of being surprised by the fleets of foreign Enemies; nor is it annoyed by the moist Vapours of the Sea; yet it is near enough to have Ships of the greatest Burthen brought into its very Bosom, by the Help of Tide every Twelve Hours."[12] Foreign visitors were astonished by the amount of shipping that crowded its narrow waters. Because at the beginning of the century some 80 per cent of all England's imports came to London and nearly 74 per cent of her exports left from that port, the congestion was not surprising. As outports like Bristol and Liverpool were devel-

[12]Maitland, *op. cit.*, Vol. 2, p. 713.

oped to handle the Slave Trade and to import the cotton needed for Lanceshire's growing industry these proportions declined somewhat, though the volume of London's seaborne trade grew. In 1700 imports into London were valued at £4,785,000 and exports at £5,388,000; in 1792 they were £12,072,000 and £14,744,000 respectively. It was not of course a steady growth. Trade was enormously affected by the wars of the century: in 1756 imports were less than they had been in 1737. In broad terms, however, the commerce of the port had doubled between 1700 and 1792 and was to double again in the next thirty years.

This growing volume of commerce put a heavy burden on the facilities of London as a port, which were becoming increasingly inadequate. For this at least some of the blame must be put on the continuation of older practices, restrictions, and privileges. The stretch of river between London Bridge, which presented a barrier to further progress upstream to any vessel too large to shoot its arches, and the Tower was the famous Pool of London. Here ships could find safe anchorage and firm banks on which wharfs could be built for the discharge of their cargoes. In 1558, to prevent the evasion of customs duties, a law had been passed which confined the unloading of foreign goods to twenty specified quays. Even here unloading was to be permitted only between sunrise and sunset. The inevitable consequence was the creation of a new monopoly. The ownership of one of these "legal quays," as they came to be called, was a valuable property, and attempts to increase their numbers were energetically resisted, though later "suffrance quays" with restricted privileges had to be allowed. As these quays were all situated between the Tower and London Bridge, a distance of some 1419 feet, the congestion can easily be imagined. The Pool was crowded with shipping—ships with sugar, ships with wine, ships bringing the furs of the Hudson Bay Company, British ships, foreign ships, all had somehow to be accommodated in this restricted space. Custom had imposed some sort of order on this apparent confusion. Most homebound ships anchored between Limehouse and London Bridge. The coasters and small craft got as near to the bridge as possible. Colliers lay between Radcliffe Cross and New Crane Stairs; ships from Hamburg anchored off St. Katherine's Church. Bigger vessels of 300 to 400 tons moored off Deptford while the still larger East Indiamen

anchored between Deptford and Blackwall, from where their
cargoes had to be conveyed to the legal quays in covered barges.
To modern readers the word "port" conjures up a picture of acres
of docks fitted with devices for loading and unloading, but until
the beginning of the nineteenth century London lacked any such
facilities. There was a small wet dock at Blackwall, and at Rotherhithe there was the Howland Great Wet Dock, called after the
family who had once owned the land on which it was situated.
These docks, however, were for repairing ships and not for the
routine business of loading or unloading them. The Howland
Dock, which covered some 10 acres, had a lock 44 feet wide and
150 feet long and at spring tides a depth of 17 feet, which meant
that it could be used by even the largest ships.

To discharge cargoes, the practice was to unload them from
the anchorage in the river into barges and to unload these onto
the legal quays. Even had the system been operated with efficiency and honesty, congestion and delay were inevitable. In addition
to the ships at anchor, space on the crowded Pool had to be found
for some 3500 barges and lighters to ferry the cargoes to and fro.
Labour costs were high as a result of the double loading and
unloading. Also, because of the system of the legal quays vessels
might have to lie in the river for weeks waiting their turn. On
some occasions the confusion was made worse by the fact that the
goods might be piled up on the quays for lack of warehouse
space. This tended to happen at certain periods of the year. The
sugar importers, for instance, had storage space for somewhere
around 32,000 hogsheads, whereas the annual import was between 100,000 and 120,000, most of which arrived within a stretch
of three months. In time of war, when the fleet from the West
Indies sailed in convoy and arrived together, the chaos was at its
peak, with hogsheads piled six to eight feet high on the quays.
Such a system encouraged exploitation of every kind. It was
common knowledge that the first cargoes to reach the saleroom
after the delays of the winter would command the best prices,
and in such circumstances graft and bribery to secure the quick
discharge of the cargo was only to be expected. More open were
the depredations of the river thieves, each specializing in his own
method. There were the River Pirates who cut the lighters adrift
and, when they went ashore, plundered them. Scuffle Hunters

prowled round the quays filching what they could. Watermen of
bad character were known as Night Plunderers; the name is
sufficient description of their activities. Mates of ships and revenue officers, acting in collusion, were nicknamed Light Horsemen;
the Heavy Horsemen were porters and labourers. The Mud Larks
worked with both. The former threw the goods overboard at high
tide, the latter retrieved them from the mudbanks at low tide. In
spite of the persistent pilfering that went on, and in spite of a
parliamentary inquiry, it was not until 1799 that a new dock was
planned on the Isle of Dogs. Over all this confusion the Customs
House, with its end on Thames Street and its front facing the
river, presided like a dignified matron. In its famous Long Room
the commissioners sat with their clerks and officers. Here, too,
were opportunities for graft and bribery. Customs officers were
underpaid for their responsibilities, much of their income being
derived from fees rather than from a salary, and to undervalue a
cargo in return for a consideration was a constant temptation.

Quays specialized in the products landed on them, a choice
often dictated by their immediate economic hinterland. At Billingsgate fish was landed and sold in the nearby market, also salt
and oranges and lemons for the fruiterers. In summer small craft
brought in cherries from Kent. At Smart's quay the principal
cargo was wheat or other grain. The wharf at Puddle Dock must
have been an unsavoury place for it was used as a Laystall for the
soil and rubbish of the streets. Here the lighters and barges came
to collect it and take it away for farmers to use to manure their
fields. The congestion that lay behind the legal quays must have
rivalled that of the river that they served. For goods unloaded at
the quays had to be once again reloaded onto carts, or delivered
to porters, to take them on the next stage of their journey to the
warehouse. Maitland describes Thames Street, which ran from
Puddle Dock east to the Tower, as being "much pestered with
Carts, for lading and unlading of Goods." St. Benet's hill was
similarly congested. Thames Street, which was "inhabited by
large and eminent Dealers in heavy goods,"[13] Leadenhall Street,
and Threadneedle Street were the heart of commercial London,
with so much blood pumping through its narrow arteries that it is

13Maitland, *op. cit.*, Vol. 2, p. 855.

surprising that it managed to function as well as it did, hampered as it was by bad town planning and outdated privileges and practices.

The congestion of the streets was made worse because London's domestic needs were still supplied in large measure by a series of markets in which individual householders might buy if they so desired but which more and more supplied the wholesalers and the shopkeepers. Many of the medieval trading regulations were, in theory at least, still in force. In the fish market at Billingsgate only fishermen, their wives, and apprentices were allowed to sell retail and nobody was permitted to buy and sell again in the same market, the old sin of regrating. In the summer, that is, from Lady Day to Michealmas, the market opened at 4 A.M. and in the winter at 6 A.M., but sprats, herrings, and mackerel could be sold at any hour, so little were they esteemed. Smithfield was "a most capacious Market for black Cattle, Sheep, Horses, Hay and Straw,"[14] and around it were ranged inns for the drovers and "Pens or Folds, so called of Sheep there parted and penned up, to be sold on market Days." Another popular market had been established on the site of the filled-in Fleet Ditch. Here were sold butcher's meat by retail, poultry, fish, herbs, fruits, butter, and cheese. The whole arrangement was pleasant and orderly. "The Stalls range in two Rows of equal height, with a handsome Walk between the whole Length from North to South, and secured from the Weather. In the Centre is a neat Lanthorn with a Clock. The whole is paved with Rag Stones and the Fruiterers' stands are made in the Form of Piazzas, with proper Conveniences to deposit their remaining stock."[15] In the alleys and passages near the markets were further shops—butchers', fishmongers', poulterers', and bacon shops. The markets must have presented a busy and lively scene as citizens' wives or their servants chaffered and bargained over their purchases, but in hot weather no doubt they were fly-ridden places, reeking with the smell of blood and stale fish and better viewed, like so much of Georgian London, from the safe distance or two hundred years.

Many of the commodities discharged at the quays found

[14]*Ibid.*, Vol. 2, p. 987.

[15]*Ibid.*, Vol. 2, p. 989.

their way to these markets and were commodities needed by
Londoners in their daily life. Important among these was coal,
both for domestic use and to provide the fuel for the capital's
industries, many of which consumed considerable quantities. The
yearly amount imported fluctuated between 600,000 and 700,000
tons in the first part of the century, but soared after 1765 to more
than 800,000. Most of this coal was brought from the Tyne and
Wear in colliers, specially built for the trade. On arrival in the
Thames it was unloaded into lighters and stored in yards by the
coal merchants. From there it was distributed in carts to smaller
middlemen. All this shipping, unloading, storing, and distributing
employed substantial capital sums and needed a sizable labour
force. Because of this need for capital, a powerful ring of wealthy
merchants appear to have dominated the trade. Nevertheless, it
would have been difficult for Londoners to have dispensed with
their services because, though the eighteenth-century collier was
stoutly built to withstand the buffetting of the North Sea, bad
storms could delay the arrival of the ships. Moreover, in time of
war there was a danger of enemy action. London therefore required a reserve, particularly from November to March when
demand was briskest and supplies liable to be interrupted. So far
the emphasis has been on imports; the handling of exports put
further pressure on the port's facilities. Many of these were the
products of London's own industries, in particular there was a
considerable export of porter, much of which went to Ireland, but
the majority represented national rather than local productivity.
Even by the fifteenth century London merchants were contriving
to get a stranglehold on the export from the outports of many
branches of the cloth industry. By the sixteenth century Blackwell
Hall was the recognized centre to which foreign buyers and
English exporters alike came to purchase their cloth. By the
eighteenth century the individual country manufacturer bringing
his cloth for sale had been ousted by the factors who now dominated Blackwell Hall. Exporters both foreign and domestic found
this a convenient way of obtaining supplies. The result was a
large export of cloth from London. The grain trade too was dominated by the metropolitan market, which catered both to London's own requirements, to those of the neighbouring counties,

and to the export trade; in good years England still had a surplus for this purpose.

One of the major factors in the commercial life of Britain had been the acquisition and organization of her colonial empire. Within the framework of the Navigation Acts and the Laws of Trade, merchants had built a great commodity market in colonial products. Arthur Young claimed that in 1784 the import of sugar added three million pounds a year to the national wealth, that tobacco contributed a million, and rice only a little less. The figures are an opinion not a satistical exercise, nor did London have the monopoly of the trade, but the statement does reflect the important role that was accorded to the colonial trade. The list was not confined to these major imports; dyewoods of every kind and timber for furniture, for housing, and for shipbuilding were also important. In so far as colonial produce found a market in Europe and could be reexported to other countries, it was argued that it made a substantial contribution to the achieving of a favourable balance of trade. Gradually however, partly because of the increase in population and partly because more raw material was being processed in Britain, the home market came to absorb more and more of the cargoes discharged at the port. For example, in the second decade of the century at least one quarter of the raw sugar was reexported, but even when Johnson first came to London the increase in the amount of sugar refining, together with the increased consumption as standards of living rose, combined to reduce reexports drastically. The increased competition from the French West Indian sugar islands, which had lessened European demand, had a similar effect.

Whether the ultimate destination was British or Continental, London continued to be the great centre for the handling of the sugar crop of the British Caribbean Islands. In the spring, when the sugar fleet arrived, there was a great bustle as the hogsheads were unloaded, for after the long winter the sugar refiners were anxious to replenish their stocks and, as has already been said, the first casks ashore secured the highest prices. The responsibility for supplying the market devolved on certain merchant houses which acted as sugar factors, handling on commission either the sugar directly consigned to them from the planters or that bought by local West Indian merchants and shipped by them to London. The factors paid the freight and duty on the sugar, contracted the brokers, and through them sold either to the sugar refiners or to the grocers. It was important to sell as promptly as possible for the planters, without waiting to hear what their consignment had fetched, were in the habit of drawing bills on their London factors in order to meet their other commitments or to finance the goods that they wanted sent out to their plantations. Here again personal relations were the order of the day. The London factor was more than a mere handler of the planter's crop. To some extent he acted as his banker, handling his bills and providing him with loans for the extension of his estate or the increase or replenishment of his slave labour force. He was also his man of business in more personal ways. If the son of the planter were finishing his education or embarking on a social career in London, the probabilities were that the sugar factor would be payng school bills or meeting the expenses of the young man about town out of the sale of the sugar. His might be the responsibility for choosing a new gown for the planter's lady or for selecting the latest fashion in tea things. To succeed a factor needed both credit and judgement, for the market was apt to fluctuate wildly, particularly in time of war or when storms in the Atlantic held up supplies. In imagination one can recreate a day in a sugar factor's life. There would be correspondence to deal with that ranged from querulous complaints from the planter about the price obtained for the last consignment to requests to restrain the extravagance of a young son at present visiting England. Coffeehouses would have to be frequented to find out the latest news about the arrival of shipping or the possibilities of war with France or, more mundane but of everyday importance, to find the broker whose connections were likely to be most helpful in disposing of a particular load of sugar. If credit were strained or money had to be laid out, it might be necessary to get bills discounted or to get a loan on the security of the unsold sugar. Before a London grocer sold a pound of the coarsest sugar to the goodwife of some artisan or supplied the steward of a great house with sugar of the best quality, the highly organized London commodity market had been called into play.

This illustration has been taken from the sugar trade, but

every major commodity had its special organization. In general, the handling of each product that was the property of an overseas planter was dominated by some variation of the factor, with his expert knowledge of the London market. In the tobacco trade the handling of the leaf was further complicated by the fact that much of it was reexported, involving much reckoning of drawbacks and the possibility of a good bit of sharp practice. Some of this might have been eliminated if Sir Robert Walpole's attempt to transfer the collection of the duties on it from the customs to the excise had been allowed to go forward, but the measure, which was opposed for political even more than economic reasons, had to be dropped. Apart from matters of taxation, colonial opinion was extremely critical of the way in which the tobacco crop was handled, believing that the merchants who were engaged in the reexport trade were diverting into their own pockets an undue proportion of the profits. In this they probably overestimated the elasticity of the foreign market and underestimated the skill needed to handle it, for after 1783 the American exporters found that they could not at first get as good a price as the London handlers had obtained. The marketing of tea was dictated by the fact that its import both from India and from China was the monopoly of the East India Company. Tea sales were held four times a year when conditions were normal—in March, June, September, and December. The initial buyers were the tea brokers who bought for the group of tea merchants for whom they were acting.

The levers controlling this empire of trade were concentrated in the City. The machinery was complicated, with many interlocking parts, for economic functions were not as clearly differentiated as they were to become later. Men could at once be merchants, bankers, underwriters, and shipowners, using their capital wherever the prospect of profit seemed likely. This overlapping of function makes it difficult to describe the way in which the City provided the services that British commerce needed. In the main it was a question of providing credit, facilitating international payments, and bringing together the men who could do this and the men who required their services. Some method of insurance was also necessary—insurance against loss by fire at home and loss by shipwreck or enemy action at sea. Amid the seeming confusion four institutions stood out: the Bank of England, the East India Company, the South Seas Company, and much later, Lloyd's of London. At the centre of the financial system stood the Bank of England,[16] which had been founded in 1694 to lend money to the government during William III's wars with France. Its connection with the administration had always been close, and it had been able to use the latter's financial difficulties to secure for itself in 1707 the monopoly of joint stock banking, which gave it a command of capital that no private bank could rival. Its position was further strengthened by the fact that no bank with more than six partners was allowed to issue paper money. By the thirties the Bank had surmounted its earlier difficulties and occupied a commanding position in the world of finance. In 1781 Lord North described it as part of the constitution. Its government was in the hands of a General Court, a Court of Directors and a Governor and Deputy Governor, but for most of the century the control seems to have rested with the Governor and the company's Committee of Treasury, though, as always throughout the century, the personality of individual directors was important, especially when particular interests had to be pushed or safeguarded. In the first half of the century the Bank concentrated its interests more on public and quasi-public than on private business, but in the second half its private business, particularly that concerned with the discounting of bills, grew rapidly. The Bank both made loans to the government on the security of the taxes and floated public ones. Lending to the government was a profitable business. In particular, individuals within the charmed circle did well out of the fact that the Bank was authorized to contract with others for furnishing money to provide cash for the payment of Exchequer bills. The sum of £1,-500,000 was normally raised for this purpose, but in practice it was rare for more than 10 per cent of the sum nominally subscribed to be called up, though there might be calls in panic years like 1745 when London was threatened by the advancing forces of the Young Pretender. As the interest was paid on the nominal subscription, there is little wonder that the Court of Directors

[16]See Sir John Clapham, *The Bank of England,* Vol. 1 (Cambridge University Press, 1944).

limited the right to take part in "The Subscription for the Circulation" to its own members and to the company's servants. When
public loans were to be floated, it was the Bank that haggled with
the Treasury over the terms to be offered and that secured a
generous allotment of stock for its Directors and their friends,
many of whom made large fortunes. That this was bitterly resented by those who were not "friends to government" or within the
inner ring, there is no doubt. This indeed, as a subsequent examination of the politics of the City will seek to show, was one of the
great strains to which it was subjected. Yet to take the attacks of
the Bank's enemies at their face value is less than fair. The Bank
was not a philanthropic institution, and by mobilizing the resources of some of London's wealthiest citizens, by making loans,
circulating government paper, paying annuities, making remit-
tances overseas in times of war, issuing a reliable paper currency,
through its circulation seems to have been limited to a sixty mile
radius of London, and acting as a reserve for bullion, it was per-
forming services the lack of which would have most seriously
hampered the expansion of trade and of empire that did in fact
characterize the eighteenth century.

Not all shareholders could hope for these opportunities for
gain. Five hundred pounds of stock was necessary to entitle the
holder to vote in the General Court; after 1771 this had to be held
for six months in order to prevent rigging the vote on controversial issues by a fictitious sale of shares. A Director had to hold
£2000 and a Governor £4000. In terms of eighteenth-century
purchasing power these were large sums of money and insured
that the men who directed policy would feel the results of their
decisions in their own pockets. By the middle of the century 3294
persons were eligible to vote. They were drawn from many
sources. The majority were private gentlemen and London citizens whose money came from trade or industry. But Bank stock
was regarded, and rightly so regarded, as an excellent security,
and the aristocracy was well represented. Not all the stock was
held by individuals. It was a useful investment for corporate
funds: city companies and Cambridge colleges, even the Society
for the Propragation of the Gospel, held Bank stock. So did foreign investors, particularly those from Holland. Sir John Clapham
has estimated that some 1000 of the stockholders entitled to vote

in 1751 were Dutch, many of them not merchants, as might have been expected, but noblemen and gentlemen. Despite these foreign investors and a sprinkling of individuals and corporations from the English provinces, most of the stock was held by Londoners.

It was not, however, the Bank of England to which they looked for the ordinary day-to-day financial services that they required. With some exceptions the Bank of England was not interested in catering to the needs of private individuals. This function was left to a group of private bankers whose antecedents went back to the seventeenth century and whose growing numbers and technical skills were developed in response to the needs of the eighteenth. The stimulus came from two directions—the landed gentry and the business community. Because of the dissimilarity of their needs, London bankers tended to concentrate on either one or the other type of business. Even in the world of banking social fissures were deep. The more wealthy a landowner was, the greater his need for financial facilities in London, because either as a member of the Lords or of the Commons he was likely to spend an appreciable part of each year in the capital. It is perhaps not a coincidence that two of the most popular banks to handle this kind of business were Hoare's and Child's both of them descended from the seventeenth-century goldsmiths whose strong rooms and loans had been so useful to their aristocratic customers. By the eighteenth century their banks were flourishing concerns with premises in Fleet Street. At a time when the wealth of the landowning classes was drawn from their rent rolls rather than from direct participation in farming, stewards arranged for these to be transferred to London, where they could be drawn upon with ease. Many landowners had additional sources of income from their estates. Some controlled coal mines or drew royalties from them. Others possessed quarries or iron ore deposits or lead or copper mines. Woodland and coppice were a profitable source of revenue. Those who were lucky enough, as were the Bedfords, the Berkeleys, and the Cavendishes, to own the land over which London was extending made money from ground rents and leases and development schemes. In the aggregate it was no mean stream of money that flowed into such banks as Hoare's and Childs's. Much of it flowed out again in the form of personal loans and loans on mortgages. Many of these were no doubt to tide over the lean period before the next installment of rents was due. Others were to meet some particular financial emergency—a marriage settlement or a funeral or, perhaps even more common, a gambling debt. After a disastrous night at White's many a man, and woman too, was forced to seek such accommodation. In contrast many mortgages were for productive purposes. The eighteenth century was the century of the great improving landlord, and money invested in better buildings and more adequately drained land in the long run spelled higher rents and more prosperous farms. Better transport also contributed to greater ease speed in bringing agricultural produce to market or coal to an expanding island town. Child's, for example, helped the Duke of Bridgewater to finance the construction of his famous canal. In other ways, too, the banks helped their aristocratic or country clients with their investments, buying stock for them and collecting their dividends. The political and social life of the West End relied to an extent not often realized on the bankers who managed its often involved financial affairs.

The activities, and in many cases the origins, of those bankers who concentrated on the needs of commerce were very different. Most of them were located in and around Lombard Street, the financial heart of the City. Like the banks of the West End, many of the older houses originally had been practising goldsmiths, though by the eighteenth century this side of their activities had withered away. The newer ones were more likely to have grown out of some commercial partnership, the tendency being for well established merchant houses to specialize more and more in financial services and less and less in the actual handling of import and export commodities. By this time credit had long provided the sinews of trade, and the creation of credit and the payment of overseas debts were two of the vital services of the London bankers. In other words, their function was to concentrate available financial resources in those places and at those times when they could be most profitably employed. In particular city bankers specialized in discounting bills and making loans and advances to commercial or industrial enterprises. Many of them, like Martin's, handled business for country customers, crediting them with bills drawn on London or accepted by a sound London house. Some of the newcomers traced their origin to such business. Linen merchants like Barclay's or ironmongers like Lloyd's, whose financial business was extensive enough both in quality and geographical location to need a London agent, began by obliging their business associates by handling this type of transaction for them and ended by establishing their own headquarters in the City, thus becoming full-fledged bankers themselves. Their customers were drawn from almost every economic activity— from the prominent merchant or Blackwell Hall factor to the small tradesman.

Eighteenth-century banking was a highly personal business and depended on the property and financial acumen of three or four partners. The type of business done was considerably influenced by the interests and connections of these partners. For example, Francis Gosling, who had been a printer and bookseller in Fleet Street, attracted the custom of literary men. Both Edward Gibbon and Samuel Richardson banked with him. In 1743 he took as a partner Samuel Bennet, a wealthy East India merchant who dealt in diamonds. Through him the firm built up a useful East India connection; Clive and Warren Hastings both had accounts there. In a similar way the banker Richard Glyn, who was a drysalter dealing in dyes and chemicals, used his connection with the silk trade to whom he sold his dyes. This was strengthened still further when he married as his second wife the daughter of a wealthy silk mercer of Ludgate Hill. Because of the personal nature of eighteenth-century banking, partnerships were always changing. The early history of Barclay's illustrates this well. The original founder was not a Barclay but one John Freame, a goldsmith who traded at the sign of the Black Spread Eagle in Lombard Street. His father-in-law Thomas Gould was a banker, and his daughter Sally married James Barclay in 1733. Her brother Joseph then went into partnership with James Barclay, whose father was a prominent city merchant. John Barclay, Joseph's younger son, joined the partnership, which became Freame, Barclay, and Freame. In 1766 both James Barclay and John Freame died, and the partnership was reconstructed, becoming Freame, Smith, and Benning. Then six years later David Barclay Junior was taken into partnership, and the firm became Barclay, Bevan, and Benning. It is not necessary to follow further the fortunes of the business, which eventually was to achieve, under the control of the Barclay family, the status of a great bank.

Merchants with wide international connections did not necessarily look toward banking for the extension of their profits. To specialize in foreign exchange could be equally attractive, and by the eighteenth century the exchange broker, who for a commission dealt in bills of exchange, had a recognized place in city finance. Merchants requiring such accommodation had only to go to one of the coffeehouses, such as Jonathan's, where the dealers congregated, in order to find a reputable broker. Some merchants, among other activities, engaged in underwriting, as the business of insuring ships was called. Sir John Barnard, so prominent in the city's politics, included this among his other activities. It was out of this type of business that another great financial institution was born, the now world-famous Lloyd's.[17] It was very much the child of the circumstances of its time. Commerce depended on the safe passage of the ships that brought the imports and sailed away with their holds full of goods for export. This required a considerable fleet, for voyages both to distant countries and to nearby British ports; wherever possible goods were sent by sea rather than by road, for which the rates were high and the danger of breakage for fragile goods great. The shipowners themselves were a wealthy and influential body. The hazards that faced their vessels were considerable and twofold. There was always the chance of storms and of wrecks. Five hundred tons was a ship of respectable burthen, but five hundred tons in an Atlantic storm, with the sails in shreds and the decks swept by heavy seas, was a mere puppet in the hands of the gale. Lack of charts in some areas, reefs, fog, all took their toll. Added to the risks of nature were the activities of man. There was always some risk of piracy, so that most ships of any size carried a few guns and were prepared to make a fight of it. But the greatest hazard of all was war. For long stretches throughout the century France and Britain, with Spain playing an occasional hand, were struggling for overseas colonies and the command of the sea. Between 1740 and 1763, with a short intermission after the peace of Aix-la-Chapelle in 1748, and again during the American War of Independence the

[17]See D. E. W. Gibb, *Lloyd's of London* (Macmillan, 1957)

losses in shipping were heavy. The idea of protecting one's self against such crippling blows by insurance was not new; the contribution of the eighteenth century was to systematize it. The early practice was for the broker, in eighteenth-century parlance known as an office keeper, on being approached by a shipowner, to arrange insurance, that is, to make the rounds of those men most likely to underwrite some proportion of the ship in question. There was at this time no one place where underwriters were to be found, though the likeliest area was in the vicinity of the Exchange. Nor was there any effective check on their reliability. Indeed an office keeper, anxious to complete a deal and trusting that an evil fate would never put the worth of the signatures to the test, was sometimes tempted for the sake of the commission to add unsound or even fictitious names. Partly because this could be a genuine abuse and partly because shrewd men, including Sir Robert Walpole, saw a profit to be made, during the wave of speculation associated with the South Seas Bubble in 1720, two joint stock companies, The Royal Exchange Insurance Corporation and the London Assurance Company were chartered to provide a more solid financial backing for marine insurance. At the beginning individual brokers were dismayed, supposing that the new creations would put them out of business. As in the case of the Bank of England and the private bankers, this did not happen. The two new companies more and more specialized in fire rather than marine insurance.

With the growing demand for effective and sound marine insurance, good organization was as necessary as the legal right to operate. This grew, half by chance, half by design, around Lloyd's coffeehouse. No one can study eighteenth-century London for long without coming across the ubiquitous coffeehouse. In the West End its purpose was social, in Covent Garden and Fleet Street theatrical and literary, in St. Martin's Lane artistic. In the City coffeehouses were the nerve centres of the business world. West Indian merchants met at the Jamaican Coffee House; the Jerusalem Coffee House was the gathering place for men interested in the Indian and China trade. Garraways in Exchange Alley had an early connection with tea. By 1691 Lloyd's in Lombard Street was beginning to collect clients whose main interests lay in the movement of ships. Its proprietor pioneered an early newssheet that carried information about shipping in 1693, and though this proved premature and was discontinued three years later, a newssheet was again issued in 1740 and rapidly became recognized as a reliable source of information. Because of the services that Lloyd's Coffee House provided, brokers knew that there they would find men ready to underwrite their ships, and shipowners knew that there they would find the leading brokers. Its importance in the shipping world however was completely unofficial. Nor was there any guarantee that all its customers were competent brokers or even financially sound men. Moreover, because Lloyd's was a personal concern, its fortunes fluctuated with the abilities and shrewdness of its proprietor. In 1763 it had passed into the control of Thomas Lawrence, who unfortunately lacked the hardheaded commonsense of its earlier owners. London at this time was in the clutches of a gambling mania. The betting books at places like White's were full of wagers of a personal and completely incalculable nature. It was, for instance, fashionable to lay odds for or against the recovery of some well known invalid or to bet on the future sex of an unborn child. Under Lawrence, Lloyd's became badly infected by this craze. It was beginning to attract the wrong sort of patron, and the sober businessmen who came there were increasingly alienated. Apart from this somewhat ephemeral circumstance, there was also a growing feeling among them that a meeting place open to anybody, whatever his standing, no longer served their purpose. It was therefore decided to break away and start a new coffeehouse. Their first quarters in Pope's Head Alley proved too small, and a committee was elected to find bigger premises. This was not easy, for the pressure on accommodation in the City was heavy. However, in 1773 the splinter group finally managed to secure two rooms over the Royal Exchange, in many ways an ideal location in the heart of the business world. The next step was to organize it as a club with a recognized membership. The entrance fee, which was intended to keep out men of straw, was fixed at £5, with an annual subscription that varied from 2 to 4 guineas. Apart from this, there seems to have been remarkably little vetting of members for the remainder of the century. It is surprising that there were so few failures, for though the brokers and underwriters had now an official club, the actual risks were borne, then as now, by individuals and partnerships. Lloyd's was not, and did not become, a corporate body, and the strain of war with the American colonies was to prove a heavy one. In 1779, according to its register, 656 ships were captured by the enemy, and in the following year a major disaster occurred. A convoy of sixty-three merchant ships was intercepted by the joint fleets of France and Spain, and only five escaped. On this occasion many of Lloyd's underwriters found that they could not meet their obligations. Nevertheless, in spite of the occasional failure and in spite of all the pressure of war, the number of members continued to grow. Nor was their business confined to British ships, even in time of war. National enemities were still considered more the concerns of government and of professional armies and navies than of businessmen, and until after the turn of the century a surprising amount of trade and business took place between countries that were at war with one another.

Another important pillar supporting the economic life of the City was the East India Company.[18] Its ramifications were so wide that there was hardly an activity of any kind that was not in some way influenced by it. Financially the Company was entangled with the Bank of England and the government. It was itself an issuer of bonds, it represented a large segment of London's overseas trade, and it employed, in one capacity or another, many of London's citizens. Both in City politics and in those of the nation it played a considerable part. It was at once a finance and a trading corporation, although, unlike the South Seas Company, its trade was the base of its power. After a somewhat chequered career in the seventeenth century and after a period of bitter rivalry between the Old and the New Company at the close of the century, the union of the two companies in 1709 had led to a period of prosperous trading under the first two Georges. Up to the middle of the eighteenth century it had remained essentially a trading company, though even then its wealth had made it a factor in politics. With the victories of Clive and the acquisition of Bengal, combined with the defeat of the French, its character was drastically changed. Although its aim still was to manage and

[18]See L. M. Sutherland, *The East India Company in Eighteenth Century Politics* (Clarendon Press, 1952).

organize its trading activities, its hold over Bengal thrust new administrative responsibilities upon it and entangled it irrevocably with government politics, dragging it into the rivalries and controversies of the day. Its London headquarters were at East India House on the southeast side of Leadenhall Street. The old building, which had been in great danger of falling down, had been replaced in 1729 by a handsome new one designed by Theodore Jansen, who also designed the Foundling Hospital. Because of the limitations of the site, though the front had been enlarged, the building was still narrow in proportion to its depth. It was described as "supported by six Doric pilsters on a rustic basement storey. There are two series of plain windows in the inter columniations, and the top is finished with a balistrare." At the back was a garden and warehouses with an entrance for carts that opened into Lime Street. Inside the building there was a magnificent courtroom with a notable overmantle carved by Rysbrack that depicted Britannia seated on the seashore receiving the offerings of India. Here the Court met every Wednesday.

The executive power of the Company was vested in a Governor, a Deputy Governor, and a Court of twenty four Directors elected by the Court of Propriators. The Propriators were the holders of East India stock, and in the early days of the Company anyone holding stock was entitled to vote. But when other considerations beside the primary one of choosing the best men to manage the trade of the Company became of increasing importance, because of the pressure of politics, the right to vote was hedged around with qualifications. To prevent the splitting of holdings of stock in order to create a majority of votes for some political maneuvre or appointment, stock had to be held for at least six months. After 1773 it was necessary to hold £1000 worth in order to vote, though £500 entitled a holder to be present. A holding of £3000 carried with it two votes, £6000 three votes, and £10,000 four. In addition to electing the Directors, the Court framed bylaws and declared the dividend, sometimes against the advice of the directors. It was an august assembly: its procedure was based on that of the House of Commons, and, like that house at times, it indulged in some disorderly and acrimonious debates. Its Directors were always men of substance. Although men were not permitted to hold directorships in both the Bank and the East

India Company, the links between the two were close. The East India Company kept its balances at the Bank and borrowed from it the necessary loans to tide it over until its cargoes could be sold. It also went into the loan market itself, issuing Indian Bonds in order to provide itself with short-term credit. Because these bonds were negotiable and of convenient denominations, they were popular with investors at a time when the issue of stocks was in short supply. Both as men of fortune themselves and as representatives of the combined resources of the Company, individual directors therefore were influential figures in the financial circles of the City. Like the directors of the Bank, they belonged to that inner ring which handled government loans and received preferential treatment for so doing. In its corporate capacity the Company enjoyed considerable patronage, for each one of its functions involved the employment of many persons. East India House had to be staffed with clerks, porters, and warehouse men; it needed the services of carters and packers to deal with the muslins and calicoes, the silks, the pepper, spices, and tea that it imported. It had warehouses scattered throughout the City. In addition to those in the rear of East India House, there was a Bengal warehouse in New Street, saltpetre was kept at Cock Hill, pepper was stored under the Royal Exchange, bale goods at Cutler Street, tea in Fenchurch Street and other warehouses, spices in a second warehouse in Leadenhall Street. The large number of employes on the London staff was supplemented by those required for its overseas factories in Madras, Calcutta, and Bombay. Unhealthy and even dangerous as such posts would be, they were sought after because of the chance to make money that went with them. Though not well paid as far as basic salary went, one of their perquisites was the opportunity for private trade. Whether at home or abroad, therefore, employment with the Company was a source of gain for many Londoners. One of Dr. Johnson's circle worked for the Company. Today John Hoole would hardly be considered a city type. His father had been a watchmaker in Moor fields, but because the son's eyes were not thought to be strong enough for such fine work, his father obtained for him a clerkship in the accountant's office in the October of 1744 when he was hardly seventeen. From there he rose to be Auditor of the Company; it was he who had the formidable task of producing most of the accounts called for in the parliamentary inquiry of 1772 and 1773. Like a more famous East India clerk after him, Charles Lamb, his interests were literary. He had a taste for languages and in 1763 was working on a translation of Ariosto's *Orlando Furioso,* of which the Doctor thought highly.

In addition to the people employed directly by the Company, it was also closely allied to the shipping interest. Because of the length of the voyages and the value of the cargoes carried, the East Indiamen had to be specially built for the trade. Since the seventeenth century the Company had not owned its own ships, but the supplying of their needs had grown into a monopoly among certain of the shipowners. This was known as the system of permanent bottoms. When a ship was lost or grew too old for service, its owner had the privilege of building and supplying a replacement, and because the tendency was for the number of ships necessary for the trade to be overestimated for normal demand, it was all but impossible for a new owner to break into this monopolistic circle. The commanders of the East Indiamen were also organized on an exclusive basis. In addition to the shipowners there were the ship's husbands, the managers who made arrangements for the provisioning of the ships and the handling of the cargoes. This group of owners, commanders, and ships' husbands between them made up a wealthy and influential sector of the City and were sometimes known as the Company's Household Troops. If in any way its interests were threatened, they could be mobilized in its defence. The subsidiary interests of the East Indiamen shipping group were even more widely flung. There were the men who built the ships at Rotherhithe, with all the master draftsmen and apprentices, carpenters, shipwrights, sailmakers, rope yard owners and workers, gunsmiths and the ships' chandlers who supplied provisions. There were the crews who sailed in them, the lighter crews who loaded and unloaded them, the carters and porters who brought their cargoes to the warehouses. There is little wonder that the influence of the East India Company was substantial and that politicians, within or out of office, schemed to be able to direct its flow.

Less important than either the Bank or the East India Company but far from negligible in the economic fabric of the City was the South Seas Company. This, like the Bank of England, had been chartered to lend money to the government, the bait to its shareholders being the supposed profits that would accrue to it on the opening up of trade with the South Seas at the end of the war of the Spanish Succession. As a trading company it never even began to equal the East India Company, and its profits in this sphere remained modest. The hopes that men had once cherished of its so doing had exploded in the gigantic confidence trick known to history as the South Seas Bubble. Nevertheless, as a large government creditor it had a place to play in City finance, and once the chaos of the Bubble had been sorted out, its stock was one of the few open to the investing public, then largely limited in any case to London and to foreign investors. Like in the East India Company, its affairs were managed by a Governor, a Deputy Governor, and, after the act of 1753, twenty-one Directors. There were the usual regulations to make certain that the men who were in command of the affairs of the company should themselves have a substantial stake in it. Under the terms of the original charter the Governor and his Deputy were to hold £5000 worth of stock and the Directors £3000. Its headquarters, South Seas House, was situated at the northeast end of Threadneedle Street, a magnificent building described as centering in "a Quadrangle supported by stone pillars of the Tuscan order, which form a fine Piazza. There is a beautiful front of the Doric Order in Threadneedle Street. . . . The several Offices for the Business of the Company are admirably well disposed; and the great Hall for Sales, the Drawing Room, Galleries and Chambers can hardly be parallelled."[19] Although its patronage was less extensive than that of the East India Company, both in the number of persons in its employment and in the shipping that it required, its Director must be regarded as among the important financial magnates of the City, who together with those of the Bank of England and the East India Company made up the financial trinity! The remaining chartered companies trading overseas, such as the Royal Africa Company, the Levant Company, and the Hudson Bay Company, were less influential, though all had their part to play in the interlocking economic activities of the City.

Some of the shrewdest and most imaginative business brains in the eighteenth-century world of commerce and finance were to

[19]Maitland, op. cit., Vol. 2, p. 848.

be found among the men who between them controlled the desti-
nies of the City. Without their enterprise and their exertions the
colonial empire would never have assumed the proportions that it
did, and France might well have been victor in the long rivalries
between the two countries. It was fashionable among the "ton" of
the West End to sneer politely at those who, having served the
onerous and expensive office of Lord Mayor, might be knighted
on the presentation of some loyal address from the City, and to
dub them "city knights." But if ever men had earned an honour
for "services rendered" to the economy of their country, these
men had. The sovereign at least gave recognition of this fact. At
Barclay's house in Cheapside, just opposite the Church of Mary-
le-Bow, both George II and George III were occasional guests.
On a visit to the City in 1761 the latter and his Queen deigned to
take of refreshments in the back parlour and the kitchen, which
had been elegantly arranged for the occasion. George III even
showed a sympathetic consideration for Mr. Barclay's Quaker
principles by letting him kiss the royal hand without kneeling. On
more than one occasion both he and his grandfather watched the
colourful and tumultuous Lord Mayor's Show from the balcony of
the Barclay house. Benjamin Truman, the brewer, was another
city magnate to be honoured with a knighthood, given in recognition of his patriotic contribution of a large sum to the loan for
carrying on the war against France.

Such was the London to which Samuel Johnson came, in
which he lived, and where he died. It was a busy bustling and
incredibly noisy place, where the creaking of the signs above the
shops and houses, which were not furnished with the convenience
of numbers until the seventies, the clatter of horses' hooves on the
cobbled streets, and the cries of the street vendors and ballad
singers must have seemed to the newcomer an intolerable and
earsplitting din. Yet behind the noise and babble, behind the dirt
and congestion of the streets, the business of creating the national
wealth was going on. To it each stratum of the busy community
was contributing something—the porter and the labourer his
manual strength, the craftsman his industry and his skill, the
merchant and banker the control and direction and the capital—
without which London could never have become one of the
richest cities in Europe.

THREE

The City of London: Its Government and Politics

From earliest times the City had been a centre of trade, with all its interests geared to this main purpose. As in all medieval cities, the first essential had been the elimination of direct royal control in order to evade the arbitrary actions and financial exactions of the king's officers. Because of the wealth that London's citizens had accumulated, they were able to bargain with needy rulers. As early as 1131 Henry I had allowed them to choose their own chief magistrate and to undertake the farming of the county of Middlesex. Every time the state of the royal finances made the king susceptible to a bribe, Londoners increased their privileges. So step by step the City became a self-governing entity. Because trade was its lifeblood, its privileges and the organization of its government were contrived to secure the maximum of control for the men who already controlled its trade and whose wealth depended on it. The result was a series of privileges and responsibilities graded with rough accuracy to the economic position of its inhabitants.

Numerically the majority of them were excluded, as indeed they would have been elsewhere in this period, from all share in local affairs. The accepted stratification of society was justification enough for this. In eighteenth-century eyes the manual workers, dockers, labourers, porters, and pedlars who made up a casual and drifting population with no fixed abode beyond that of a

The southwest prospect of London. Notice the commanding position of St. Paul's, the spires of the City churches, the shipping in the Thames, and the many stairs down to the river.

rented room were unfit for any responsibility. The next layer was composed of men who were householders in the City but not citizens. Citizenship was an exclusive and prized status. Every one of London's privileges had been bought at a heavy price, and in return for the money the men who provided it expected to receive specific rights. One of the most valued of these was the right to buy and sell and to follow a trade free of arbitrary exactions. Such rights were necessarily exclusive ones: in their monopoly against the stranger lay half their value. By the eighteenth century in smaller cities the rights of the freemen, as the full citizens were called because they were free of the liberties of the city, had in this respect been much invaded, but in the City of London they were jealously preserved. Only a freeman had the right to practice his trade or to open a shop within its boundaries. He had other privileges also. He was free from certain tolls. He qualified for certain City charities, of which there were many, and he could not be seized by the press gang. Citizenship could be acquired either by birth or by becoming a member of one of the City companies through apprenticeship or purchase. The latter provision, by which a rich man could buy his freedom in any company that was prepared to accept him as a member, was necessary to give some flexibility to what otherwise might have been too inbred a system.

Noncitizen householders, therefore, had very restricted rights of self-government. The City, like the rest of the country, was divided into parishes, whose churches, as we have seen, were a prominent feature of its architecture, but for purposes of City government it was divided into twenty-six wards. These were divided into precincts, each containing roughly a hundred houses. Householders who were ratepayers were entitled to take some part in the management of their own precinct. They were also entitled to vote in the ward court when the business before it was solely concerned with the internal affairs of the ward, such as the annual election of the beadle, constable, and inquest jurymen. If chosen for any of these offices, they had an obligation to serve and could be fined if they did not. But when the wardmote, as the meeting of the ward was traditionally called, dealt with matters that concerned the City government they had no right to vote. This was reserved for the freemen, who in Dr. Johnson's time numbered between 12,000 and 15,000 and who played an important part in the government of the City, because the wardmote chose both the Common Councillors and the aldermen, who between them were largely responsible for its running. By the eighteenth century the main organs of government were the Common Hall, the Common Council, and the Court of Aldermen. Its chief officers were the Lord Mayor, two Sheriffs, one of whom was the Sheriff for Middlesex, the Recorder, who was the City's main legal adviser, and the Chamberlain or City treasurer. Below them came a host of minor officials chosen in Common Hall by the major livery companies—the Mercers, Grocers, Drapers, Fishmongers, Goldsmiths, Skinners, Merchant Taylors, Haberdashers, Salters, Ironmongers, Vintners, and Clothworkers.

Originally the Common Hall had been a meeting of all the freemen, but with the growth of the City even by the thirteenth century so large a gathering had become impracticable for this purpose and attendance had been limited by successive ordinances until it had been confined to the members of liveries that numbered roughly 8000. These were summoned to the Guildhall by the Lord Mayor via the wardens of their respective companies. To prevent unauthorized persons' gaining admittance, each company went through a specially erected wicket gate guarded by the company's beadle. Annually on September 29 elections were held for the officers of Lord Mayor, the Sheriffs, and the City Chamberlain. Except in moments of extreme political tension, the choice of the Lord Mayor was traditional and formal. To be eligible the candidate had to be an alderman and had to have served as Sheriff. From the persons so qualified the Common Hall chose two candidates whose names were then submitted to the Court of Aldermen; the more senior of these candidates was almost automatically chosen, though occasionally when political feeling ran high in the City the senior alderman might be passed over in favour of his junior runner-up. In addition to electing the Lord Mayor, the Common Hall also chose the Sheriffs. This was an expensive and burdensome office, which may have been one reason for decreeing that a man must serve it before being eligible for the great dignity of Lord Mayor. Having been chosen, the Sheriff elect had to appear before the Lord Chamberlain and give a bond that he would duly appear and take the necessary oaths on the September 28 before the formal appointment on the following day. A man who refused could be fined £400. On occasions this liability was used as something of a racket. When it was decided that the City must have a Mansion House, men were deliberately chosen who would rather pay the fine than serve, and the money was then invested at 3 per cent. The office of Chamberlain was more lucrative and had less burdensome duties attached to it than that of Sheriff and was in consequence more popular.

The office of Lord Mayor was one of great dignity and was the pride of the City. It was, however, very expensive, few men served more than one term. During that year the Lord Mayor took precedence over everyone except the sovereign within the City's limits. If the sovereign had occasion to visit the City, it was the Lord Mayor who met him with ceremony at Temple Bar. Outside the City the Lord Mayor ranked next to the privy councillors. No troops could pass through the City without his permission, and he was given the nightly password for the Tower. Furthermore, he was privileged to request a royal audience, at which he was entitled to present an address in person and receive a reply from the royal lips. This was no empty privilege; it could be, and on occasion was, used to give publicity to the views of the City on the political issues of the day. Very little of importance in the City's government could go on without the presence of the Lord Mayor. He summoned and presided over the Court of Aldermen, the Common Council, the Common Hall, and the Court of Hustings, and the selection of business before them was under his control. He was a judge as well as an administrator, sitting each day at the Mansion House in his capacity as a justice of the peace. All this dignity and power was dramatized in the celebrations and festivities that accompanied his assumption of office. Foreign visitors were much impressed by them. Archenholtz describes how on "The day in which he takes possession of his charge, which is a day of great festivity in London, he goes in procession to Westminster Hall, where the oaths are administered to him by the Lord Chancellor. The procession is made for part of the way by water, in boats splendidly decorated, and accompanied by a crowd of other boats; a spectacle which has a good deal of resemblance to that of the annual marriage of the Doge of Venice with the Sea. They land at Blackfriar Bridge where they

The Mansion House. The Lord Mayor's coach is in the foreground.

are met and are attended by all the corporation of London to the Guildhall."[1] It was a splendid sight: the windows along route were crammed with people, the houses were all decorated, and the City companies marched behind their streaming banners. Some were so large that it took four boys to carry them. Different companies of the City Guards lined the streets, and the Mayor himself was preceded by a company of Artillery. In the evening he gave a great banquet at the Mansion House. On the occasion of the first Lord Mayor's installation after the coronation of a new monarch, it was customary for the king to attend in person. Count Kielmansegge tells how he drove to the City "in a state coach drawn by eight splendid cream coloured stallions which had come that summer from Hanover and accompanied by the secretaries of state and principal officers of the court, in seven or eight carriages, and escorted by all the Life Guards, mounted grenadiers, gentlemen pensioners, Yeomen of the Guard and liveried servants."[2]

The office of Lord Mayor was no magnificent sinecure. Governing the City was a formidable task, because the corporation was responsible for most aspects of the City's administration and owned much property. It was responsible for paving the streets and for lighting and policing them. It controlled and regulated the great public markets such as Billingsgate, Smithfields, and Leadenhall. Hospitals and gaols within the City were its concern, and so were numerous charities. It controlled the river, the wharves, and the port. On whether its work was well or ill done depended the welfare and prosperity of its inhabitants. The two main bodies for the exercise of this responsibility were the Common Council and the Court of Aldermen. The former represented the more democratic, by eighteenth-century standards, element in the City because the Common Councillors were elected by the freemen in the wards. When Dr. Johnson came to London, the Common Council had 234 members drawn from the middling sort —shopkeepers, prosperous craftsmen, and a sprinkling of apothecaries, surgeons, and attorneys—and its outlook tended to be antiministerial and anti-big-business. Most of the radical move-

[1] J. W. Archenholtz, A Picture of England (1797), p. 150.

[2] Kielmansegge, p. 151.

ments in the City had support of the councillors. But although the freemen had a majority in the Council, their power, at least to some extent, was restrained by the presence of the twenty-six Aldermen and the Lord Mayor. Business was conducted with a dignity and ceremony worthy of the House of Commons. Within the City the Common Council had the power to make by-laws, and these were discussed with frankness and skill before emerging as an act of Common Council. Through its power to levy rates it controlled a substantial revenue. Like in the House of Commons, much of its business was referred to select or standing committees. The Court of Aldermen represented the oligarchical element in the corporation. Although the aldermen were originally elected by the wards and were thus the choice of the freemen, they, unlike the Lord Mayor, held office for life. It was they who supplied the element of continuity and also of unity, for, representing the wards as they did, they were able to see the problems of the City as a whole. Because aldermen were also automatically justices of the peace, they, like the Lord Mayor, combined powers of police and of justice with their administrative functions. Because aldermen were nearly always drawn from the wealthier city merchants and as liverymen played an active part in the internal affairs of their own companies, they could wield considerable influence in local politics and during the second half of the century, in national politics as well. Between the Court of Aldermen and the Common Council there was always latent and sometimes very active animosity. In 1737 in an attempt to muzzle the Common Council Sir Robert Walpole, in conjunction with the wealthy financial section of the City, had pushed through an act of Parliament which gave legislative backing to the claim of Court of Aldermen to have the right to veto the acts of the Common Council. This was bitterly resented by the Council, and Henry Pelham, when carrying through a big conversion loan in 1746, had thought it wiser to arrange for its repeal. By the second half of the century the pendulum of power was swinging the other way, and the Common Council played an increasingly effective part in London politics.

One of the major responsibilities of the corporation was to provide for the policing of the City. By modern standards this was done very inadequately, because men found it difficult to get away from the older conception that to protect his person and his property was the responsibility of the individual citizen. Any householder might be called upon to act as the constable of his parish for a year. Acceptance was compulsory, under pain of a fine, and there was no salary. Because the duties were frequently unpleasant and, if executed with vigour against desperate criminals, could be dangerous, it was not a popular office. The City constables were formally chosen at the wardmote, each parish contributing its quota. It was, however, possible to pay a deputy to serve instead, and this was the course more usually followed if the householder could afford to do so. This was done at the cheapest rate possible, and the parish constable was rarely a man of much vigour or determination. There were exceptions, however, when a public-spirited citizen served in person or when the deputy meant to make something in the way of bribes by using the opportunities his office gave him to harry and bully persons too defenceless to oppose him. In addition to the constables, the corporation paid Marshalmen and Night Watchmen. The City Marshall had wide powers over the semicriminal activities of the City's inhabitants, powers that it was a constant temptation to abuse. Because he could make life hard for the keepers of disorderly houses and gambling dens, a corrupt Marshall could collect a large income from them in return for ignoring their activities. He and his assistants were always a force to be reckoned with within the City's boundaries, but they were not necessarily the force for the protection of law-abiding persons that they should have been. Much depended on the integrity of the man chosen for the office; also there were degrees of corruption, and a marshal who went too far, as did Charles Hitchen, the associate of Johnanthan Wild, would be stripped of his office when exposure overtook him. Of much humbler rank were the Watchmen. They were supposed to patrol the streets and call out the hour as they did so. Originally, this too had been a demand made on the householder, though it was usual to meet it by paying a substitute. Understandably this also was done at the cheapest possible rate, with the result that the quality of the Watch was hardly likely to deter anyone bent on mischief. In 1737 the corporation tried to make more efficient arrangements. The Aldermen and Common Councillors of each ward were authorized to nominate and choose "honest and able bodied men" who from March 10 to September 10 were to patrol the streets between 10 P.M. and 5 A.M. and from September 10 to March 10 between 9 P.M. and 7 A.M. The money to pay them was to be raised by a rate levied on each ward. It was to be collected by the parish constables and beadles, and failure to pay meant that the amount owed could be collected under duress or in the form of goods; nonpayment could also be punished by a month's imprisonment. In an attempt to prevent the watch from skulking in some alehouse and shirking their duties, the constable whose tour of duty it was, was ordered to make rounds himself at least twice every night on penalty of a twenty shilling fine for every default.

Very closely allied with the problem of policing the streets was the problem of lighting them. In 1736 it was declared that "Till this Time the Streets of London were perhaps worse illuminated by Night than any other great City."[3] This too had originally been the responsibility of the individual householder, but by the time that Johnson came to London contractors in return for 6 shillings a year from every house worth £10 a year and paying poor rates agreed to keep their lanterns lit on dark nights up to midnight from the Michaelmas to Lady Day. They were not, however, obligated to do so on those nights when officially there was a moon, that is, from the sixth day after the new moon to the third day after the full moon, whether in fact it was obscured by cloud or fog or not. Also, individual householders could if they liked continue to hang up their own "Lanthorn and Candle before their respective Houses," in which case they were excused from making the annual payment to the contractors. As a result the contractors seem to have been responsible for some thousand lights, private householders supplying the rest. But whoever provided them, the illumination given out by one candle in a lantern, often of thin horn rather than of glass, can have done little to reveal the hazards of piles of rubbish, pools of water, and uneven cobblestones, quite apart from the danger of lurking thieves. In 1737 this responsibility too was taken over by the Mayor, Aldermen, and Common Council. Under the new arrange-

[3]Maitland, *The History of London* (1756), Vol. 1, p. 568.

[4]*Ibid.*, p. 566.

ments the lights were to be kept burning "from the Setting to the Rising of the Sun, throughout the year."[4] This service was to be paid for by a carefully graduated rate. A house worth £10 per annum was to pay 7 shillings a year, between £10 and £20, 12 shillings, and so on until an annual value of more than £50 carried with it a charge of £1. In 1744 this rather elaborate tariff was amended to a straight payment of 6 shillings in the £1. The money was to be collected half yearly and paid to the City Chamberlain, safeguarded by the proviso that no collector should have more that £50 in his "Hands for the Space of ten Days." After the new arrangements came into operation, it was generally agreed that the lighting of the City was much improved.

This seems to have been true also of those parts of London that came under authorities. Well-to-do parishes promoted local acts, which gave them the authority and the funds to improve or provide such amenities as paving and lighting. Westminster and the adjacent parishes procured such a measure in 1761. The result of these and similar efforts was that the lighting in metropolitan London as a whole was much improved. Foreign visitors instead of being derogatory now were impressed, and people from the provinces gaped with astonishment at what today would seem streets plunged in gloom. On a visit to London in 1774 Thomas Yeoman, up from Somerset, wrote that ". . . in the Night it is more surprising with the Lamps. You can travel along the Streets and they are so straight and so many Hundred crossways & every street with the Lts Look so Long. Its beyond (des)cription of My Thick (brains to ponder on, I'll assure y(ou)."[5] There were, however, some occasions when the whole town must have seemed like a blaze of lights, for it was the custom to celebrate any great public event, such as the news of some naval or military triumph, by putting candles in the windows, so that all the street was illuminated by their little pricking flames.

Lighting and police were not the only problems that the City Fathers had to face. There was also the chaos of the streets. Today there is a rather naïve assumption that traffic congestion and noise and the maiming of pedestrians in their lawful pursuits is a

[5]John Yeoman, *The Diary of a Visit of John Yeoman to London in the Years 1774 & 1777* (Watts & Co., 1934), p. 30.

modern phenomenon. Nothing could be further from the truth. When Samuel Johnson knew the City first, there was no provision to protect the pedestrian from the surging traffic. In an attempt to improve the situation the corporation declared that "from the great Increase of coaches, Carts and other Carriages, and their frequent passing through the Streets, Lanes and Passages of the said City, it is to become necessary for the safety and Convenience of all Persons passing within the said City, that Posts should be set up in many Streets, Lanes and other Passages to preserve a Foot-Passage."[6] This was done, and from 1737 the pedestrian ran less risk of death or injury, although the splatter of dirt from the traffic was beyond remedy. Householders were supposed to keep the space before their dwelling swept, and the City had its scavengers, but the volume of traffic made such efforts of little use. The shouting of carters and coachmen, the clatter of hooves, and the rumble of wheels over the cobbles, combined with the calls of street vendors and the clamour of the crowds, must have made the narrow streets a bedlam of noise, to which on a windy day was added the creaking noise of the shop signs as they swung to and from. The traffic made a great impression on Thomas Yeoman. "Ther is no Shuch thing as a Pack Horse to be seen nor a Woman a Horse Back," he wrote, "everyone that Keeps a Horse keeps a Cart. Ye People which Brings goods to ye Marketts they all Brings it in their Carts there is not a horse to be seen with anyThing of that kind on his back as I have mention'd before, even People who has but a Jackass will have a Cart."[7]

Foreigners were astonished not so much by the volume of the traffic as by its comparative orderliness. Grosley, though usually sparing of his praise, declared that in spite of the numbers and sizes of the vehicles using the streets, ". . . they never give rise to any disturbance: which may be accounted for thus; the carriages move constantly in opposite directions, which never cross or disturb each other. The heaviest and those that move most slowly, directing the march of each of the files, the best carriage in London, as soon as it finds itself engaged with the others, is obliged to

[6]Maitland, *op. cit.*, Vol. 1, p. 575.

[7]Yeoman, *op. cit.*, p. 45.

follow the way pointed out by the file it belongs to."[8] In view of other accounts of cursing, swearing, and fisticuffs when traffic jams occurred, this seems an oddly favourable verdict. Even so it is interesting to notice that the rule of the road was already being tolerably well observed in London streets. Grosley attributed this comparative order to the fact that "the English do not seem to have that eagerness to arrive at their journey's end, so general among people of other countries and apparently take this into consideration when planning their journeys." Even though some kind of order was preserved, the traffic problem was serious enough to crop up again and again in the business before the Common Council. As we have seen, London Bridge was a constant headache, and in 1760 the old gates had to be removed. One of the leading spirits in tackling the city's traffic problems was Sir Robert Taylor, who, as an alderman, promoted works that he as an architect was able to appreciate; but, as many modern improvers after him have found, traffic congestion was not easily remedied. As roads were improved, the number of carts, carriages, and coaches seemed to multiply, and since the city had been rebuilt after the fire on its medieval plan, major reconstruction was impossible. Even today in the rush hour the city remains a motorist's nightmare.

The provision of water was a less serious problem and was, by contemporary standards, surprisingly well managed. Originally London had been well supplied with springs, but by the seventeenth century these alone were becoming insufficient for the growing population, and a combination of private benevolence and commercial enterprise now supplied the Londoner with this essential commodity. Water from the New River was brought to Islington, where it was stored in great cisterns. "And from the said cistern", wrote one of London's contemporary historians, "the Water is dispensed in large wooden Pipes into most Streets, and from there leaden Pipes are fixed to convey the Water into the Houses of such as become Tenants to the Company Propriators." Several companies were engaged in supplying London with water, so that "there is not a street in London", he declared, "but one or other of these waters run through it in Pipes, conveyed under-

[8]P. J. Grosley, A Tour of London (1772), Vol. 2, p. 37.

ground; and from these Pipes there is scarce a House, whose rent is 15 or 20 per Ann. but hath the Convenience of Water brought into it by small leaden Pipes laid into the great ones. And for the smaller tenements, such as are in Courts and Alleys, there is generally a Cock, or Pump common to the Inhabitants; so that I may boldly say, there is never a City in the World that is so well served with Water."[9] Aside from the water brought in from outside or pumped up from the Thames, there were waterworks at Chelsea and at Westminster; he also claimed that London had, "abundance of excellent Springs everywhere within itself; the waters whereof are much commended, particularly the Pump at St. Martin's Outwich church . . . The pump in St. Paul's Churchyard." Grosley was less impressed with the quality of Londons water, which he described as "indifferent." Today it would merit a harsher adjective, for, though plentiful, it was far from pure, any water not obviously dirty or stinking being considered fit for consumption. Much of it came from the Thames, which became more polluted each year, or from springs into which all manner of filth was liable to drain. It was perhaps fortunate that Londoners were not great water drinkers. Even so, the convenience of having water piped into so many houses was undoubtedly great. Thomas Yeoman was once again impressed, declaring that ". . . the Water is another Curious Article." He was impressed, too, by the fire-plugs at regular intervals in many streets, so that ". . . if you pull that up the water flows up all over the Street in case of fire." Throughout the eighteenth century fire remained a grim hazard, and the history of London is studded with accounts of notable blazes. The Building Act of 1774 ordered every parish to equip itself with one large and one small fire engine, one leather pipe, and three or more ladders that could be used for first, second, and third stories.

By eighteenth-century standards the Lord Mayor, Aldermen, and Common Councillors ran their city well, and during Johnson's lifetime policing, lighting, and pavement cleaning were all much improved, even though, as will be seen later, terrible abuses and evils remained, and all this was not done without many

[9]Stype, *A Survey of the Cities of London and Westminster Enlarged by Careful Hands* (1754), Vol. 1, pp. 28, 29

conflicting views and clashing interests. The remainder of the metropolitian area lacked administrative cohesion and control. Although Westminster was designated as a city, it never developed the administrative machinery appropriate to the title. Originally, under the Abbott and Convent of Westminster in Elizabeth I's reign, it had acquired a Court of Burgesses primarily to deal with the nuisances inseparable from urban living. But the sovereign had no desire to see a second City of London, with all its privileges and claims to independence, growing up on the doorstep of the royal palace. As a result, the burgesses were not given anything approaching the powers of the Court of Aldermen. They were not, for instance, placed on the commission of the peace; the city of Westminster remained under the jurisdiction of the Middlesex justices. By the eighteenth century the Court of Burgesses had, in practice, lost to them even much of the limited control and functions that it had once enjoyed. Westminster was a curiously contradictory conglomeration of rich and poor, aristocracy and democracy. The presence of the Houses of Parliament and the offices of administration made it the centre of the national government and, therefore, of aristocratic power. Yet the franchise for the parliamentary constituency was one of the most democratic in the country; every potwalloper, that is, householder who could boil his own pot on his own fire, had a vote. Elections in Westminster were rowdy and tumultuous proceedings.

Outside the City, therefore, the normal parish machinery of vestry, churchwardens, overseers, and constables functioned, supervised by the justices of the peace. It was not an administrative machine geared to the changing conditions of London. Overseers and justices could discharge their responsibilities in a rural area, where the population was limited and the tempo of life slow, but these became an impossible burden in those parishes where the poor congregated. Much depended, therefore, on the social composition of the parish. The normal organ of parochial government, the vestry, in which all rate-payers had a voice, was too large for efficient administration, and in well-to-do parishes it was more usual to entrust executive power to a select vestry composed generally of the more substantial parishioners. So long as its members were regular in their attendance and public-spirited in their attitude, this arrangement worked well: St. George's,

Hanover Square, for instance, had a high reputation for integrity and efficiency. But where select vestries were captured by a small clique, the opportunities for corruption were alarmingly great. In parishes in which tradesmen predominated, contracts to supply the workhouse were regarded as their perquisites, persons receiving alms were pressurized to spend their parish pay at the vestrymen's shops, and the conduct of business was accompanied by much eating and drinking at the expense of the parish. Unpaid service proved far from cheap, and those parishes were fortunate where gentlemen of private means were prepared to give their services for influence rather than for more tangible rewards. Such parishes were also more interested in securing local improvement acts, which gave them considerable powers to raise rates and provide amenities such as decent paving, the scavenging of household refuse, and the cleansing of the streets. Lighting could be provided and the local watch more carefully supervised. St. George's organized their own watch with thirty-two men and levied a special rate to pay them, which, with few exceptions, was the general practice among the Westminster parishes.

The contrast between the City and the rest of the metropolis is therefore striking; on the one hand a fully organized and integrated administration with its apex of power concentrated in the Lord Mayor; on the other, a series of loosely knit communities. The contrast is equally striking in the sphere of politics. In the City the canalization and concentration of power inevitably meant that men, or groups of men, struggled to control it. Out of these struggles came the politics of the City, which in turn became entangled with the politics of the nation. To ignore these aspects of the City is to ignore something that was vital both in its life and in that of the nation as a whole. The government of a great city, then as now, can never be divorced from politics. High office within the City, as we have seen, represented power to shape the City's policies in the interests of the ruling clique. It represented the spoils of office, patronage, and the ability to promote the interests of one's friends. In less tangible form it represented dignity and was the outward manifestation of the respect of the community. Just as the successful politician at Westminster hoped for office under the Crown, so the successful merchant and banker hoped to become Lord Mayor of London. Here the fountain of power was the Court of Alderman, where the initial grooming for office took place; some of the fiercest struggles in City politics were concerned with the election of aldermen and with the control of that court. In these contests the freemen tended to fall into two main groups, the membership of both being largely dictated by economic interests. The numerically smaller group was made up of the wealthier merchants, bankers, and industrialists, at this time largely the big brewers. Many of them were directors of the Bank of England, the East Indian Company, and the South Seas Company. Between them they represented a tight interlocking of financial power. The other group was composed of the lesser merchants and smaller financial partnerships, prosperous tradesmen, and small-scale manufacturers who enjoyed the support of the mass of the shop-keepers and artisans who, as we have seen, supplied the City with its food, drink, and consumer goods. In practice, however, the division was not always so clean-cut: in the struggle for power men whose economic alignment would have been with the first group might see more political advantage in leading the second in order to secure their votes in an aldermanic contest or in the Common Council.

It was probably inevitable that the domestic politics of the City should become entangled with those of the nation. Because London was the greatest trading centre in Britain, the prosperity of its citizens was closely bound up with questions of peace and war, with questions of taxation, particularly those concerned with custom and excise, and with the financing of government loans. In all these matters the City must lobby for the measures it desired and oppose those it feared or disliked. It is clear that it could not speak with a united voice on all issues. The government finance that suited the large-scale financier might seem gross favouritism to the smaller one; insurance agents and underwriters found opportunities for gain in a situation in which the shipper saw only additional costs and hazards. Nowhere was this division of interest clearer than in the management of the nation's finances. Loans were needed to fill the gap between the granting of taxes and their collection even in peacetime; in war the necessity for additional revenue made the cooperation of the City essential. As we have seen, lending to the government was an extremely profitable business, which, because the loans were secured on the taxes and were therefore regarded as the best of securities, was much sought after. Here the less important merchants found themselves at a disadvantage. Normal government practice was for the Treasury to negotiate privately with a small group who usually handled such business. The sums to be raised, the interest to be paid, and the general arrangements for the loan were all negotiated with them. Each intimated how much he was prepared to take up, and because the terms on which he did so were favourable, his profit could be considerable. But because of the way in which these loans were raised, the lesser bankers, or those who had not succeed in joining the limited group that had the ear of the Treasury, were excluded from the profits of loan promotion. Understandably, they resented it and looked for allies among the shopkeepers and small masters. Members of a livery company were not necessarily large-scale businessmen. Many of them represented the middling group of the freemen, and some found the struggle to earn a living hard. These were the men who voted in the Common Hall for candidates who, they believed, would espouse their interests, and who pushed for acts of Common Council to protect the small master against the dominant merchant rings. There was, therefore, a permanent division in the City between the rich and the not so rich who could count among their allies the poorer citizens.

This close alliance between the Treasury and the City made ministers the natural allies of the powerful inner rings and therefore the natural enemies of their excluded rivals. Because of their dependence on its wealth, the ministry of the day could never afford to let the control of City politics slip into unfriendly hands if by management and manipulation they could prevent it. Since it was a recognized part of contemporary ethics to reward one's friends with whatever spoils were available, government patronage and influence were used to provide political support for candidates favoured by it. Among Henry Fielding's numerous pamphlets is one entitled *A Dialogue between a Gentleman of London and an Honest Alderman,* printed in 1747. The gist of it is the attempt of the gentleman to support the ministers of the day. After a long argument the alderman admits: "I am almost ashamed to own it; but, O my Friend, mutual Promises have

passed between us. I have promised my Vote, and Mr. Toastum
hath promised whenever his Party comes into Power to provide
for my Son." To this the gentleman replies: "As to the Conscientious Part, I think I have convinced you on which side that lies;
and as to the interested, I believe, I need very few Arguments to
satisfy you, that my Friends are most likely to have it in the
Power to serve your Son."[10]

In spite of the influence exerted by the administration, the
antiministerial element in the City was always formidable. The
vote of the freeman in the wardmote was in essence the vote of
the little man, although in many cases it would not be exercised
without some regard to the consequences. To defy an influential
merchant by voting against him when a new alderman was being
chosen for the ward was an act of some personal courage; also,
because any prospective alderman had to be a person of substance, it might well be a choice between King Log and King
Stork. But when political passions ran high, as they did over John
Wilkes, ministerial influence was not sufficient to prevent his becoming an alderman. The ambitions of politicians out of office
provided another reason for the close connection between the
politics of Westminster and those of the Guildhall. If ministers
could not afford to ignore the City, neither could those who found
themselves out of favour. The antiministerial feeling in the City
could be a very useful weapon in their hands. The Common
Council could be incited to present petitions to the House of
Commons, so whipping up public opinion and airing grievances.
Again, the right of the Lord Mayor to present a petition in person
to the King could be a genuine embarrassment if the Lord Mayor
were unfriendly to the Court. Politicians out of office therefore
strove by every means in their power to increase their influence
over Common Hall, Common Council, and the Court of Aldermen and aimed if possible to carry the election of the City's four
members against the ministers of the day.

Intimate though the relation between the City and Westminster was, it varied considerably from decade to decade. On occasions the antagonism that flared up was demonstrative and row-

[10]Henry Fielding, A Dialogue between a Gentleman of London and an
Honest Alderman (1747), p. 89.

dy, sometimes cooperation prevailed for long periods; though the underlying tensions were there, the political situation was so undramatic that they went unnoticed. During Johnson's sojourn in the City these relationships went through three phases. The first was dominated by a hatred of Walpole, the second by an admiration for Pitt, and the third embraced the struggle with George III that is associated with the name of John Wilkes. In the first of these Dr. Sutherland has suggested that the driving force behind the demonstrations was provided by those politicians at Westminster who were the bitter opponents of Sir Robert Walpole; in the second the explanation lay in the personality and policy of Pitt; in the third the City had become a political entity in its own right, able to treat its rather feeble political allies at Westminster on an equal basis.[11] By this time the City was no longer concerned only with problems of finance and trade; it was developing a radical outlook on matters connected with parliamentary representation and the franchise.

The first crisis, that over the Excise Bill, occurred just before Johnson settled in London. How far the City had genuine grounds for its opposition to this measure it is difficult to judge. Certainly the tobacco brokers, who had long enjoyed a control over the importation of tobacco that had been much resented by the growers in Virginia, had no quarrel with the old and long-established practices of the trade whose abuses Walpole was trying to eradicate. But though the merchants of the City might have had little love for the measure, it is at least doubtful if they would have reacted against it so violently without the active instigation of Walpole's enemies in the House. For years William Pulteney in his speeches and the *Craftsman* in its articles had been spreading tales of Walpole's graft and corruption, so that the City had become a hotbed of anti-Walpolian feeling. The average citizen had reasons for disliking him. Sir Robert was the friend of the Bank of England and had earned the title of the Skreen Master as a result of his efforts to shield the Directors of the South

[11]See L. M. Sutherland, *The City of London in Eighteenth Century Politics in Essays*, presented to Sir Lewis Namier, edited by R. Pares and A. J. P. Taylor (1956), and The City of London and Opposition to Government (Creighton Lectures in History, 1959) on this subject.

Seas Company from complete financial ruin after the collapse of the Bubble. Men who come between the duped investor and his prey are rarely popular. He had added further to his unpopularity by persuading several prominent aldermen to petition the Commons in 1724 to strengthen the Court of Aldermen by recognizing their right, always hotly contested, to veto the acts of Common Council. So it was not difficult to mobilize the City against him over the Excise Bill, particularly because many shopkeepers must have had a genuine and justified fear that excisemen searching their warehouses for goods that might have reached them through illegal channels could prove to be high-handed and corrupt in the pursuit of their task. A petition presented by the corporation and asking to be heard by counsel against the bill was brought to Westminster with great pomp and publicity. But though by then Walpole had made up his mind that the measure would have to be dropped, he was determined not to give the City Fathers the satisfaction of thinking that he had been influenced by their pressure. The petition was left to lie on the table, and by a majority of seventeen their plea to be heard by counsel was negatived. In spite of this snub the citizens celebrated the defeat of the hated bill and the hated enemy with bonfires, the ringing of bells, and the illumination of windows. Taverns and coffeehouses were full of merrymakers drinking the health of the King, the Lord Mayor, and the Common Council, and the windows of any known supporter of the bill were gleefully broken by the surging crowds. On 18 April the Common Council expressed its gratitude in more formal fashion to the City's M.P. and to the Lord Mayor for their exertions in opposing the bill. Walpole's supporters lost more than their windows: in the subsequent City election the votes went to those candidates who had actively fought against the bill, and in the general election of 1734 antiministerial candidates were returned to Parliament.

All this was very recent history when Samuel Johnson first came to seek his fortune in London. Nor was the fight between Walpole and the City over. Its chief champion was Sir John Barnard who from 1720 had led the antiministerial forces. In the election of 1722 he was returned as one of the four City members and showed himself to be an able and persuasive speaker. The son of a wine merchant, he came of good City stock and by his integrity and religious principles gained and kept the respect of his fellow citizens. He was knighted in 1732, served as sheriff in 1735, and became Lord Mayor in 1737. By then cracks were beginning to appear in the facade of Walpole's power, and Sir John Barnard and Micajah, who was Lord Mayor in 1738, were both active in the campaign against him. Whether it believed in Pulteney's constantly reiterated charges of corruption and betray-al of the national interests, as Sir John seems to have done, or not, the City was closely concerned with the minister's handling of commercial affairs. Trade with Spain was important, and by 1738 Anglo-Spanish relations were working up to one of their periodic crisis. Walpole, always a firm believer in peace, was straining every nerve to reach a negotiated settlement. Neither the Spanish nor the English governments wanted war and hoped that in the Convention of Prado they had found a workable compromise. This might well have proved to be in the best interests of the commercial community, but Walpole's opponents were able to argue that his failure to uphold the British claim to sail freely in the Caribbean, a claim that Spain had always rejected, was a gross betrayal of them. Patriotic fervour against Spain was always easily aroused. Once again the City was in an uproar and the machinery of parliamentary petition was put into motion. At a meeting of the Common Council in February, Sir John moved that a committee be appointed to draw up a petition setting forth "the fatal consequences that must attend the Trade and Naviga-tion of Great Britain on the American Seas, if the pretensions of the Spaniards . . . be admitted of." When presented, it was accept-ed by the House of Lords where opposition to Walpole was well led, but rejected, though by a small majority, by the Commons. In the previous debate on the petition ministers exasperated the City still more by deliberately making fun of the petitioners, holding up to ridicule their trades and crafts, and sneering at their compe-tence to express views on matters of state. Walpole had some justification for his bitterness because the agitation was in many ways a manufactured one, but it was successful in that the City and the parliamentary opposition between them dragged the country into a war that Walpole mismanaged, and so facilitated his resignation in 1742. When the bells of the City rang out to celebrate the declaration of war, he made his oft quoted remark: "They are ringing their bells now. Later they will be ringing their hands." He was right. City merchants had expected the Spanish colonies to be an easy prey and British harbours to be full of Spanish prizes. After some initial successes this proved to be a pipe dream. As the war with Spain merged into the war of the Austrian Succession in 1740, British merchants found themselves for the next eight years involved in a war that became increasingly unpopular and ended in a peace that completely ignored the problem of the right of search for which they had clamoured so fiercely in 1739. That, however, was in the future. In 1739 the antiministerials were in full cry and feeling was so intense that Sir George Champion, who as senior alderman should normally have been elected Lord Mayor, was passed over for his junior because Sir George had supported Walpole's policy. In the election of 1741 candidates hostile to Walpole were returned by the City, and before Common Hall adjourned the radical suggestion was put forward that a paper of Instructions be delivered to the new M.P.'s. Few better instances can be found of the interaction of City politics on the fate of ministers and of national politics on the career of City magnates. Johnson himself was caught up in the general feeling of the City; his poem *London* is full of anti-Walpole sentiments, though in later life he was more prepared to give that statesman his due.

The fall of Walpole was followed by much easier relations between ministers and the City. Henry Pelham, in whose hands the general direction of policy came to rest, particularly after 1745, aroused none of the antagonism that Sir Robert had pro voked. Conciliatory by nature and anxious to restore the finances after the long drain of the 1739-1748 war he was determined to win the cooperation of the City. To do this he carried the repeal of Walpole's much hated act, which had given the Court of Aldermen a veto over the Common Council, and worked closely with Sir John Barnard and his friends by agreeing that loans should be raised, as they had always advocated, by open subscription. It is also significant that during Pelham's period of control, opposition in Parliament all but disappeared, for whereas Sir Robert had driven able ambitious men into opposition, Pelham found room for them in the administration. As a result there were few disappointed politicians anxious to stir up trouble for the ministers in the City.

An even greater change took place during the ascendancy of William Pitt, later Earl of Chatham, to whom the City gave its wholehearted allegiance. The reasons for this were varied. In 1756 war had once again broken out with France. Merchants tended to prefer a naval war with its hope of prizes and the chance to acquire new colonies that might increase the supply of raw materials in which they dealt and extend their overseas markets. To their disgust the Duke of Newcastle and his colleagues were mismanaging this aspect of the war and seemed in danger of getting bogged down in the usual Continental campaigns that pivoted on George II's possession of Hanover. Pitt, forthright and sweeping in his denunciations of this policy, was dismissed, once from his office of Paymaster General and again after his brief tenure of power as Secretary of State and effective head of the administration. London, like many other cities, presented him with its freedom contained in the traditional gold box, and when the King was forced to take him back, with Newcastle as First Lord of the Treasury, and the direction of the war was at last in Pitts' hands Londoners supported him loyally. There were other reasons of a more personal and social character. Although in the past the City had acted with the leaders of the opposition to Walpole, men like Bolingbroke, Pulteney, and Lord Carteret, there was a deep social and even emotional gulf between its prosperous citizens and the nobility and gentry. The latter tended to be jealous of the solid wealth of the merchants and to make fun of their lack of social polish; they were "the cits." A gentleman might borrow from them, might marry their daughters if the dowry were large enough, might even mix with them on a social level in a condescending way, but they remained inferior beings. Archenholtz commented on "This difference which holds even in the hours of eating and drinking, in the kind of amusements, the dress and manner of speaking etc. has given rise to a degree of mutual contempt by the inhabitants of each of these quarters for the other. Those of the city reproach them of the other end for their idleness, luxury, manner of living, and desire to imitate everything that is French: these in their turn never mention an inhabitant of the city but as an animal gross and barbarous, whose only merit is his strong box . . . this mutual dislike is sung in the streets, it is introduced upon the stage, and even in parliament it is not forgotten."[12] One satirical example might be quoted from the *Gentleman's Magazine* for January 1753, where under the heading "The Engagements of a polite lady" appeared the entry "To dine with my husband's uncle, the city merchant—Comment city politeness intolerable! Crammed with mince pies, and fatigued with the compliments of the season! Play at Pope Joan for pence! O the Creatures."[13] Such comments convey an exaggerated impression. Relations between citizens and gentlefolk were often friendly and even cordial. The great city magnates were men of culture, far removed from "an animal gross and barbarous." Ministers, lords and ladies, gentlemen, all attended the great civic functions and Lord Mayor's banquets. Yet basically the tension was something of which everyone was aware, and citizens resented the attitude of their social superiors.

Pitt too was something of a lone wolf in the political society of the day. Though he had plenty of aristocratic connections and friends, he never fitted easily into the world of patronage and jobs. Either temperamentally he could not use them or he despised them; whatever the reason, his aloofness appealed to the citizens of London. Moreover, he had close friends among them, in particular Alderman Beckford. The son of a Jamaican planter, William Beckford was a man of wealth and ambition who had had the imagination to realize what a political asset the support of the City would be. In 1752 he contrived to be chosen as alderman for the Billingsgate ward and next year was returned as one of the City's representatives to the Commons. His colonial interests and knowledge drew him to Pitt, and the two men became friends. Until Beckford died in 1770 the relation between them remained a close one, and Beckford was recognized as Pitt's spokesman in the City. This was not Beckford's only claim to be remembered, for in the new phase of city politics, which was ushered in with the accession of George III and the resignation

[12]Archenholtz, *op. cit.*, p. 122.

[13]*The Gentleman's Magazine*, January 1753, p. 36.

of Pitt in 1761, he became one of the leaders of that opposition
to King and ministers associated with the cry of "Wilkes and
Liberty" that marked the beginnings of a radical movement that
was to end in demands for parliamentary reform.

The resignation of Pitt and the kind of peace that Lord Bute
seemed likely to conclude with France threw the City back into
opposition. In part this was the product of their loyalty to Pitt,
which they demonstrated by voting him their official thanks as
ostentatiously as possible in Common Council. Ordinary Londoners expressed it less formally but equally emphatically by the
ovations that they gave him when on ceremonial occasions he
appeared in the City's streets. Even before his resignation when,
as was customary, the new king George III attended the first
Lord Mayor's banquet after the accession Kielmansegge who
was there recorded that "Although the King and Queen were
greatly cheered by the people as they passed, the cheering was
nearly exceeded by that raised in honour of Pitt, who had some
difficulty in moving on as the populace clung to his carriage and
horses in order to see him."[14] Personal loyalty, however, is not
enough to account for the rather subtle change in the character of
this opposition. In the days of Walpole the impetus seems to have
come from the politicians at Westminster, who needed it for its
nuisance value. It was the politicians who dominated the tactics,
in alliance with the City. But since those days the close cooperation of Pitt and Beckford had given the City a greater sense of its
own importance in the affairs of the nation. In consequence,
though it continued to work with those politicians who found
themselves opposed to the King and his ministers, it no longer
felt the need to defer to them. It was now sufficiently experienced
in the world of contemporary politics to let its latent resentment
against aristocratic leadership have full rein. In the years to come
it was Lord Rockingham who had to accept a policy of which he
was little enamoured in order to keep the unity of his attacking
forces.

The first ten years of George III's reign were marked by a
series of clashes between the royal ministers and the City, where
the growth of a radical movement for a time succeeded in captur-

[14]Kielmansegge, *op. cit.*, p. 152.

ing the administrative hierarchy. Many ingredients went into its formation. There was loyalty and sympathy for Pitt, though this was badly shaken when he returned to office in 1766 as the Earl of Chatham; there was a dislike of an executive that was sometimes high handed and more often inept; and there was the skillful propaganda of the opposition. All these things combined to make the City increasingly critical of the composition of the House of Commons. It seemed patently unjust that the City, Westminster, and Southwark should only be represented by eight members, while Devon and Cornwall returned seventy. When a barren site like Old Sarum, which contributed nothing to the wealth of the nation, sent two members to the Commons, for the City with all its wealth to have only four could not be defended on any logical principle and seemed to give a quite disproportionate influence to the aristocracy and gentry. The reality was perhaps not quite so unfair. Rotten boroughs were not the monopoly of the gentry. Old Sarum itself had once been the property of Diamond Pitt, the mercantile grandfather of William, who at the beginning of his parliamentary career had himself represented it. Many prominent City personalities were in the Commons where, though technically the members for some small and obscure boroughs, in practice they spoke for the financial and commercial interests of the City. James Townshend was the member for West Loe, and John Sawbridge, the antiministerial champion, sat for Hythe. But though it had its practical convenience, the system could hardly be defended on theoretical grounds, and when William Beckford, standing for election for one of the City seats in 1761, declared that ". . . our Constitution is defective only in one point, and that is, that little piteful boroughs send members to parliament equal to great cities, and that it is contrary to the maximum that power should follow property,"[15] he was appealing to a good deal of latent resentment.

The man around whom this half-unconscious discontent crystallized was John Wilkes, since 1761 the member for Aylesbury. Wilkes was one of the most colourful and notorious characters in eighteenth-century political life. Contemporaries com-

---

[15]*Memoirs of William Beckford of Fonthill* (1859), Vol. 1, p. 33, cited in I. Christie, *Wilkes, Wyvill and Reform* (Macmillan, 1961).

mented alike on his ugliness and his personal charm. His origins were middle-class, his education that of a gentleman, his extravagant tastes those of the nobility. The one thing he was determined never to tolerate was obscurity, and the growing tensions as the negotiations over the Peace of Paris drew to their close gave him his opportunity. On the one side was the King, young and inexperienced, and his also inexperienced First Lord of the Treasury, his former tutor Lord Bute; on the other side were the elder statesmen who had directed the triumphant war, William Pitt and the Duke of Newcastle, now in opposition and bitterly resentful of the new regime. In order to attack the impending peace Lord Temple, Pitt's wealthy brother-in-law, financed a new paper, the *North Briton*, and made Wilkes its editor. No eighteenth-century journalist had an overscrupulous regard for truth, and the conventions of the day accepted a degree of personal abuse that now demands a more sophisticated presentation. As a ranking political journalist Wilkes was superb. The details of his long struggle with the Court are complicated, and only the barest outline can be given here. After an attack on the King's speech at the opening of Parliament, Wilkes and the printers and publishers of the *North Briton* were all arrested on a general warrant on the charge of having committed a seditious libel in No. 45 of the newspaper. After some maneuvering on the part of his powerful friends he was brought before Lord Chief Justice Pratt, a school friend of Pitt's, who released him on the legal grounds that as a member of Parliament he was covered by his parliamentary privilege. Wilkes had a wonderful gift for publicity and by posing as the victim of a high-handed executive, for in time of peace general warrants were of doubtful legality, he was able to make himself a symbol of personal liberty. He proclaimed in the course of these proceeding that if he were condemned, the liberty of all Englishmen would be in peril, stressed for propaganda reasons that the people of the middling and inferior set, who were most in need of protection, would be the chief sufferers, and declared with a flourish that the underlying issue was whether in future English liberty should be a reality or a mere shadow. George III and his ministers were alike furious with this self-styled champion of "Liberty". By 273 votes to 111 the House of Commons declared No. 45 *North Briton* "a false, scandalous and seditious libel" and ordered it to be burnt by the Common Hangman at the Royal Exchange. It was an unwise step. Londoners seized the opportunity to demonstrate their antiministerial feelings, pelting those whose duty it was to supervise the proceedings with pieces of wood and the filth that lay everywhere at hand. The glass of their coach was broken, and the copy of No. 45 was rescued from the ignominious flames.

Londoners might make their city echo with the cries of "Wilkes and Liberty," which at intervals during the next ten years was to be their watchword, but Wilkes had no hold as yet over the City's administration, and popular clamour was a poor defence against government. Wilkes was expelled from Parliament, and a writ was issued for his arrest both for republishing the offending number and for printing privately a parody of Pope's *Essay on Man* under the title of *Essay on Women* with notes purporting to be by Bishop Warburton, the contents of which may be inferred from the title. Wilkes never pretended to be a saint and before his rise to political notoriety had been a member of the Medenhamen Abbey circle. Having lost the protection of his parliamentary privilege, he retired to France and in his absence was convicted, though not sentenced, for his writings. By 1768, hounded by his French creditors, as previously he had been by his English ones, he was anxious to return to England, hoping that some of his old political allies who were now in power would secure for him a royal pardon. When they indicated that though they might be prepared to help him with his debts, they had no intention of facilitating his return, Wilkes returned to London, determined not to drag out his days in obscurity and poverty and defying his former political associates. Immediately he made it clear that he intended to look for support to the antiministerial faction in the City, and his first step was to apply for membership in the Joiners' Company in order to obtain the necessary qualification to stand as a candidate in the parliamentary election of 1768. In his address to the City electors he declared that he presented himself to them as a private man, unsupported by connection and looking for no other support than that which they would accord to him. This appeal was greeted with wild enthusiasm by the small masters and craftsmen. The City was full of latent discontent; the previous winter had been very hard, the Thames had frozen over, the price of bread had risen sharply, the coal heavers and the Spit-alfields weavers were engaged in turbulent strife with their employers. In such circumstances the memory of John Wilkes as a man unjustly victimized by the authorities was one to appeal to all who felt themselves to be in a similar case. Wilkes and his supporters knew well how to use such popular feeling and how to augment it by skillful propaganda and well-timed publicity. On his public appearances his sedan chair was hoisted high on the shoulders of his supporters; on one occasion they hired him a hackney coach bearing the sacred number 45 and drawn by six black horses with long tails. Everywhere men were wearing his colours, a blue cockade, and everywhere crowds were crying "Wilkes and Liberty." If the huzzahing and shouts of the multitude could have carried the election, the issue would have been in little doubt. Unfortunately for Wilkes only freemen had the vote, and they for the most part had already been promised to William Beckford or Barlow Trecothick, who represented the "patriot party," or were pledged to candidates who had the favour of the ministers. When the results were declared after a week's polling, in which, as was the custom, each elector had to give his vote publicly and in person, the influence of the administration had proved strong enough to carry the two Court candidates Thomas Harley, the Lord Mayor, and Sir William Ladbroke at the head of the poll. Beckford and Trecothick came third and fourth. Wilkes was the last of the seven candidates. Undismayed, he immediate-ly declared his intention of standing for Middlesex, where the election had not yet taken place.

Here his chances were better, for Middlesex, being a county seat, depended on the vote of the forty-shilling freeholder. This meant that many of his supporters, small masters, small shop-keepers, and the like, were enfranchised. Once again his personal appearances were greeted with scenes of almost delirious approv-al. On the day the poll took place the road out to Brentford was crowded with his supporters, and, according to some reports, persons not wearing his colours could not get to the hustings to vote. This time there was no disappointment: Wilkes was de-clared to be at the head of the poll. That night, and for some subsequent nights, the mobbish part of the town went mad. Crowds swarmed through the streets, breaking the windows of any house not illuminated in Wilkes's honour. Horace Walpole recorded that even the Austrian ambassador was dragged from his coach and the number 45 chalked on the soles of his shoes! It was a significant example of the mass hysteria that a demagogue could arouse and of the way in which public order could be swept into violence. These jubilations were only the first of a series of mob reactions that engulfed the City and the West End alike. Wilkes's position was now peculiar: even though the member for Middlesex, he was still an outlaw and a man convicted, though not yet sentenced, for seditious libel. Scenes amounting to farce accompanied his efforts to clarify the situation. When he surrendered to his outlawry at King's Bench, he found that he must wait to be formally arrested. When in due course this was done, the crowds mobbed the carriage in which he was being conveyed to King's Bench prison, took out the horses, and, turning the coach around, drew it along the Strand and back into the exultant City. Only after dark and in disguise was Wilkes able to elude his faithful supporters and give himself up. In the subsequent proceeding his outlawry was quashed on purely technical grounds, but he was fined £1000 and sentenced to twenty-two months' imprisonment for seditious libel. Meanwhile London once again had been seized by wave after wave of disorder as his adherents gathered outside his prison and staged noisy demonstrations. On May 10 the troops that had been called out to guard it, after considerable provocation and the reading of the riot act, fired into the crowd. Altogether eleven people were killed in what became known as "the Massacre of St. George's Fields." Wilkes and Liberty had now been hallowed by martyrs' blood; American readers may see some parallel with the Boston Massacre. With the shedding of blood the disorders grew worse rather than better, to the alarm of more staid citizens.

Up to 1769 Wilkes's cause had been espoused chiefly by the ordinary freeman of the City and the freeholders of Middlesex, though earlier the parliamentary opposition, under the rather uneasy leadership of the aristocratic Rockingham and of Pitt, now Earl of Chatham, had argued that the use of general warrants had constituted a genuine threat to individual liberty. In 1769 the situation changed, and the affair of Wilkes passed out of the sphere of London politics into that of the nation. He was not a person to languish unnoticed in gaol and succeeded in arousing the fury of ministers to such a pitch that they once again secured his expulsion from the House of Commons. So far their action was legal; the sequel was to demonstrate its political folly. If the Commons were within their rights in expelling Wilkes, the Middlesex electors were equally within theirs in reelecting him. Three times the farce was repeated until at the fourth election his opponent Colonel Luttrell received 296 votes to Wilkes's 1143 and was declared by the Commons to be the rightful member. The result was a first-class constitutional issue, which was promptly taken up by the aristocratic Rockingham faction and by Chatham. Once again the City found itself in alliance with the opposition leaders. The situation was, however, very different from that which had prevailed in the days of Sir Robert Walpole. Now these uneasy allies were divided in their outlook, for Londoners were adopting a critical and radical attitude toward the basic composition of the Commons, whereas the Rockinghams argued that the best safeguard for English liberties would be to restrain the influence that the Crown could exert over the House by its use of patronage. In the past the parliamentary leaders had called the tune. In 1769 the City politicians paid little attention to aristocratic susceptibilities, and though both wings organized petitions to the Crown, their tone was markedly different.

Here the ancient privileges of the City—to present a petition to the King in person through the Lord Mayor and to receive a reply from the royal lips—furnished them with a formidable instrument of publicity. Such petitions were presented with considerable ceremony, the Lord Mayor being accompanied by the Sheriffs and many of the aldermen and other City dignitaries and received by the King in state. In 1770 Beckford, who was Lord Mayor for the second time, used this privilege to stage a dramatic act of civic defiance against George III himself. The object of the maneuver was to force a dissolution of Parliament, and on May 23 Beckford presented a petition to this effect. Archenholtz, who was there, gave a graphic description of the incident. "It is the custom after a solemn audience of this sort," he wrote, "for the deputation to kiss the king's hand and to retire. But Beckford, who had not come with an intention to undergo a ceremony so little suited to the objects of a free people, resuming the discourse, entreated the king with a respectful firmness, not to look with indifference on the petition of the first city of his kingdom but to yield to the reiterated solicitations of his people. This apostrophe of the particular mayor was unexpected and unexampled. I was one of the spectators, and I own that in my life, I have never been witness of a more extraordinary scene. The trouble and agitation of the courtiers was visible in their faces, while the citizens showed by marks equally unequivocal how much they applauded the courageous patriotism of their first magistrate. He in the meanwhile stood with a noble tranquillity before the throne expecting an answer from the king. As none was prepared a deep silence reigned for a considerable time over the whole hall, during which the spectators looked at one another with astonishment. Beckford then saw that it was time to put an end to this strange scene; he bowed and retired. It may be guessed how much offense this conduct gave at St. James's; it was called insolent, and the Mayor threatened with the Tower. In the city, on the other hand, nothing was heard but solemn thanks to him for his conduct."[16] A month later Beckford was dead, but the patriotic section of the City were determined that his memory should not be forgotten and subscribed for a statue to be erected in front of the Guildhall.

To suppose, however, that this intransigent attitude on the part of the City Fathers sprang from any personal loyalty to or even liking for Wilkes would be to oversimplify and misunderstand a much more complicated situation. Wilkes's wrongs were a convenient stick with which to beat the minister and bombard the Court, but Beckford and his friends were by no means grieved that Wilkes himself should be safely immured in prison. They were far more sincere in developing radical views than Wilkes, who was chiefly interested in using such views to further his own career. In consequence there was a fierce struggle within the City between the Court party, which was always a force to be reckoned with, the more radical group, and Wilkes's personal following for the control of the official hierarchy. With the death of Beckford and with his release, Wilkes, who while still in prison had been chosen as alderman for the ward of Farrington Without, was able to strengthen his own power within the City. The Court,

[16]Archenholtz, *op. cit.*, p. 151.

however, proved to have sufficient influence over the Court of Aldermen to prevent his being chosen Lord Mayor in 1771, even though the Common Hall had voted for him. He was blocked again in the following year, but in 1774 he at last attained his twin ambitions. He became Lord Mayor of London, and when he was again returned for Middlesex in the general election of that year, he was allowed to take his seat without further opposition. Wilkes had won, but paradoxically it was the end of Wilkes and Liberty. With success his appeal and his popularity waned. It had served its purpose; he is reputed to have said: "I never was a Wilkite myself." Dr. Campbell who waited more than an hour to see him, drew an unattractive picture: "He Wilkes was rather worse than I had expected to find him, for he labours under baldness, increptitude and want of teeth (from the hedge of his teeth being removed his tongue is for ever trespassing upon his lips; whereof the undermost together with his chin projects very far)."[17] Though they disagreed on politics—indeed Wilkes once told Boswell that "Liberty is as ridiculous in his mouth as Religion in mine"[18]—and though the Doctor had supported the Commons in expelling him in 1769 and had written a pamphlet, *The False Alarm*, in defense of this action, the two men were friendly. Johnson declared that "Jack is a scholar, and Jack has the manners of a gentleman, he has always been at me but I would as soon do Jack a favour as not."[19]

The tussle with the House of Commons over the printing of debates in 1771 furnishes still another example of the determination of the City to defend its privileges. The eighteenth-century House permitted no reporting of its proceedings; it was to be as independent of the public as it was of the king. In practice Londoners were too keenly interested in politics to submit to this ruling, and, under transparent devices that deceived nobody, the London newssheets contrived to print more or less accurate accounts of the debates. Because the Middlesex election and the petitioning movement had left the Commons particularly resentful of criticism, they decided to call some of the offending print-

[17]*Dr. Campbell's Diary of a Visit to England in 1775,* newly edited from the MSS. by James L. Clifford (Cambridge University Press, 1947), p. 74.

[18]J. Boswell, *Life of Samuel Johnson* (1934), Vol. 3, p. 224.

[19]*Ibid.,* Vol. 4, p. 183.

ers, who had dropped even the convention of pretence, to the bar
of the House; Wheble of the *Middlesex Journal*, Thompson of the
Gazetteer, and Miller of the *London Evening Post*, all Wilkites,
refused to appear and took refuge in the City. Here an attempt
was made to arrest them without the warrant having been signed
by a City magistrate, which was an infringement of a much valued privilege. The situation rapidly degenerated into the same
near farce that had marked Wilkes's attempts to surrender to his
outlawry. Alderman Oliver freed Thompson; Brass Crosby, the
Lord Mayor, arrested the offending messenger of the House of
Commons; the House in turn retaliated by committing Oliver and
Crosby, who were both members of the House, to the Tower for
contempt. The whole affair aroused the greatest feeling in the
City. Tumultuous crowds unharnessed the horses and drew the
coach, in which Oliver and Crosby were driving to Westminster,
themselves. Lord North in contrast was singled out as the object
of their spite. The glass of his coach was broken and he and his
supporters pelted with dirt, a favourite reaction of the London
mob. Once Oliver and Crosby were safely shut up in the Tower,
popular demonstrations took a different form. On April 1 a mock
ceremony was held on Tower Hill, the place of execution for
traitors, where dummies of the Dowager Princess, Lord Bute, the
Speaker, and the Foxes, father and son, were beheaded. A few
days later the dummies of other unpopular ministers suffered a
similar fate. Meanwhile in the Tower the champions of liberty
were being ostentatiously visited by opposition members. Their
imprisonment did not last long. Because Commons' power to
imprison for contempt is confined to the period in which the
House is sitting, the proroguing of Parliament automatically set
them free on May 8. Their release was celebrated by a salute of
twenty-one guns fired by the Honourable Artillery Company, and
they were escorted back to the City with a triumphial procession
of some fifty-three carriages containing most of the Common
Councilmen. Once again the City patriots had demonstrated their
power. By doing so they had gained a victory of national rather
than merely civic importance. Though the Commons did not
abandon their claim to prohibit the publication of reports, they
made no further attempt to enforce it. Brass Crosby, Oliver, and
Wilkes, who had been the third alderman involved in the strug-

gle, had secured a significant extension of the freedom of the press.

The years since Johnson had come to reside there in 1737 had been momentous ones for the City. In every way it was a better-administered, cleaner, and lighter place. It had been adorned with many new buildings, such as the new edifice of the Bank of England and the provision of a Mansion House, which were a tribute alike to its growing financial strength and to its civic pride. Transport congestion had been eased by the removal of the old gates and the building of Blackfriars Bridge, though the overcrowded river still awaited the building of new docks and the abolition of the legal quays. In a material sense much had been achieved before Johnson's death in Bolt Court in 1784. In the field of politics London's contribution was increasingly important. In 1737 its role in national affairs could still be regarded as a subordinate one; ministers depended almost automatically on the support of the City magnates, and politicians in opposition found the resentment of the lesser merchants a useful weapon in their armour against the administration. From the sixties the City had become much more a political entity in its own right. Though government influence remained strong, ministers had to fight hard to retain it and were not always, as we have seen, successful in so doing. Nor were the opposition more so. They lost an easily controllable weapon and gained an ally who insisted in any clash between them on taking its own course. By the seventies the City had become the hotbed of radical political thought, and when, on occasion, the radicals did capture the civic machinery, they used it, as in the petitioning movements, to promulgate notions of reform that were nearly as unpleasing to the Rockingham Whigs as they were to Lord North. Fighting from the bastion of their privileges, they were able to make a dent in the political thought of the day. It was, however, a dent and not a breakthrough. The violence and destruction of the Gordon Riots, when the old prison of Newgate went up in flames, cured many of its citizens of their radical views, and the end of the American War of Independence and the long ascendency of the younger Pitt removed much that was contentious from the politics of the City and of the nation. Within ten years of Johnson's death the threat of revolutionary France stilled all lesser animosities.

FOUR

The Politicians' London: Lords, Commons, and Court

Though the wealth and independence of the City gave it great influence, the hub of national politics nevertheless lay in Westminster. Here were the Court, the main government departments, including the dominant Treasury, and above all Parliament. Everybody who counted socially was almost certain to have some connection with one of these three. In summer, when Parliament was not sitting and the king had abandoned St. James's for one of his country residences, in the case of George III usually Richmond, Horace Walpole writing to his numerous correspondents moaned again and again that town was empty and nobody was left. Hot weather made London a place of intolerable stench and dust; whoever could, fled from it—the citizens to the neighbouring villages of Highgate, Islington, and the like, the gentry to their country estates. For the Quality it was the prorogation of Parliament and the absence of the Court that made this possible. Perhaps this is to reverse cause and effect. Courtiers and politicians alike had no intention of enduring the summer in London, and therefore Parliament had to be prorogued. It was difficult enough to get a respectable attendance in the early autumn when the country gentlemen were shooting their pheasants and grouse or in the early summer when they began to hanker after their estates. Adroit politicians were apt hold up controversial measures until these members had gone home, leaving only placemen and professional politicians on whose votes the administration could depend. One of the major difficulties of opposition leaders throughout the century was to keep their supporters in London. So, though the labouring poor, the artisans, and the small shop-keepers remained in London, those who could departed.

The House of Lords and the House of Commons between them represented the cream of British society. Neither was a very large assembly. The number of the Lords fluctuated somewhat according to the number of minors or aged among the peers. Others were out of the country on diplomatic missions or serving with the army or navy. In 1759 the effective attendance seems to have been two royal dukes, twenty nonroyal dukes, one marquis, eighty-one earls, two viscounts and fifty-eight barons. Probably some 220 peers could normally be considerd potentially active members, though their actual attendance varied enormously. Bishops also sat in the Lords, and though many of them owed their position to their political usefulness or administrative abilities, many of them were cadets of those families already represented in the person of the head of the family. The number of the Commons, on the contrary, was fixed. There were 558 members, including forty-five for Scotland and twenty-four for Wales. Until the Act of Union of 1801 Ireland had its own Parliament in Dublin. Even including the bishops and the Law Lords, effective legislative power lay in the hands of not much more than 800 persons. Had they been indeed isolated individuals, their presence or absence would have had little effect on the fullness or emptiness of town. This, however, was far from being the case. When a peer or a member of the Commons came to Westminster, he was accompanied by his family, his friends and dependents, and a host of servants and hangers-on. It was these groups that made up the world of the politicians and the world of pleasure. It was they who made London at once a centre of fashion and a centre of power.

Neither the Lords nor the Commons was housed in a way comparable with the dignity of these bodies. The exterior of the Lords was very plain, except for some pinnacles ornamenting the front of the building, which faced Abingdon Street and was connected with Westminster Hall by an outside lobby. The chamber itself was eighty feet long, forty feet wide, and thirty feet high. Housed in the same building was the Princes' Chamber, where the king put on his state robes, and the Painted Chamber, so called from old frescoes on the wall. Grosley, though hampered by his more than limited knowledge of the English language, contrived to be present at the opening of Parliament. He was not impressed by the chamber itself. "Nothing is wanting to this august assembly but a place answerable to its majesty, a place that might vie with the grandeur and magnificence of Ranelagh. The house of peers, in which it is held, is a narrow hall of so little extent, that often times part of the lords, finding it entirely occupied, either remain confounded with the people who crowd the outside of the bar, or are under a necessity of retiring. . . . The furniture is suited to the simplicity of the place: the four wool packs and plain benches fill the enclosure; the panels which separate the windows formed of little panes, are adorned with old tapestry of the sixteenth century on which is depicted the defeat of the invincible armada. The throne, raised upon a few steps and covered by a canopy is the only ornament that strikes the eye. The king never sits on it except with the crown on his head, the sceptre in his hand and the royal mantle over his shoulders."[1] Though Grosley was not impressed by the architectural beauties of the Lords, the ceremony connected with the state opening of Parliament affected him deeply. Even by the eighteenth century it had become rooted in long tradition: today the procedure is still the same that Grosley witnessed, though the old Parliament buildings were burned down in 1834, and the present mock Gothic but dignified pile was erected. "The union of the three powers in the house of peers," he wrote, "is the grandest sight which England can present to the eye of a foreigner." What impressed him particularly was the absence of any military guard or security precautions. "The king, invested with all the ornaments of his dignity, and accompanied by his brothers, mounted his throne without any other guard than that which surrounds a father in the midst of his family, confidence and respect." Grosley then went on to describe the general seating arrangements. "The lord chancellor and the judges were seated at his feet upon four great wool packs, in a quadrangular figure. On the right of the throne stood

[1]Grosley, *A Tour of London* (1772), Vol. 2, p. 191.

the spiritual lords: the temporal peers filled the remainder of the enclosure, at the bar of which stood upon a step the speaker and other members of the house of commons."[2] It was a colourful scene, the peers wearing their full robes, coronets, and decorations and the bishops like fluttering birds with their rockets or lawn sleeves.

De Saussure, when he attended a formal prorogation, was plainly fascinated by the picturesque scene and described the costumes worn with careful detail. The robes of the peers were "very long and ample, scarlet in colour and bordered with ermine. The dukes' robes of state have five bands of gold across the sleeves, from shoulder to elbow, divided by as many bands of ermine. Counts or earls have three bands, viscounts two and barons two. Those noblemen who belong to the Order of the Garter or the Order of the Thistle wear the golden collar of those orders over their robes, fastened on the shoulders with wide black ribbons. The princes of the Church wear their episcopalian garments, which are ample white surplices of cambric, and over these their scarves. Instead of hats they wear flat square black caps, trimmed with a thick tuft of black silk."[3] He was much impressed by the ceremonial procession with its grenadiers, its yeomen of the guard, and the officers of the Houshold. In particular his fancy was caught by the footmen "with swords at their sides, and with sticks in their hands, their livery being scarlet with vests and facings of blue, braided on the seams with two rows of gold braid, between which there are two rows of velvet. Instead of hats they wear small flat caps of velvet." But to him, as to most of the onlookers, the highlight of the procession was the state coach "all the woodwork of which is carved and doubly gilt, the doors being beautifully and delicately painted. The front and sides have large mirrors, and the back and outside are lined with red leather, ornamented with gilt nails, the inside being crimson velvet embroidered in gold with heavy gold fringes. The King only makes use of these eight splendid horses and of this magnificent coach when he goes in state to Parliament."[4] Londoners

[2]Grosley, *op. cit.*, Vol. 2, p. 192.

[3]Cesar de Saussure, *A Foreign View of England in the Reigns of George I and George II* (John Murray, 1902)

[4]*Ibid.*, pp. 57, 58.

enjoyed such spectacles, which added colour to lives that were often drab and squalid and emphasized alike the dignity of Parliament and the splendour of the monarchy.

When Lords was engaged in ordinary business, its general atmosphere was much less formal. Peers wore their normal clothes, though eighteenth-century fashions must have made their meetings more colourful than the dark-hued lounge suits of today. Most of them would probably have agreed with Grosley on the shortcomings of their chamber. The benches were traditional rather than comfortable, and in winter it was notoriously a cold, draughty place in spite of the great fireplace on the left wall. Peers were supposed to sit according to their rank—the dukes nearest to the throne, then the earls and viscounts, and facing them, on the left of the throne, the spiritual peers. The barons sat on the crossbenches. In a full house the earls were overcrowded on their benches, and the barons less so. These rules with regard to seating were often disregarded, for individual peers were apt to maneuver to get a seat as near to the fire as possible; in the absence of the judges even the woolsacks were invaded in the pursuit of warmth and comfort! Generally it was possible for persons with the necessary credentials to obtain admission to listen to the debates, but this was a privilege that both Lords and Commons could withdraw at will. In May 1738 the peers decided to exclude all strangers in order to prevent any record of their speeches being passed on to the press and published. This move on the part of their husbands much annoyed some of the peeresses. With the Duchess of Queensbury and Lady Huntingdon as their ring leaders, a group of them went to the House and demanded admission to the public visitors' enclosure. When this was refused and the doors shut against them, dignity and restrain were abandoned; the noble ladies banged on the doors and shrieked their annoyance, but all in vain. The doors remained locked. Next they resorted to stratagem. A sudden calm fell, and for half an hour the guileful peeresses made no sound, thereby lulling their husbands into the belief that they had abandoned their intentions and gone home. Accordingly the doors were opened, and in rushed the triumphant ladies, who, once inside, listened to the debate with every mark of interest.[5] Grosley,

[5]*The Letters and Works of Lady Mary Montagu* (ed. Lord Wharncliffe, 1837), Vol. 2, p. 248.

having succeeded in listening to a debate, had the doubtful pleasure of hearing "the old duke of Newcastle speak: the latter delivered himself as he was leaning on two young lords, who sat before him on the second bench."[6]

In the politics of the day the influence of the Lords was very great. Though the peers had lost the right to amend money bills sent to them by the Commons, they could, and frequently did, reject other measures. Indeed it was a ministerial device to let some measure that was popular with the country gentlemen of the lower house pass through all its stages there without attempting to obstruct it, secure in the knowledge that it would be defeated in the upper one. It was not so much the opposition of the City as the fear that his enemies were undermining his influence in the Lords that made Sir Robert Walpole withdraw his excise bill in 1733.[7] Invariably some of the most important ministers were drawn from the peerage, because their wealth and family connections gave them control over so many of the borough constituencies and considerable patronage, which they could use to further the ends of government. Leading opposition politicians were in the Lords for the same reason, namely, that they were wealthy enough and could exercise enough political patronage in their own right to be able to collect around them members of the Commons who, for public or private reasons, were prepared to resist government measures. Such men did not need oratory. Lord Rockingham, for instance, was a miserable speaker and had hardly opened his mouth in the Lords when he became First Lord of the Treasury at the age of 32. He had, however, extensive estates in Yorkshire and Ireland and a very large rent roll. In the same way, it is unlikely that the Duke of Grafton would ever have been called upon to undertake the responsibilities of the Treasury and to act as leading minister of the Crown had he not been a duke. Newcastle himself, though a much abler politician than he is sometimes given the credit for being, came into politics not because he was an eloquent speaker, which he certainly was not, or an efficient administrator, but because he was a peer and a

[6]Grosley, *op. cit.*, Vol. 2, p. 107.

[7]See J. H. Plumb, *Sir Robert Walpole* (Crescent Press, 1956), Vol. 2, for details.

very wealthy landowner. In eighteenth-century London therefore the peers provided the nucleus of the ministries and the Court; the world of politics and the world of fashion were an integrated whole.

By the eighteenth century, however, it had become clear that the successful management of the House of Commons was a *sine qua non* for any stable administration, and from the time of Walpole at least one of the leading ministers had been a member of the lower house. Because it held the power of the purse, there the ultimate fight for power must take place. For foreign visitors the Commons was also an irresistible attraction, for nothing quite like it was to be found in Europe. Because of its importance in the life of the nation, men like Grosley were surprised by the simplicity of its setting. It resembled, he wrote, "an ancient chapel; it is of an oblong form. . . . At the farther end of the saloon, there is a large glass casement, which, as in most buildings of this sort, lets in too great a glare so as to dazzle the eyes of the assembly, their faces being turned towards the speaker's chair." In his opinion "The majesty of the people of England but ill displays itself in this place," which, he thought, when compared with the magnificence provided for the councils of Venice and Genoa, had "no better appearance than a rustic grotto."[8] Charles P. Moritz from Berlin, who visited England in 1782, was also disappointed in the setting, which he described as "a rather mean looking building, that not a little resembles a chapel." Having managed with the aid of a two-shilling bribe to get a place in the strangers' gallery, he provided his readers with a graphic picture of the scene. "The speaker, an elderly man, dressed in an enormous wig, with two knotted curls behind and a black cloak, with his hat on his head, sat opposite to me on a lofty chair, before which stands a table, like an altar; and at this there sit two men, called clerks, dressed in black with black cloaks. On the table, by the side of the great parchment acts, lies a huge gilt sceptre, which is always taken away and placed in a conservatory under the table, as soon as ever the speaker quits the chair . . . All round, on the sides of the house under the gallery, are benches for the members, covered with green cloth, always one above the other, in order that he who is

[8]Grosley, *op. cit.*, Vol. 2, p. 288.

speaking, may see over those who sit before him. The seats in the gallery are on the same plan."[9]

Foreign visitors were puzzled by the lack of gravity and almost disorderly behaviour in the House. "They even come into the house in their great coats, and with boots and spurs. It is not at all uncommon to see a member lying stretched out on one of the benches while others are debating. Some crack nuts, others eat oranges, or whatever else is in season. There is no end to their going in or out; and as often as anyone wishes to go out, he places himself before the speaker and makes his bow, as if, like a school boy, he asked his tutor's permission." The majority of speeches also seemed to lack the dignity that the foreign observer expected. Moritz goes on to describe the typical behaviour of the House: "Those who speak seem to deliver themselves with but little, perhaps not even with a decorous gravity. All that is necessary, is to stand up in your place, take off your hat, turn to the speaker (to whom all the speeches are addressed), to hold your hat and stick in one hand, and with the other to make any such motions as you fancy necessary to accompany your speech. If it happens that a member rises who is but a bad speaker, or if what he says is generally deemed not sufficiently interesting, so much noise is made, that he can scarcely distinguish his own words . . . on the contrary, when a favourite member, and one who speaks well, and to the purpose, rises, the most perfect silence reigns: and his friends and admirers, one after another, make their approbation known by calling out *hear him!*"[10] Grosley received much the same impression: "The meetings of the house are very noisy and tumultuous. Every member talks to the person next to him, and scarce seems to give any attention to what is said at the bar, except when the friends of the question command silence and attention by crying Aye, Aye."[11] "The little less than downright, open abuse, and the many really rude things, which the members says to each other," Moritz writes, "struck me much. For example when one has finished, another rises and immediately taxes with

[9]C. P. Moritz, "Travels through Various Parts of England in 1782," in *The British Tourist*, Vol. 4, edited by W. F. Mavor (1798), p. 27.

[10]Moritz, *ibid.*, p. 27.

[11]Grosley, *op. cit.*, Vol. 2, P. 289.

absurdity all the Honourable gentleman (for with this title the men of the house of commons always compliment each other) had just advanced. It would indeed be contrary to the rules of the house flatly to tell each other, that what they had spoken, is false, or even foolish: instead of this, they turn themselves to the speaker, and so, whilst their address is directed to him, they fancy they violate neither the rules of parliament, nor the good breeding and decorum, by uttering the most cutting personal sarcasms against the member or the measure, they oppose."[12]

Despite such criticism, the House certainly had a sense of occasion, and important speeches from ministers, or from opposition speakers, were listened to with close attention. The modern party organization had not yet taken shape; though the man who saw in politics at once his career and his major interest was likely to belong either to a group of ministerial supporters or to one opposing them, the country gentleman, who owed his seat either to the regard in which he was held by neighboring county families or to his control of a pocket borough, was sufficiently independent to need convincing by argument. Sir Robert Walpole indulged in few flights of oratory—he left those to William Pulteney—but generally speaking he had the feel of the House and complimented members' understanding by the carefully argued and well informed speeches in which he put his proposals before them. Pitt, unlike Walpole, was an orator. Johnson compared the former to a fixed star, the latter to a meteor flashing across the sky. His speeches had the brilliance of the genuine parliamentary spellbinder. Even as a young man he could stir and delight the House, but after his triumphs in directing the Seven Years' War a major speech by Pitt was accorded a special reverence. Count Kielmansegge was lucky enough to be able to listen to a debate in which Pitt spoke and was of the opinion that "There can be no denying that he is one of the most powerful speakers of our time, he had undoubtedly prepared his speech before hand, but he answered categorically, and in a very thorough manner all the reproaches which had been levelled against him during the day and the arguments brought against his opinions. When he speaks a look of fixed attention is promptly visible upon the features of all present

[12]Moritz, *op. cit.*, p. 30.

and absolute silence reigns in the whole House especially among the strangers, so that you do not lose a word."[13] He was much less impressed by George Grenville who followed him. This was one of the periods when the two brothers-in-law were estranged. Pitt it will be remembered had married Lady Hester Grenville. Because George Grenville had been opposed to Pitt's resigning the Secretaryship in 1761 after having failed to get the cabinet to agree to an immediate declaration of war on Spain. Generally the House listened to him with respect, for even though he was pompous in manner and extremely legalistically minded, his arguments were sound and his speeches well informed. But against the oratory of Pitt he cut a poor figure. On one famous occasion, during a period of strained relations, when Grenville in a speech on taxation paused to ask dramatically where the necessary money could be raised without recourse to the measures he was proposing, Pitt maliciously filled the silence with the refrain from a popular song, "Gentle Sheppard tell me where?" Inevitably the unfortunate Grenville became known as "The Gentle Sheppard." It was such episodes that drove Grosley to ask: "Who would not, upon seeing the greatest personages in England treating the most important state affairs in this manner, who would not I say, be tempted to look upon the English as the gayest, most jovial, and most addicted to buffoonery of all nations?"[14] There was apparently very little light relief in the speech to which Kielmansegge listened, for George Grenville was not good at that kind of things, and the Count found it "so inferior to the previous one, and so very long, and had so little sequence that it was hard to know what he was driving at beyond the point that everything was obviously intended to damage his brother-in-law, without reference to the previous debate. Consequently he began to bore not only myself, but apparently all the others who left during the speech."[15]

In spite of much outward flippancy, which at times made the Commons seem more like a collection of noisy schoolboys, a character that it has not altogether lost even today, than the chief

[13]Kielmansegge, *op. cit.,* p. 163.

[14]Grosley, *op. cit.,* Vol. 2, p. 208.

[15]Kielmansegge, *op. cit.,* p. 165.

representative council in the land, the members took themselves and their speeches seriously. Burke once told Dr. Johnson that "it is very well worth while for a man to take pains to speak well in parliament. A man, who has vanity, speaks to display his talents, and if a man speaks well, he gradually establishes a certain reputation and consequence in the general opinion, which sooner or later will have its political reward. Besides, though not one vote is gained, a good speech has its effect. Though an act which has been ably opposed passes into a law, yet in its progress it is modelled, it is softened in such a manner, that we plainly see the Minister has been told that the members attached to him are so sensible of its injustice or absurdity from what they have heard, that it must be altered." Moreover, he added, "There are many members who generally go with the Ministers, who will not go all lengths. There are many honest well meaning country gentlemen who are in parliament only to keep up the consequence of their families."[16] These observations show a very sound insight into the attitude of the Commons. He added also the characteristic comment: "And, Sir, there is the gratification of pride. Though we cannot outvote them we will out-argue them. They shall not do wrong without it being shown both to themselves and to the world."[17]

Political feeling through much of his London stay ran high, but basically, except for such episodes as the Middlesex election, until the revolt of the American colonies, which produced sharply differing and bitterly conflicting views, the struggle was for power rather than for policies. As the Doctor caustically observed, "Politicks are now nothing more than a means of rising in the world. With this sole view do men engage in politicks, and their whole conduct preceeds upon it."[18] Politics were a game that combined the excitement of the contest and the solid rewards of success. No account of Dr. Johnson's London would be complete that ignored the fascination that the political intrigues and fortunes of the day had both for the contestants themselves and for the closed society in which they operated. In the absence of or-

[16]J. Boswell, *Life of Samuel Johnson*, Vol. 3, p. 233.

[17]*Ibid.*, Vol. 3, p. 233.

[18]*Ibid.*, Vol. 2, p. 69.

ganized parties to regiment men into two opposing camps, the political situation was perpetually fluid. Ambitious men grouped themselves around their chosen political patron. They were "the friends of Lord Rockingham" or "the friends of the Duke of Newcastle," and it was from such groups that ministries were formed. Inevitably some were unsuccessful in obtaining office, and from them came the spearhead of opposition in the Lords and Commons as they tried to oust their successful rivals by making it impossible for them to carry on the king's business. Such a naked fight for power could hardly be acknowledged when political convention banned consistent and organized opposition to the royal government as disloyal and well nigh treasonable. Causes and consciences were required. General warrants and the Middlesex election helped Rockingham and his friends to proclaim themselves as the defenders of the liberty of the subject; at times political bitterness and strife rose to a shrill crescendo of abuse not only against the ministers but even, in the case of George III, against the king himself. Charges of corruption were the stock-in-trade of politicians in opposition who disseminated the belief that by his use of influence and patronage the king was subverting the independence of Parliament itself. The fact that a large proportion of the Commons was composed of country gentlemen, who were uninterested in obtaining places and whose votes and cooperation had to be won by persuasion and argument, was something that politicians out of office preferred to ignore. Johnson thought that "a certain degree of crown influence over the Houses of Parliament was very salutary, nay, even necessary, in our mixed government" and that the charges of corruption and undue influence were much exaggerated. Recent research has shown that he was right.

It is not easy today to recapture the flavour of the eighteenth-century House of Commons, though much of the procedure is remarkably unchanged. Moritz would still find the speaker quitting the chair "as often as the house resolved itself into a committee. A committee means nothing more than the house puts itself into a situation freely to discuss and debate any point of difficulty and moment, and, while it lasts, the speaker lays aside his power as a moderator. As soon as this is over someone tells the speaker that he may now again be seated; and immediately on the speaker's being again in the chair, the sceptre is also replaced on the table before him."[19] Because there was much less business to be got through, parliamentary sessions were shorter than they are now, and such devices as the guillotine and the closure were unknown. Debates were allowed to take their leisurely course until the patience of the members was exhausted and they chorused out "The question, the question," demanding the formula that "The question now be put" and the division taken. A modern observer transported back would probably be surprised at the limited nature of the business before the House. The eighteenth century felt no need to sponsor a continual programme of new legislation. By and large members not only accepted but approved of the social structure. The whole conception of remaking society by the legislative power of Parliament would have been abhorrent to Lords and Commons alike. So would any attempt to liberalize the Constitution. Most of the measures discussed were related to either the raising of revenue or the implementing of foreign policy. In addition there was a great deal of local legislation that dealt with the carrying through of some enclosure project, or the setting up of a special authority to manage the poor in some particular town, or authorizing the creation of a turnpike trust to improve local roads or, in the seventies and eighties, a company to make a canal. The majority of members were completely uninterested in such matters; only the member from the constituency and his friends were concerned. Very occasionally the conscience of the House would be stirred by some particularly glaring exposure of social injustice and cruelty, such as the state of the prisons in the early years of the century, the desperate position of persons imprisoned for debt, or the appalling death rate of infants in workhouses. Then a select committee would be appointed to collect evidence and make recommendations. Generally they were more successful in the first than in the second task, because revolting as was the state of things revealed by the committees, both administrative and psychological difficulties made the subsequent legislation, even if any was attempted, very largely ineffective. What generated the greatest interest were the debates on foreign policy, when the opposition could ask that the

[19]Moritz, *op. cit.*, p. 27.

papers most likely to be embarrassing to ministers be laid before
the House, and financial debates when the opposition could drop
endless hints of corruption, demanding details that no contemporary government department, hindered by almost medieval methods of accounting, could produce. Perhaps the greatest moments
of excitement and tension came when a new House met after a
general election; charges of improper practices and corrupt bargains could then be hurled around and petitions presented to
unseat successful candidates on these charges. No one expected
the investigating committee to be impartial; it was a way of testing
the amount of support the House was prepared to give to the
minister of the day. It was because these petitions began to show
a steady drift against his friends that Walpole was finally driven
to resign after the election of 1742. Viewed from this angle, they
were the parliamentary opinion poll of the day.

A modern observer would also find the style of the speeches
very different from the fashion of modern-day debates. This was
partly because the eighteenth-century House of Commons was
socially an extremely homogeneous body. The greater part of its
members had received the standard education of a gentleman,
whether it had been acquired at one of the great schools such as
Eton, Winchester, or Westminster, or at home with a private
tutor. Most of them had probably put in a little time at one of the
universities or at the Inns of Court or had made the Grand Tour
on the Continent. This education was severely classical. Some
members had reached high standards of scholarship, others had
no more than had been flogged into them by their schoolmasters.
But all had some acquaintance with classical tags and mythology
and were expected to adorn their speeches with the fruits of their
learning. They all shared much the same background of culture
and taste—their houses, their pictures, their gardens, their furniture, all conformed to a general pattern. So did their social as-
sumptions. It was this shared heritage that gave Parliament its
particular character and lessened political animosity. In the cut
and thrust of debate members could lambast their honourable
opponents with whatever invective sprang to their lips and later,
once the House had risen, drink and dine together as the best of
friends. Also, what was said in debate was not in theory for public
consumption. As we have seen, both houses considered the re-

porting of their debates a breach of privilege. This did not, in
fact, prevent its being done. Journalists in the public gallery took
surreptious notes and filled in the gaps from memory or imagination as best they might. Often members who were proud of a
speech or who wanted their sentiments to reach a wider public
furnished copies themselves under a seal of secrecy. Sometimes
the debates were published under transparent disguises. Between
November 1740 and February 1743 Dr. Johnson furnished these
for Cave of the Gentleman's Magazine under the title of "The
Senate of Lilliput." Sometimes he was able to get skeleton information about what was actually said; sometimes he knew no more
than the names of the speakers and the part they had played in
the debate and had to fall back on his imagination for their oratory. He seems to have regarded these fabrications as a form of
literary exercise, and when he discovered many people believed them to be genuine, he refused to continue his contributions. Despite the difficulties, and the danger of legal prosecutions
until the Commons' unsuccessful brush with the Lord Mayor
Crosby, so avid was London's reading public for news of parliamentary proceedings that accounts of the debates, more or less
complete and more or less accurate, continued to be published.
Today the historian is better placed than the reader of London's
newssheets to obtain an accurate picture of what really happened
on the floor of the House in those days, because many of the
members themselves kept parliamentary diaries in which the
substance, if not the more flowery oratorical flourishes, of the
more important speeches was noted down.

Westminster was not only the home of the politicians, but
also the headquarters of the lawyers. Criminal cases were dealt
with at the Old Bailey, near the great gaol of Newgate, but the
four great judicial tribunals of the country—King's Bench, Common Pleas, Chancery, and the Court of the Exchequer—all ad-
joined the great Hall of Westminster that was part of the original
palace of the medieval kings. During the legal term the Hall was
a busy place. Lawyers in their wigs and gowns sauntered around
looking at the stalls of the booksellers, printers, and picture
dealers who occupied the booths that lined its sides, or stood in
groups discussing some nice legal point, or hurried purposefully
into one of the four Courts. Within these walls vital decisions

The First Day of Term; a typical view of Westminster Hall.

were taken that affected the lives and liberties of British subjects
everywhere. The eighteenth century saw some great lawyers, and
their decisions played a major part in politics. Ambitious lawyers
played the political game with anxious care in the hope of landing
one of the prizes of their profession—the Solicitor General's or
Attorney General's office or, greatest prize of all, the coverted
position of Lord Chancellor with its power, dignity, and political
importance. As in earlier periods, the law was still the most promising professional ladder for social and political advancement;
several of the century's great Lord Chancellors came from undis-
tinguished families. Philip Yorke, later Earl of Hardwicke, was
the son of a country attorney; politics were to make him the
lifelong friend of the querulous and self-conscious Duke of Newcastle. To read his correspondence is to be impressed by his wide

political knwledge and balanced point of view as he picked his
way through the labyrinth of maneuver and intrigue and comfort-
ed or cautioned his noble friend. Indeed so active and influential
was he as a politician that it is easy to forget his great contributions as a lawyer. Another great lawyer-statesman was William
Murray, better known as Lord Mansfield. At heart he disliked
political life; though he was a brilliant speaker, he argued as a
lawyer, not as a House of Commons man, which, although it
listened to his arguments, disliked his style. It was unfortunate for
him that as Attorney General under Walpole he had to endure the
raging, biting eloquence of young Pitt, and it was with thankful-
ness that in 1757 he was able to exchange his political post for the
more congenial position of Lord Chief Justice of the King's
Bench. There as Lord Mansfield he established his reputation as
one of the great lawyers of his day. It was by one of his famous
judgments that a slave setting foot in England was declared to be
free. It was he, too, who sent John Wilkes to King's Bench prison
for his seditious libel: in general and by temperament Mansfield
was a supporter of law and order as interpreted by George III
and his ministers, being himself of a conservative cast of mind.
Very different in temperament and outlook was his great legal
rival Sir Charles Pratt, later Lord Camden. Pratt and Pitt had
been at Eton together and politically continued to act in concert
in the tumultuous years after 1761. Pratt's views were Whiggish in
the sense that in his interpretation of the law the safeguarding of
a subject's liberty, which in practice tended to be political liberty,
loomed large. It was he who freed John Wilkes on the ground
that parliamentary privilege covered seditious libel, Wilkes'
friends having had the foresight to apply for a writ of habeas
corpus in Common Pleas, over which Pratt presided, rather than
in his rival's Court of King's Bench. It was Pratt who took the
stand against general warrants and finally gave his judicial opinion against them. Unlike Mansfield he was a political animal, and
his ambition was the Great Seal, which Pitt was determined to get
for him when, as Earl of Chatham, he formed his disastrous
ministry in 1766. This determination was the prelude to a personal tragedy because Charles Yorke, Lord Hardwicke's younger son,
had a compulsive urge to succeed his father on the Woolsack. The
rivalry between the two men illustrates well the personal nature

of much of eighteenth-century politics. Men like Lord Rockingham, who had grown up in the Newcastle-Hardwicke connection, championed Yorke while Pitt championed Pratt. The result
was to divide the Whig faction that was opposing George III and
his ministers and thus make their cooperation more uneasy. In
1766 Pitt carried his point, and Pratt, as Lord Camden, became
Lord Chancellor. Then tragically in January 1770 Yorke achieved
his ambition: Camden was dismissed by an indignant George III
who offered the Great Seal to his rival. To refuse was to lose his
lifelong dream forever; to accept was to ruin the plans of his
friends. Torn betwen ambition, a genuine loyalty to the king,
and loyalty to his friends, he wavered, accepted, and three days
later was dead. London buzzed with rumours, and most people
believed that, distraught by the burden of choice, he had taken
his own life.

Not all attempts to combine politics with the law ended so
tragically. Many famous lawyers divided their time between the
Courts and the Commons, passing and repassing through Westminster Hall in their daily routine. There was Dunning who is
remembered more for his famous resolution that "the power of
the Crown has increased, is increasing and ought to be dimin-
ished" than for his judicial decisions, "Bully" Norton who, it is
reported, with a leer asked a prisoner whom he had just sentenced to death, "When will it be agreeable for you to be executed?" and Lord Thurlow of the black brow and sarcastic tongue
who nevertheless in his young days was much admired by the
fair. A student of law might have been interested to catch a
glimpse of Blackstone, the first Vinerian professor of English Law
at Oxford who had been returned for Hindon in Wiltshire in the
1761 election. He became even better known after 1770 when the
last of his famous volumes of *Commentaries on the Laws of
England* was published. Blackstone was not attracted by the
excitements and rewards of a political career, though ministers
were favourably disposed toward him. He preferred to devote his
talents and his time to the law, and in 1770 became Sir William
and a justice of the Court of Common Pleas.

Being so much at the centre of the centre of the nation's
political life, Londoners not surprisingly were keenly interested in

the doings in Parliament, and even ordinary citizens were rather well informed as to what was happening in the world of politics. This was a source of perpetual astonishment to foreign visitors who, for the most part coming from countries where government was a mystic institution reserved for the few, did not expect ordinary citizens, much less artisans, to concern themselves with such matters. Grosley was surprised to find a debating club presided over by a baker and composed of such men as masons, carpenters, and smiths where "Public affairs, and even religious topics, equally claim the attentions and speculations of this meeting at which the subjects that occasion most debate in parliament are often discussed."[20] This society, which met at the Robin Hood tavern twice a week, was well known, and for an entrance fee of 6 pence a night nonmembers were permitted to listen to its discussions. According to Archenholtz, this interest in politics was widespread. He declared that "It is often with the greatest difficulty that you can prevail on an Englishman to speak; his answer is seldom more than *yes* or *no:* but if one has the address to turn the subject to politics, his face immediately brightens up, he opens his mouth, and becomes eloquent, for this topic, if we may use the expression, is combined with his existence."[21] One proof of this political awareness on the part of Londoners was seen in the constant demand for newspapers and political pamphlets on every conceivable subject and from every conceivable point of view. Indeed Archenholtz was inclined to attribute the "excessive moroseness and unsociable temper of the English" to "this extreme eagerness to read these immense quantities of Gazettes and political papers which are printed every day." Perhaps this eagerness is more explicable when it is remembered that the politicians at Westminister were not remote figures cut off from the everyday life of the capital. They attended the theatres of Drury Lane and Covent Garden, they strolled in St. James's Park, their coaches were seen in the streets, and many Londoners, either directly or indirectly, were dependent on them for a livelihood. Their footmen and servants mingled with the craftsmen in

[20]Grosley, *op. cit.*, Vol. 2, p. 150.

[21]Archenholz, *op. cit.*, p. 63.

the taverns. Not only were they real people, but the laws they
passed at Westminster might have a very direct bearing on the
fortunes of ordinary folk; therefore for those of them who were
literate political journalism played an important part in their life.
Earlier in the century the favourite medium had been the pamphlet, but for the quick cut and thrust of politics the weekly or
even daily newspaper was found to be more serviceable. When
Johnson first came to London, the weekly journal *The Craftman*,
under the control of Walpole's enemies, was pouring out its
stream of abuse, which the *Daily Gazetteer*, subsidized by the
administration, did its best to counteract. In the early days of
George III's reign these roles were sustained by the notorious
North Briton and *The Briton*, written by Smollett, both of them
weeklies. Under the influence of the mounting political crisis of
1769, the *Middlesex Journal* was published in April of that year
with the express purpose of attacking the ministry, as its subtitle,
Chronicle of Liberty, proclaimed. Other newspapers, founded for
avowedly less partisan purposes, provided more objective political news. By the fifties the leading dailies were *The Publick
Advertiser*, *The Gazetteer*, and *The London Daily Advertiser*; the
chief evening newspapers, published three times a week, included
The London Chronicle, to which Johnson was a contributor, and
the *London Evening Post*. In 1771 the editor of the latter was
John Almon who, by defying the ban on publishing undisguised
accounts of the debates in the House of Commons, precipitated
the conflict between the City, in the persons of Lord Mayor Brass
Crosby and Alderman Oliver, and the Commons that we mentioned before. Another of the offending papers was the *Morning
Chronicle*, also founded in 1769, whose editor William Woodfall
was the owner of so prodigious a memory that without taking a
single note, after listening to a debate from the gallery, he could
write it up with astonishing accuracy in the columns of his paper.
Before Johnson died there were six main daily papers, though
some were more interested in commercial than political news, and
nine evening papers. None had what today would be described as
large circulations, except on special occasions, as when *The Publick Advertiser* published the mysterious and vitriolic "Letters of
Junius," whose authorship still remains one of the best kept
secrets in the history of journalism. Few rose above 3000, al-

though through the media of the coffeehouses they reached a much wider public than that figure would suggest.

There was also an almost insatiable market for topical comment in the form of satirical prints, which were skillfully used by the opponents of the ministry to inflame public opinion against it. During Johnson's early years in London the campaign against Walpole was being conducted by a flood of prints illustrating his misdeeds and his corrupt practices with a wealth of allusions that could only have been meaningful to men thoroughly familiar with politics of the day.[22] Each political crisis produced a new outpouring. In 1756, with the loss of Minorca, the anger of Londoners at the incompetence of Newcastle and the failure of Admiral Byng made them eager purchasers of antiministerial prints, which appeared on the stalls and in the shops by the hundred. Mathew Darly, a well known dealer in such wares, gave his caricatures an even wider circulation by reproducing many of them on cards, some 2½ by 4 inches, that could easily be sent by post. In these prints many ministers were represented as animals—Fox almost inevitably by that cunning animal, Newcastle as often as not as his dupe, a goose, while poor Britannia and the British lion were depicted as the victims of every kind of folly, corruption, and exploitation. Later, in the early years of George III's reign, contemporary caricature reached new depths of scurrility in their attacks on Bute, symbolized as a jackboot, and his supposed liaison with the Dowager Princess of Wales. Long after his effective influence over the king had disappeared, he remained the subject of the political cartoonist, and the impact that this constant stream of political abuse made on public opinion did much to perpetuate the legend of the minister behind the curtain. Later Lord North and Charles James Fox were the targets of a bitter campaign that helped to create a most unfavourable political atmosphere for them before the general election of 1784. Undoubtedly the Londoner was a political animal; otherwise he would never have parted with his sixpences and his shillings for such merchandise.

Their interest in politics was not confined to reading pamph-

[22]See M. D. George, *Political Caricature to 1792. A Study of Opinions and Propaganda* (Clarendon Press, 1959).

lets and newssheets or to laughing over some particularly apt cartoon. All classes and all sections of the metropolis were prepared to demonstrate if they thought that their special interest were likely to be adversely affected by some proposal before Parliament. The protests and petitions organized by the City itself were, as we have seen, impressive and dignified occasions. The protests of the workers ranged from the pathetic march of the Spitalfields weavers, accompanied by their wives and children, to the tumultuous gatherings of the coal heavers, but all shared a common belief that injustice should not be suffered supinely and that it was the business of Parliament to redress their grievances. Not all these demonstrations were as spontaneous as they seemed, however. Often they were stirred up by political opponents of the ministers in order to embarrass them. An outstanding example of such tactics was the use of the mob by Walpole's enemies during the debates on the excise bill. Every instrument of propaganda—editorials, broadsheets, squibs, cartoons and rabblerousing choruses—was used to stir the citizens to action. On the day that the hated bill was postponed, which, as everyone knew, meant its end, the mob swarmed around Westminster in an ugly mood, looking for trouble and refusing to disperse even after the reading of the Riot Act. Walpole, as he left the Commons, was hustled and insulted and had difficulty in getting away. During the Wilkes crisis similar scenes were enacted. When attempts were made to alter the calendar, to provide for the nationalization of foreign Jews, or to alleviate the legal position of the Roman Catholics the London tradesman and artisan demonstrated his innate conservatism or his contempt for the men who sat at Westminster with his lungs, his fists, and his feet.

Even elections were more democratic in London than in most parts of Britain. In the City elections the liveryman was entitled to vote and so enjoyed a brief moment of importance, though the ordinary householder was debarred from doing so. This was not the case in Westminster where the franchise was a remarkably wide one: it was one of the few constituencies with an electoral roll of more than 10,000. As a result the contest was always lively and could be tumultuous. It might be thought that men who could have found some safe and secure pocket borough elsewhere would have preferred to do so. This was not the case.

To be one of the two members for Westminster conveyed a certain prestige, and the Westminster electors showed a preference for a well known name. Generally their sympathies were antiministerial. Charles James Fox was their darling. Dr. Johnson, who knew him well, in the crisis of 1784 described him as the man "who has divided the Kingdom with Caesar; so that it was a doubt whether the nation should be ruled by the septre of George III, or the tongue of Fox."[23] Even after his dismissal by the king, when the full force of the official machine had been used against him in the election of 1785, Westminster sent him back to Parliament as their representative. Though the old tavern that once stood there has long been replaced by a modern building, a Soho pub still bears the name of *The Valiant Fox* in his honour.

German and French visitors found the business of choosing a representative to serve in Parliament a particularly British phenomenon. Pastor Moritz has left a graphic description of a by-election in Westminster in 1783 when Sir Cecil Wray was returned, which is worth quoting. "The election was held in Covent Garden, a large market place in the open air. There was a scaffold erected just before the door of a very handsome church, which is also called St. Paul's but is not to be compared to the cathedral. A temporary edifice, formed only of boards and wood nailed together, was erected on the occasion. It was called the hustings: and filled with benches; and at one end of it, where the benches ended, mats were laid: on which those who spoke to the people stood. In the area before the hustings, immense multitudes of people were assembled; of which the greatest part seemed to be of the lowest order. To this tumultuous crowd however, the speaker often bowed very low, and always addressed them by the title of *gentlemen*. Sir Cecil Wray was obliged to step forward, and promise these same *gentlemen*, with hand on heart, that he would faithfully fulfill his duties as their representative. . . . The moment that he began to speak, even this rude rabble became as quiet as the raging sea after a storm; only every now and then rending the air with the parliamentary cry of 'hear him! hear him!' and as soon as he had done speaking, they again vociferated a loud and universal huzza, everyone at the same time waving his

[23]Boswell, *Life of Samuel Johnson*, Vol. 4, p. 292.

hat."[24] It was events of this sort, rare though they were, that made Englishmen boast of their liberty, and elections were eagerly welcomed, not only because treating was universal and beer flowed freely but because for a brief period the vote of the ordinary man was solicited, hat in hand, by his betters.

The London of the politicans was also the London of fashionable society. When Parliament reassembled in the autumn everybody with any pretensions to social importance flocked to London and the season began. Wealthy peers usually owned substantial town houses which, if they had not quite the magnificence of the Paris hotel, were nevertheless splendid settings for lavish entertainment; predominant among them was Northumberland House, near Charing Cross. One can easily imagine the bustle of activity in these mansions as the skeleton summer staff was augmented by the hordes of servants that are needed in any great establishment and all was made ready for their aristocratic owners. The arrangements made by members of the lower house, or by the visitors who came to London either for pleasure or for gain, followed a less uniform pattern. Those members who were merchants in the City had in most cases their permanent home in London, perhaps in the City itself or in the parishes to the East but often in the fashionable area of St. James's or Hanover Square. The majority of country gentlemen either took a furnished house or, if resources were limited or the family small, furnished lodgings. Both were to be found in the most fashionable parts of the town. Archenholtz was impressed by the ease with which this could be done. "In a few hours," he wrote, "a house may be hired and in a day or two completely furnished. Persons who are not willing to purchase furniture, may take a furnished house by the year or the month. This is very generally practised, for no family of distinction, coming up to London from the country, ever take up their abode in an inn."[25] Kielmansegge found it difficult to secure lodgings at a reasonable price when he arrived there in 1761, which he attributed to the fact that "The arrival in London of so many foreigners, as well as people from all parts of England, had

[24]Moritz, *op. cit.,* p. 33.

[25]Archenholtz, *op. cit.,* p. 228.

raised the price of lodgings a little, especially in this district and we had to pay for one room, not over large, consisting of a bedroom and dressing room combined, with common mahogany furniture, which is found in most houses here, and a room for the servant 35s a week; our two fellow travellers for a somewhat bigger room paid 3½ guineas."[26] The influx of visitors was due to the forthcoming coronation of George III. Once established in their temporary residences, friends renewed old contacts, the ladies of the family inspected the latest fashions, ordered fresh mantles and bonnets or hats, and generally prepared themselves for the round of pleasures that provided the background to political life.

Such social activities were far from being politically unimportant. At balls, routs, and dinners problems were discussed and strategy was planned. By adroit social attentions waverers might be won over and political followings increased. One reason for this close integration of political and social life was the important part played by patronage in contemporary politics. In the absence of any organized party system this was the cement that gave cohesion to parliamentary life. The administration itself only controlled a very limited number of seats. Sir Lewis Namier estimated the number in the Parliament of 1761 as about 30.[27] Ministers could also count on the support of the placemen, who held some position of profit under the Crown, to provide them with a solid block of dependable votes. But the members who could be directly controlled in this way were not sufficiently numerous to give the ministers the majority that they needed if the king's business was to go forward smoothly. For this they relied on the goodwill of the independent members, many of whom represented their own pocket boroughs or owed their seat to a patron. Though many of the country gentlemen were completely uninterested in anything that the Crown had to offer, it was understood that a member who gave consistent support to the administration expected his loyalty to be rewarded by some

[26]Kielmansegge, op. cit., p. 7.

[27]Sir Lewis Namier, The Structure of Politics on the Accession of George III (Macmillan, 1957), p. 162.

attention to his wishes and interests in the disposal of government patronage. The voters who had returned him to Parliament expected to have their compliance recognized not so much by direct bribery as by his willingness to further their interest. If he were to maintain his control over the borough, he had to be able to demonstrate his power to serve them. Even though this in some cases might not be necessary, in an age when the relationship of client and patron was a perfectly respectable one he expected, through his influence with ministers, to be able to help his family or his friends. Such favours were a status symbol: to receive none, whether they were in fact necessary or not, was to display one's political unimportance to the world. The song

> Nothing is for nothing,
> Nothing is for free,
> I look after you Jack,
> You look after me.

sums up well enough the patronage rat race of the eighteenth century. This had side effects. Ministers dispensed patronage only to those who were great enough or important enough to be "obliged." Therefore anyone who wanted a commission in the army or navy, or looked for preferment in the Church, or even wanted some minor administrative post was forced to badger and solicit the help of some social superior, who either had such gifts at his own disposal or whose political importance was such that ministers would consider favorably his application on behalf of a client. Much of Boswell's first visit to London was employed in the search for a patron who could secure for him the commission in the footguards that he so much coveted. At first he had hopes of the Duke of Queensbury; then, when he proved unhelpful, he tried to enlist the support of the Duke of Northumberland, but despite fair words and high hopes the quest was unsuccessful. For ministers the whole business was a minor but unavoidable nightmare that absorbed time and energy. There were never enough offices, sinecures, pensions, commissions, contacts, and livings to satisfy all claimants, never enough "pasture for the sheep." When the incumbent of a rich living* was known to be at death's door, or merely only ill or ailing, if the living was in the gift of the Crown, half a dozen men, all of them with some political influence, were certain to begin to bombard ministers with requests for the office for some friend or relation. Even the smallest post in the customs or excise could never be disposed of without anxious thought, because for every gratified man half a dozen displeased men would remain. Once this essential fact of political life has been grasped, it is easy to see why men whose careers were at stake "waited on" or attempted to cultivate those with favours to give. Before the day of the competitive examination the great man's levee was the door to a successful career.

The lack of an organized party system had the further effect of increasing the importance of personal relationships even at the highest ministerial levels. Cabinets were not so much homogeneous political entities as collections of political chieftains, whose deliberations were presided over by the leading minister of the Crown, who by the middle of the century was generally recognized as the Prime Minister, and whose every member had his own followers and was able to bargain for places and favours for them. Government was not so much a matter of what policy should be followed as what man or group of men should hold office. For this reason political patterns were constantly changing. As soon as some politician out of office seemed to be getting too great a hold over the House, a place in the ministry had to be found for him and a subordinate office for his more important followers. The result was constant reshuffles. One minister might be induced to resign on the promise of a pension, another might be gratified with a title. In this way places were found for the troublemaker and his friends; the process was known as "storming the closet." Governments regularly had to be strengthened in this way, and much of the politics of the day revolved around such intrigues. For example, the early months of Lord Chatham's administration were bedevilled by the problem whether Lord Rockingham and his friends or the Duke of Bedford and his "Bloomsbury

*The term living is used in England to denote the benefice of a clergyman and the holder of such a living is the incumbent. The right to present to a living is known as an advowson and is often in private hands.

gang" should be taken into the administration. In the small, closed world of eighteenth-century society, from which the personnel of politics were drawn, matters of this kind were very much part of London's social life. Men met at breakfasts, they met to dine, they met to gamble or watch a cockfight or attend a racemeeting. Women schemed and charmed to help the political ambitions of a husband, a son, or a lover. London society was politics, and politics was London society.

In this world the king had an important part. No politician could afford to offend him or leave him out of his calculations. The revolutionary settlement had aimed at keeping the royal activities within the law; he was forced to cooperate with his Parliament, which alone could grant the necessary taxes or authorize an army, but within these limits the king was the acknowledged head of the executive branch. The choice of ministers was his. Though he could no longer force a favourite minister on an unwilling Parliament, he could still hamper and thwart the rise to power of a man he disliked. Only the pressure of an unsuccessful war forced George II to entrust the control of affairs to the elder Pitt in 1757, and until 1746 he had been able to prevent his holding office at all, declaring that if he were forced to take him as Secretary at War, he would refuse to speak to him! In the same way Charles James Fox was again and again denied office because of the dislike of George III. When George II became king in 1727 everybody expected that he would withdraw his favour from Sir Robert Walpole, whose levees were significantly deserted as politicians rushed to pay their court to the new king and his presumed new chief minister Sir Spencer Compton. If Walpole triumphed, it was because he had the foresight to win the favour of the new queen and the financial acumen to win for George II a larger civil list than his father had enjoyed. He was too valuable to be discarded, but it had been a near thing, and at every rumour that Sir Robert had lost the confidence of his new master London society buzzed with the expectation of his impending fall. If therefore politics was at the heart of Dr. Johnson's London, the king, his wife, if she was as able as Queen Caroline, and his mistresses were at the heart of politics. Even a man as capable as Sir Robert was well aware that he could never disregard the Court; hours of his time and stores of his patience

were spent briefing the queen or placing his policy before the
king. The reward was another fifteen years of office. If even so
capable a minister as Walpole depended to this extent on the
royal goodwill, men with less ability needed it still more, since
their chance of office depended on the royal inclination. Unlike
their modern counterparts, eighteenth-century prime ministers
did not choose their own colleagues, though they did their best to
influence the royal choice. Often the leading minister had to work
with men for whom he had little liking and less trust, because it
was for the king to select the men to serve him. Moreover, he
enjoyed a good deal of patronage untrammelled by the need to
consider the wishes of Parliament. Court offices were much
sought after, partly for the honour, partly for the emoluments,
and partly for the influence that those near the royal person might
hope to acquire. Although ministers tried to persuade the king to
use this patronage to build up support for them in Parliament,
they were not always successful. While so much power and so
much patronage remained there no man desirous of playing an
active part in public affairs could afford to ignore the Court.

In the world of fashion the Court had a formal importance,
but was not its genuine centre. This was largely because of personal factors. The English had little attachment to the House of
Hanover, particularly during the reigns of the first two Georges.
George I, an elderly foreigner who spoke little English, disliked
living his life in public, and was given to the choice of plain and
greedy mistresses while his wife was condemned to spend the
remainder of her life as a prisoner because of her indiscretions,
aroused little enthusiasm. He was a political necessity, to be
courted by the politicians but to be treated with some contempt
by fashionable society. George II was never much liked; he was
irascible, obstinate, and boring. De Saussure, who came to England while George II was still Prince of Wales, described him as
"about forty three. He is taller than his father, his figure well
proportioned and he is not as stout; his eyes are very prominent.
He looks serious and even grave and is always richly dressed,
being fond of fine clothes. I am told that the Prince is not as
kindly as his father, and he is not as popular, being very hasty and
easily angered." Luckily he had married a woman who was able
to make up for his deficiencies, both intellectual and social. "She

has been one of the most beautiful princesses in Europe," continued the same commentator, "but has grown too stout. She is witty
and well read, and speaks four or five different languages, and she
is gracious and amiable, beside being very charitable and kind."[28]
When Caroline became Queen, she did much to enliven court life
and to attract some interesting people to it. Among other interests
she was a keen theologian and enjoyed using her wits against
those of learned men. But because she loved power and worked
closely with Walpole, helping him to make the policy that he
wished to follow acceptable to the King, she had to sacrifice her
personal inclinations to his dull routine and fussy personality, and
with George II as its centre the Court of St. James was never
likely to be a stimulating or even amusing rendezvous for society.
The record of its intrigues, its jealousies, and its tedium has been
preserved for all time in Lord Hervey's "Memorials." As a close
friend of both Queen Caroline and Walpole he was well placed to
observe it all. The picture that he left is malicious, but lively and
well informed. We see the King erupting into the gallery, where
the Queen was drinking her chocolate, and dealing out criticism
with a lavish hand. His wife was stuffing herself as usual, his
daughter Caroline was getting fat, his son, the Duke of Cumberland, was standing awkwardly, and his other daughter did not
appear to hear a word of what he said. The Queen had long
learned that a soft answer turns away wrath. She took her irate
spouse for a walk in the garden, since walking was a favourite
method of his for working off his irritation and his energy.
"Whenever," wrote Lord Hervey, "in public or private, I have
seen her with the King, she has always behaved with the obse-
quiousness of the most patient slave to the most intemperate
master."[29] Yet in spite of his outbursts, his mistresses, and her
tribulations the bond between this oddly assorted pair was one of
deep and genuine affection.

This affection neither parent extended to their eldest son
Frederick, Prince of Wales. An almost perpetual feature of English
Court life, at least until the death of the Prince in 1751, and one

[28]De Saussure, *op. cit.*, pp. 45, 46.

[29]W. Croker, *Some Memorials of the Reign of George II* (1848), Vol. 2,
p. 45.

that provided London with endless gossip, was the continuous tension between the reigning monarch and his heir. In the years following Johnson's arrival there were a series of crises. The natural jealousy of an aging father for the son who had little occupation but to wait for dead men's shoes had something to do with it. Politics acerbated this situation. The parliamentary rivals of those ministers who currently enjoyed the royal confidence turned almost inevitably to the "reversionary interest" of the heir, with the result that the Prince of Wales, almost whether he wished to be or not, became the figurehead leader of a band of political malcontents. Frederick was something of a lightweight, the tool rather than the manipulator of politicians, but he had a surface charm, easy generosity, and some artistic appreciation. It was easy for him to court popularity with the crowd and the middling citizens. His magnificent barge, designed and decorated by William Kent, rowed by his watermen in their gold-laced red and blue liveries, and adorned with his white silk standard and with the Prince of Wales feathers, which billowed in the breeze, was a popular spectacle as it made its stately way up and down the Thames. Because of its importance, the goodwill of London was a matter of concern to ministers and the Crown, so that during its anti-Walpole phase, when it was choosing its officials from the ranks of his opponents, the happy flirtation between the Prince and the City could not but cause misgivings. He had either the knack or the good fortune to remain popular. Sometimes he would mingle incognito with the crowd to watch a Lord Mayor's parade. On one occasion, when one of the perpetual fires that were forever ravaging the City broke out, he hurried to the scene and stayed until the early hours helping to deal with the blaze. He became Perpetual Master of the Sadlers' Company and was given the freedom of the City in a gold box. He dined with the Lord Mayor and Aldermen at the Guildhall and entertained them in his turn. His mother declared that "Fritz's popularity makes me vomit." When they could keep him out of the limelight, his parents did so. Even on his wedding day the Princess was not allowed a state drive through the City from Greenwich and was refused a detachment of Guards. No wonder tongues wagged!

They were to wag still more with the birth of the Princess' first child. The young couple had no establishment of their own, merely occupying apartments in the various royal residences. The fact that the Prince and his friends had tried to obtain an independent settlement from Parliament, against the wishes of Walpole and the King, had not eased the situation, and though public relations were formally correct insofar as the Prince dined with his parents in public and attended the royal drawing rooms, rarely did a word pass between them. So bitter was the undercurrent of feeling that when the Princess was known to be pregnant, Caroline declared her belief that so eager was her son to produce a male heir that the young pair were quite capable of smuggling in a suppositious child and that as a precaution she intended to be at the bedside herself throughout the labour to ensure the authenticity of the royal baby! With such insinuations flying around, the Prince seems to have been determined that his first child should not be born under the parental roof. When Princess Augusta's pains began, the Court was at Hampton Court. It was early evening, and without the knowledge of either the King or Queen the Princess was bundled into a coach, and the couple drove in haste to St. James's. It was a nerve-racking drive, even though the Prince's *valet de chambre* was a midwife and a surgeon, for the Princess nearly gave birth on the way. The excuse they gave for their hurried departure was the need to be nearer the medical skill available in London, but this his parents refused to believe. The Prince and Princess of Wales were ordered to leave their apartments in St. James as soon as she was fit to be moved, and as a sign of the depths of his displeasure George II ordered the diplomatic representatives of foreign states not to wait on them. It was also made clear that anyone who did so would be not be received at St. James. At first the ostracised couple found a refuge at the White House, Kew; then, after a short spell at Norfolk House, behind the Haymarket, where the future George III was born—the first baby, object of so much drama, was a girl—they found a permanent home at Leicester House. London now had two courts: the one official and patronized by supporters of the administration, the other unofficial and the haunt of opposition politicians.

With the death of Frederick his widow found it expedient to make her peace with George II and Caroline, but the young Prince George was never allowed to take much part in public life until the death of his red-faced, fiery grandfather in 1760 made him King. At the beginning of his reign he was immensely popular and, by straining a little the indulgence accorded to monarchs, could be called handsome. He was tall, well made, with fair fresh colouring, blue eyes, good teeth, and light-auburn hair. It is true that his eyes, like those of his grandfather, were somewhat protuberant, and even in his youth he was fleshily jowled, but at least he had good manners and no German accent. Indeed he told his people that "Born and bred in these Islands I glory the name of Briton." Londoners would have preferred him to glory in the name of England, but, in spite of a weakness for the Scottish Lord Bute, he was thought at first to be a great improvement on his grandfather. Soon society was buzzing with rumours that he was greatly attracted to the lovely Lady Sarah Lennox. On the occasion of the King's Birthday Ball he was so engrossed in conversation with her that he quite neglected his other guests. In the end duty overcame inclination, and he allowed himself to be convinced that it would be impolitic to make a subject his wife, particularly one who was the niece of that very complete politician Henry Fox, and he married Princess Charlotte of Mecklenburg. Under George III the Court took on an air of decency and decorum, though it remained very dull. Unlike his predecessors the new King had no mistresses, either official or unofficial; his domestic life was above reproach. To this extent the possibilities of intrigue were cut down, though for a time politicians remained suspicious that the dowager Princess of Wales might exert undue influence over her son's political decisions. Moreover, for many years there was to be no Prince of Wales old enough for a rival Court to coalesce round. However, before the death of Dr. Johnson the old familiar pattern had repeated itself in the person of George, Prince of Wales, later Prince Regent and finally George IV. He was a more colourful figure than his father, something of a rake, certainly a dandy, the friend of Charles James Fox, and the darling of one section of the opposition. George III in paying his debts and extracting him from compromising situations could only reflect on the contrast with his own early manhood.

The early months of the reign were taken up with the pageantry of the royal wedding and the coronation, and the populace was looking forward to the spectacles that it so much enjoyed—

the progress of the state barges on the Thames, the cavalcade of coaches, horses, and the Guards. The coronation did not apparently come up to expectations. There seems to have been a general muddle over the arrangements, and the route was far too short for all the people who had wanted to see the procession to do so. Indeed, many failed to catch a single glimpse of the King and returned home in a mood of discontent. But though some may have been disappointed, loyalty and enthusiasm for a time continued. Kielmansegge described how on a visit to Drury Lane "Between the first and second piece the gallery and pit made a great noise, calling out the orchestra to play God save Great George the King and they would not desist until Garrick ordered it to be played, when everybody joined in and sang the well known anthem in a loud voice, which amused the King and Queen not a little."[30]

In the early months of the new reign everybody flocked to Court to pay respects. There was a royal levee every Monday, Wednesday, and Friday; on Thursdays and Sundays the Queen held a reception at which the King was also present. Count Kielmansegge, whose social position gave him the entree to Court circles, attended regularly, having been presented by Baron Munchausen. On these occasions he found "The Court exceptionally full as everyone had come to town, and it was with great difficulty that we at last succeeded in getting through to the first drawing room where the crowd was no less."[31] On New Year's Day he went to hear the traditional ceremony, an English ode set to music and played by the Court band, which, he condescended to admit, "was not badly done." Once again the Court was crowded. On the January 11 he went again, because it was the Queen's birthday. Then as now royal birthdays, or rather their official ones, were movable events. It was customary to appear in a new suit both for that of the King and for that of the Queen, and unfortunately Queen Charlotte's real birthday, like that of George III, fell in the summer. However, in consideration of their subjects' pockets "the celebration of the Queen's has been fixed for the winter: otherwise everybody would have to get two new

[30]Kielmansegge, *op. cit.*, p. 225.

[31]*Ibid.*, p. 27.

summer costumes, besides having to get one for the winter. As matters now are arranged you can do with one new suit for each season."[32] With everybody resplendent in their new outfits, it must have been a colourful scene. Once again it was certainly a crowded one, for it took the Count and his party a long time to reach the ballroom. There formal etiquette reigned. "The place for dancing is divided from the rest of the room by a railing; inside this space nobody is admitted except the royal family and suite and those who dance minuets. All the rest of the room is occupied by benches and a gallery runs all round for the onlookers and the band. Only one couple dances the minuet at a time."[33] Persons who wanted to dance sent in their names to the Lord Chamberlain the previous day and were then called out according to their rank, starting with the duchesses—a frustrating process for dancers of less exalted station. It all sounds incredibly dull, though no doubt the onlookers relieved their tedium with some lively gossip about the stately dancers!

Though St. James was the official residence where the Court was held, the sovereign generally preferred to live elsewhere in greater comfort and privacy. Kensington Palace and Hampton Court were favourite retreats for the first two Georges; George III preferred Richmond where he lived with something of the simplicity of a country gentleman. Grosley was surprised to find that he travelled "in a very plain equippage, escorted by a few light horse."*He was even more surprised to discover that "coachmen and carmen, never stop at his approach, and that they take a pride in not bowing to him: 'Why should we bow to George?' say the insolent rabble 'he should bow to us: he lives at our expense.'[34] Other visitors to London had the same impression. Dr. Campbell, the diarist, met the King near Richmond. He was "with a single gentleman and two of the Princes. I did not know him until I was cheek for jowl with him and then took off my hat." Dr. Campbell had hired a youth to carry his coat on the walk, the

---

*This is the regular description of a type of cavalry regiment. Horse is used here in the plural sense.

[32]*Ibid.*, p. 235.

[33]*Ibid.*, p. 199.

[34]Grosley, *op. cit.*, Vol. 1, p. 221.

day being warm, and after encountering the King he asked the lad "if he knew who that was—He answered in the negative—I then told him that it is the King. He showed no emotion but turned round and said leisurely 'is that the King?' An Irish boy would have dogged him at the heels as long as he could."[35] This attitude of Londoners toward authority was characteristic of their independence. Rank itself was accepted as part of the social order, and the man of rank was treated with a deference that amounted to fawning in personal relationships. Nevertheless, Londoners cherished the image of their freedom and their dignity. Grosley thought the ordinary people "haughty and ungovernable," though he admits that they could also be "good natured and humane," as when at public spectacles children and persons of low stature were pushed to the front so that they might have a good view. But on ordinary occasions he found the lower classes full of a robust disrespect for not only foreigners but also for well-dressed English people. Poverty had not reduced them to subservience. Although the majority had no vote and therefore no choice over their representative or the policy of ministers, they took every advantage that their residence at the seat of political power gave them. In a town as comparatively small as eighteenth-century London ministers and M.P.'s were as familiar figures as the television screen has made them today, with the added advantage that, being there in substance and not in shadow, they could be the object of cheers or jeers as it pleased the craftsmen and apprentices of London. No one can understand Dr. Johnson's London who forgets how large a part politics played in its normal life.

[35]*Dr. Campbell's Diary, op. cit.*, p. 82.

FIVE

The Pleasures of London

Dull though the Court might be, outside the confines of St. James diversions of every kind, reputable and disreputable, elegant or brutish, were at hand. To many of its visitors London was first and foremost a city of pleasure, where, during the season when Parliament was sitting, they could give themselves up to the sophisticated amusements that country life denied them. One of these was simple enough—to see and be seen, to wear one's smartest clothes and to quiz those of one's acquaintances. This was not a pleasure confined to the so-called "fair sex": the eighteenth-century dandy was as clothes-conscious as any film star. He was a man who devoted his life to the business of dressing and adopted in its extreme form the latest craze. It is salutary to remember that the eighteenth century also had its beatniks, its Teddy Boys, and its Mods and Rockers in the world of fashion. Earlier in the century it had been fashionable to adopt a pose of extreme slovenliness, dressing as carelessly as possible in long loose coats, leaving breeches unbuckled at the knee, and sometimes even appearing with curl papers in their hair. While this phase lasted, fashionable young men aped their social inferiors, dressing like jockeys in black caps and jackets and leaving their boots deliberately dirty. By the seventies the mode was all for a lavish embellishment of buttons, shorter waistcoats and cutaway coats with a low-slung pocket, a large three-cornered hat, and a long pigtail wig. The sloven had become a dandy again. Women's fashions changed as rapidly. In 1735 skirts were comparatively

149

short, showing a provocative amount of ankle; ten years later hoops were sweeping the ground. Styles in hairdressing changed just as rapidly, reaching a climax of absurdity in the seventies— great erections were built on frames and decorated with feathers, flowers, and jewels, so that getting into a coach or sedan chair was a matter of some difficulty. Even the most cursory student of the eighteenth century has heard the horrifying story of the lady who kept her coiffure undisturbed so long that a mouse made its nest therein! No wonder that dressing was a major occupation for both men and women of fashion; ordinary citizens had better things to do.

It was not only an occupation; it was also a social ritual. Great men, like kings, held their levees, and gentlemen considered it an honour to attend the toilette of a well known toast. Beaux received their visitors in the same way. Once dressed, the fashionable place for promenading was the Mall in St. James's Park. It was a curiously mixed throng, for though in theory it was one of the royal parks, public access to it had long been a matter of right. Nobody's social credentials were scrutinized; women of the town and servants in second-hand finery mingled with great ladies and well-bred gentlewomen. This almost democratic attitude to public places of amusement was indeed something that characterized eighteenth-century London. Anyone who was decently dressed and had a few shillings to squander could in such places mix on equal terms with the greatest in the land. Foreigners invariably commented on the spectacle that this fashion parade provided. Earlier in the century de Saussure wrote: "Society comes to walk here on fine warm days, from seven till ten in the evening, and in winter from one to three o'clock. Englishmen and women are fond of walking, and the park is so crowded at times that you cannot help touching your neighbour. Some people come to see, some to be seen, and others to seek their fortune, for many priestesses of Venus are abroad, some magnificently attired, and all on the outlook for adventures, and young men are not long in reprenting that they have become acquainted with such beautiful and amiable nymphs."[1] As he indicated, St. James's Park was a well known place for assigna-

[1]de Saussure, op. cit., p. 48.

tions; here an admirer could make the advance courteous, the acquaintance apparently accidental, often finding a willing, if mercenary, accomplice in the waiting woman or servant whose task theoretically was to protect her mistress's privacy. The situation is described in contemporary plays and novels and often had its counterpart in real life. Apart from the crowds in the Mall, there were other things to see. Then as now there were the ducks and water birds to amuse, though today one can no longer buy a draught of milk straight from the cow. In Johnson's day the milk-maids and cows near Spring Gardens added a pleasantly rural touch, though some people did complain that they turned the area into a dung heap! Other parts of the park had more sombre associations. Rosamond's pond was a favourite place for suicides, and it was within the park that soldiers were flogged, as well as drilled, on the parade ground. Not all visitors were favourably impressed. Pastor Moritz declared disparagingly that "This cele-brated park is nothing more than a semicircle, formed of an alley of trees, which enclose a large green area, in the middle of which is a marshy pond. The cows feed on this green turf, and their milk is sold here on the spot, quite new. In all the alleys, or walks there are benches on which you may rest yourself. When you come through the Horse Guards, into the Park, on the right hand is St. James's Palace, or the King's place of residence, one of the mean-est public buildings in London . . . but what again greatly com-pensates for the mediocracy of this park, is the astonishing num-ber of people, who, towards evening, in fine weather, resort hither; our finest walks are never so full, even in the midst of summer. The exquisite pleasure of mixing freely with such a concourse of people, who are, for the most part, well dressed and handsome, I fully experienced here."[2]

Grosley, usually so critical, approved of the park where, he said, "nature appears in all its rustic simplicity: it is a meadow, regularly intersected and watered by canals, and with willows and poplars, without any regard to order. On this side, as well as on that towards St. James's palace, the grass plats are covered with cows and deer, where they graze, or chew the cud, some standing, others lying down upon the grass: this gives the walks a

[2]Moritz, *op. cit.*, Vol. 4, p. 7.

lively air, which banishes solitude from them when there is but little company: when they are full they unite in one prospect, the crowd, the grandeur, and the magnificence of a city, as wealthy as populous, in the most striking contrast with rural simplicity. Agreeably to this rural simplicity, most of the cows are driven about noon and evening, to the gate, which leads from the Park to the quarter of Whitehall. Tied in a file to posts at the extremity of the grass plat, they swill passengers with their milk which, being drawn from their udders on the spot, is served, with all the cleanliness peculiar to the English, in little mugs at the rate of a penny a mug."[3] There is no record of how clean the mugs were in which they were served!

At night the park was less reputable. It was unlit and, except on moonlight nights, darker than even the murky gloom of the surrounding streets, which made it the haunt of soldiers off duty and their molls. Though its gates were supposed to be locked each night at ten, keys were widely available on payment of a guinea, and for those who grudged or could not afford this sum, illicit keys were not hard to come by. Respectable people were always complaining of the indecency that took place in the park, and this was not always confined to the hours of darkness. On Sundays in particular it made a convenient playground for the populace of the surrounding areas, many of them distinctly insalubrious; the consequence was gambling, bathing in the ornamental waters, and running races. In a hard winter the canal froze over and made a wonderful place for skating, a popular amusement but not a particularly quiet one, for people laughed and shouted, roaring their applause or shouting their jeers at the performers on the ice. When this happened on a Sunday, the day when the unruly crowds were at their greatest, so that the time of divine service was ignored and the peace of the royal family disturbed, complaints grew even stronger. As a result of the turbulence and disorder of St. James's, persons of quality began to frequent another of the royal parks, Kensington Gardens.

Kensington had been the favourite residence of William and Mary, who had adapted the original mansion to their use and had laid out the gardens. It was also popular with the early Hanoveri-

[3]Grosley, *op. cit.*, Vol. 1, p. 8.

View of the Canal in St. James's Park.

153

an kings: George II and Caroline spent a good deal of time there. Landscape gardening was fashionable, and the Queen took much pleasure in transforming the gardens, which had reflected earlier canons of taste. In doing so she made skillful use of its natural features, particularly of a little brook known as the West Bourne, whose winding waters were controlled and enlarged to make the modern Serpentine. The result was a controlled beauty, artificially contrived but natural-seeming, that to eighteenth-century taste was the height of elegance. Because Kensington still lay a little ouside London, it was easier to keep its visitors a select group without giving offense to "the mobbish part of the town," who if affronted were apt to show their resentment in a forceful fashion. Even servants were excluded, being left at the gates, to prevent any unsuitable person gaining admission. Here ladies might walk unattended without being confused with the "ladies of the town," and all was decorum and peace. In spite of these advantages, or possibly because of them, the Gardens never gained quite the popularity of St. James's as a place of promenade; on one thing foreign observers were agreed, whether they wrote at the beginning or the end of the century—that at the fashionable hours the "ton" were to be seen there taking the air on its main walks.

London was indeed particularly well furnished with parks that afforded opportunities for recreation. On the other side of Kensington Gardens lay the mighty Hyde Park. At the beginning of the century much of it was still wild enough to provide some sport for an occasional royal hunt, but the main attraction was the famous "Ring" which since the time of Charles I had been used for riding and for driving the equipages of the young bloods. Eighteenth-century gentlemen prided themselves on their capacity to handle their horses as well as any professional coachman, and the "Ring" provided a good opportunity to display their prowess. Further west still lay the gardens of Kew. These were a later creation, being very largely due to the enthusiasm of George III's mother for gardening. After he became King, George III spent much of his time at the palace at Kew, preferring it to the residences nearer to London. Like the other royal parks Kew was open to the public, but remained a specialized haunt rather than a playground for the rabble. The great attraction was the floral display. When John Yeoman visited London in 1774, he recorded in his diary on March 25: "We took a walk to Kew Where we saw the Kings Flower Gardens, there was Roses and Pinks and Carnations all in full Bloom. Mr. Green the Gardener Said he gathers Some 3 Times a Week all the Year Rownd, there was Oranges and Leomons all in full Groath, also Tea Trees, also Divers other things." He then proceeded to describe the great event of the expedition, explaining with the aid of his rather peculiar spelling that "we was all Ledaufied a Thing its Impossible to describe. Its composed of a Mixture of conbustables that If you Touch it the Fire flys out of it, besides you have Shuch Shudden Shock with it. We all hold hand in hand about 7 of us When I toucht it, and the Moment I was struck so hard in the Stomack that I could not Stand, the Rest felt it as well as me. If there was 500 it would be all the same. They would all feel the Shock the Same Instant."[4] One can almost hear his countryman's voice describing the wonder of modern science to his cronies as we read his account with its emphatic use of capitals to convey the importance of his key words.

If St. James's provided the beauty and the fop with the chance to display their attractions and their taste, the gossip with the raw material for the latest scandal, and the wit with the wherewithal on which to exercise it, the middling sort and the craftsmen and their families were equally addicted to semirural pleasures. London was ringed by less pretentious pleasure grounds and tea gardens. Kalm wrote that "A multitude of people now stream out here from all sides of London to enjoy their Sunday afternoon and take the fresh air. In all the aforesaid villages there was a superfluity of beershops, inns, and such like houses, where those who come from the towns rested. There were also small summer houses, built in the gardens, with benches and tables in them, which were now all full of swarming crowds of people of both sexes."[5] In view of the stench and dirt of London, particularly in hot weather, which made the heaps of refuse and the inadequate drains especially offensive, this partiality for the countryside is easily understood. The pleasures they sought were surprisingly

[4]John Yeoman, *op. cit.*, p. 18.

[5]P. Kalm, *An Account of a Visit to England* (1892), p. 87.

simple—a garden laid out with arbours and furnished with benches and tables where tea could be taken seems to have been the chief attraction. More elaborate were the tiny spas, so characteristic of the period. In addition to the facilities for drinking the waters, these usually provided evening entertainments in a long room or gallery, often equipped with the fashionable organ for concerts. A painting of Bagnigge Wells in 1772 shows a room crowded with fashionably dressed people, some parading to and fro, others drinking tea at tables along the walls. Overhead the candles blaze in the hanging chandeliers, while through the long windows the night shows black, throwing into relief the brightness and gaiety within. White Conduit House was another favourite centre, where in the daytime patrons could play cricket with bats and balls provided by the landlord. By Johnson's time cricket was already well established. In the seventeenth century it had been one of the games of the masses; then the gentry and even aristrocracy had adopted it, as they adopted so many of the sporting activities of their social inferiors, and it was played by all classes. Even in London there was no shortage of fields for this purpose, though they were far from being the beautifully tended pitches of today. One place, popular because it was free and without restriction, was the Long Field that lay behind Montague House, now the British Museum. The competition among tea gardens and spas around London was fierce, and most of them offered more than the pleasures of drinking tea. In addition to cricket, some provided facilities for fishing and others for skittles, the ancestor of the bowling alley of today.

Marylebone Gardens, noted for its plum cake and its evening concerts, attracted custom also by a fireworks display, which was always popular. But in the English climate such an attraction had its perils. So famous were these displays that Dr. Johnson himself sallied forth to Marylebone to enjoy them. Alas he had chosen a showery evening; the small company was informed that "the conductors to the wheels, suns, stars, etc. were so thoroughly watersoaked, that it was impossible any part of the exhibition should be made." Johnson was suspicious. It was, he said, "a mere excuse to save their crackers for a more profitable company" and suggested to his companion that they should "both threaten to hold up our sticks and threaten to break those coloured lamps that surround the Orchestra, and we shall soon have our wishes satisfied. The core of the fireworks cannot be injured; let the different pieces be touched in their respective centres; and they will do their offices as well as ever."[6] Some young men who were standing by heard the Doctor and promptly started to follow his advice. Johnson proved a true prophet insofar that an immediate attempt was made to save the lamps by lighting the fireworks, but otherwise his suspicions proved unjustified—the fireworks obstinately refused to go off!

Another pleasure gardens that was already well established when Johnson first came to London was Sadler's Wells, now the home of popular ballet. Its method of attracting customers was to provide them with free entertainment. De Saussure described it well. "An entertainment is given here all the summer through, which lasts from four o'clock in the afternoon till ten o'clock at night. You first see rope dancers, tumblers and acrobats; after that tricks of skill and daring are performed, among others that of men going up ladders that lean against nothing, their heads downwards and their feet in the air, and all kinds of tricks of equilibrium and diversions of that sort. The entertainment ends with a pantomime, acted on a very pretty little theatre with good scenery. Beside this there is quite a good orchestra; but best of it is you pay nothing for this entertainment, you need only throw the actors a few coins. Each party of spectators sits in a kind of box which contains a little table on which to place plates and glasses, for everyone must have something to eat and drink, as none are allowed into the house for the diversion of the eyes and ears only, enjoyment must also be given to the palate. You may order any sort of wine, cold meats, and sweetmeats which are not dearer than elsewhere the only difference being that the bottles contain about a glass less than in other places. Not withstanding the cheapness the proprietor is quite satisfied with the profits for many persons come daily and much wine is drunk."[7]

Many of these pleasure gardens, such as the previously mentioned Bagnigge Wells, owed their start to the discovery or possession of a local spring of real or supposed medicinal quality,

[6]J. Boswell, *Life of Samuel Johnson*, Vol. 4, p. 324.

[7]De Saussure, *op. cit.*, p. 139.

which some enterprising man or group had exploited by providing the social amenities necessary for the drinking of the waters, which had become a favourite English pleasure by the eighteenth century. Families or individuals who could afford the expense went to Bath or Tunbridge Wells, where the routine of the cure was combined with an active and elegant social life. Tradesmen and artisans could spare neither the time nor the money for such luxuries, though they, or at least their wives, were as avid as their social supervisors to benefit by this fashionable cure and to enjoy the social amenities associated with it. So they flocked to the local spa. That at Islington earlier had even, somewhat optimistically, been known as the New Tunbridge Wells. They rarely had a long or successful life as spas, though the development of pleasure gardens and tea houses provided them with plenty of customers. Most of them remained reputable establishments whose patrons were largely made up of family parties, ranging from the gentry, or near gentry, to the less sophisticated clientele of the gardens around Stepney and Mile-End that catered to the rougher population of the riverside parishes. Here the attractions were more brutal: sailors preferred beer to tea and dogfighting or badger baiting to the elegance of a musical evening. Some, though they started well, as did the Dog and the Duck on the South side of the Thames, became the haunts of highly questionable characters or lapsed into thinly disguised brothels. Nevertheless the general impression of such places remains a pleasing one. Clearly Londoners had not lost their taste for simple pleasures or the capacity to enjoy themselves on family outings. In a century sometimes better known for its vices than its virtues the picture they present is that of the family as a unit for pleasure as well as for work, relaxing and enjoying itself on a Sunday after the toils of the week. The stricter Sabbath of Victorian times had not yet laid its all-restraining hand on popular entertainment, even though the authorities might, and constantly did, bewail the license of the times and even though the fashionable world kept away from those places where ordinary Londoners sought their pleasures on Sundays.

This absence did not, however, apply to two celebrated places of amusement, Vauxhall and Ranelagh, which were more elegant and sophisticated but offered basically the same kind of diversion as the smaller respectable spas, though there was no pretence of drinking the waters. As befitted pleasure gardens in the English climate, they were opened only during the spring and summer months and shut in October. To fill this gap the Pantheon was established in 1772 to provide indoor entertainment of a similar kind, namely, music, light refreshments, and the opportunity to see and be seen. These three establishments were considered to be among the most important sights of London, and no visitor to the town, most certainly no foreign visitor, would fail to spend an evening at each of them. As a consequence descriptions of all three abound in contemporary writing. Fanny Burney's heroine Evelina visited them all, and perhaps the place they have in that novel, as seen through Evelina's eyes, gives as clear an impression of their attractions as can be found. Vauxhall was the earliest of them, the most popular, the gayest, and the least select. It was situated on the south bank of the Thames in the parish of Lambeth. Before the completion of Westminster Bridge the only approach from the City or the West End was by water; afterward one could go by coach or on foot. In the centre of the Gardens was a large orchestra so that, as Moritz noted, "As you enter the gardens you immediately hear the sound of vocal and instrumental music."[8] Around the orchestra were boxes in the form of Chinese "kiosques," furnished with chairs and tables. Here parties supped while listening to the music and watching their friends and acquaintances as they strolled past. On a summer evening it was a pleasant way of spending a few hours and was correspondingly popular. Unlike at Sadler's Wells, the refreshments here seem to have been on the expensive side; at any rate the frugal Scandinavian Kalm thought so, writing that they were all "tolerably dear, so that those who sell them do not seem to lose anything by it."[9] Moritz, too, estimated that it would cost half a guinea to take supper there. The gardens themselves were laid out in formal walks of elm and lime. "The avenues and trees," wrote Kielmansegge, "are all planted in good taste, with vistas of fine high trees and hedges between them. Some of the vistas end with representations of old ruins amidst the landscapes, and

[8]Moritz, *op. cit.*, p. 18.

[9]Kalm, *op. cit.*, p. 65.

A contemporary representation of the pleasures of Vauxhall. Notice the alcoves for refreshments at the side.

others are decorated with triumphal arches."[10] Evelina, however, while acknowledging that they were very pretty, thought them too formal and would have been better pleased "had it consisted less of straight walks where 'Grove nods at grove, each alley has its brother.' "[11] By the time *Evelina* was written in 1778 the approved style in gardens was changing, and a less mannered layout was more in favour. Even so, as it grew dark and the lamps were lit, it must have been delightful to see some 1500 of them glimmering through the trees, illuminating the dresses of the company as they sat in their boxes or took the air. Not all the walks were well lit. The "dark walks" where groups of gallants looked for adventure and prostitutes looked for custom were notorious. Apparently the ladies of the town did not always confine their solicitations to these parts. Even in the main walks, crowded with people, they rushed up to parties of men "by half dozens, and in the most shameless manner"[12] importuned them for wine. Doubtless such behaviour was encouraged by the fact that most men unaccompanied by respectable females had come there themselves for the purpose of enjoying such company.

This mingling of the classes, so characteristic of Vauxhall, was characteristic of London as a whole: it was not merely a rich man's town, even in its pleasures. In private life people tended to mix only with those of their own station when in pursuit of social pleasure, but in public places there was no such distinction, though in practice the leaders of society were less likely to be found at White Conduit House or Bagnigne Wells than the wealthy tradesman or the middling sort. But to places like Vauxhall everyone who could pay the shilling entrance fee was admitted, from the aristocratic party supping sumptuously in a box to the apprentice in his best clothes out for an evening's fun. Kalm was not sure that this was wholly desirable, commenting cautiously that "Its use by folk may in a certain way be good, but then it is certain it is also in some ways harmful because the youth is not a little ruined through it when he gets into a habit of coming here every evening. He gets accustomed to do no work,

[10]Kielmansegge, *op. cit.*, p. 166.

[11]F. Burney, *Evelina*, Letter XLVI.

[12]Moritz, *op. cit.*, p. 19.

and, on the other hand, to squander money in various ways. Young ladies, also, might not always be improved to the pitch of perfection here."[13] Certainly if they were rash, or innocent enough, as Evelina was, to venture into the "dark walks" they would not. Any woman who did so was tolerably certain to be molested or at least kissed and fondled, which again illustrates the very clear distinction that society made between a respectable woman, who was in effect a woman protected by the conventions of her class, and one not so protected, who was considered fair game. With drink flowing freely, with women for the asking, and with high-spirited, tipsy men who wore their swords or later in the century carried sword sticks if they were gentlemen and who were well accustomed to use their fists if they were not, it is hardly surprising that fights and brawls occurred frequently, especially in the less lit parts of the gardens. The last night of the season was notorious for its rowdiness. As young Branghton told Evelina, "Why Lord, it's the best night of any; there's always a riot,—and there the folks run about,—and then there's such squelling and squalling!—and, there, all the lamps are broke,—and the women skimper scamper.—I would not take five guineas to miss the last night."[14]

Ranelagh was very different. Johnson thought it an innocent recreation and went there often. Vauxhall was already an established institution before Ranelagh had even been projected. Like the former, it lay on the outskirts of the town, almost in the open country, on the north bank of the Thames in Chelsea. By the eighteenth century this had become a fashionable district, and from 1714 Walpole's house there became his main retreat when business forced him to be in London. As Paymaster-General he controlled the Royal Military Hospital, which was situated there, and occupied a smallish house, previously used by his predecessor, known as Orford House. It was delightfully situated, with a garden that ran down to the Thames, and Walpole, with his flair for building, improved the property immensely. He built a terrace with an octagonal summerhouse at one end, where he could sit and look over the wide expanse of the river. He added, as was

[13]Kalm, *op. cit.*, p. 66.

[14]Burney, *op. cit.*, Letter XXIII.

fashionable, an orangery and an aviary of singing birds. He enlarged his garden at the expense of the hospital and planted it with expensive shrubs and flowers. With the aid of Sir John Vanbrugh, the architect of Blenheim Palace, he turned Orford House into a beautiful dwelling. His neighbour was Lord Ranelagh, who, when he was Paymaster in 1768, had secured some seven acres of land from the Crown. Later he extended this in order to enlarge his garden. By the time that Walpole moved to Chelsea Ranelagh was a dignified house, surrounded by magnificent gardens. Walpole was soon to have a very different neighbour. In 1733 the house and gardens were divided into lots and sold to speculators. Lacy, the patentee of Drury Lane, seems to have contemplated taking over the house and garden and turning them into a very superior tea garden, though eventually a William Crisp appears to have undertaken the venture. In so doing he overstrained his resources and went bankrupt. The idea was nevertheless not dropped; the property was divided into thirty-six shares of £1000 each, of which Sir Thomas Robinson held the majority. Under his direction Ranelagh flourished.

Its glory was not so much its gardens, which were less extensive than those of Vauxhall, but its rotunda, which impressed by its spaciousness and elegance. Evelina thought it "a charming place" and was astonished by the brilliance of its illuminations. Almost every visitor from the Continent described it minutely. Looking through the eyes of the Frenchman Grosley, it is easy to reconstruct the scene that he saw. "In the midst of these gardens is a rotunda, or a round saloon, of about a hundred and eighty feet in diameter, capable of containing five or six hundred persons. In the centre, there is a chimney, supported upon four pillars, and a braiser, with four faces, on which the different beverages are warmed for the company. The braiser defuses less heat than that of a stove, and emits a brilliant lustre: it is the centre of motion, and the sanctuary of this elegant temple. Sconces of a vast size, and rows of lamps, distributed throughout the hall, form the rest of the illumination. Opposite to one of the fronts of the braiser, is an amphitheatre composed of seats, gradually rising above each other: and here a band of excellent musicians is employed the whole evening, in playing grand symphonies, and pieces both of Italian and English composition, alternately. The inside of the

The inside of the famous Rotunda at Ranelagh, with a view of the orchestra and the tables for refreshments.

saloon is divided into three stories. The first, adorned with pillars, is distributed into boxes, all furnished with a table and seats for ten persons. The second order, formed of pilasters, is cut into galleries, which correspond with the boxes upon the ground floor: before these galleries there are moving lattices by means of which one may see and enjoy all the pleasures of the place unperceived."[15] Kielmansegge, with an eye for detail, noted that there were forty-eight recesses around the hall and that the forty-eight boxes above them were rarely used except for large parties or on special occasions. On ordinary nights the entrance fee was half a crown for which, he informed his readers, "you have from eight o'clock to half past ten some pretty good instrumental and vocal music, and you can drink as much tea with bread and butter as you like, without any further charge except perhaps a shilling to the waiter."[16] The main diversion seems to have been to walk round and round the central fireplace, gossiping, quizzing the company, listening to the music, and, when weary or bored, refreshing oneself with tea and bread and butter.

It was all very decorous and sounds a little dull. There was none of the rowdy element that patronized Vauxhall. The world of fashion went there, but so did sober citizens and their wives, dressed in their best clothing and doing their utmost to copy the airs and manners of the Quality. Good pastor Moritz thought that "the incessant change of faces, the far greater number of which were strikingly beautiful, together with the illuminations, the extent and majestic splendour of the place with the continued sound of music, makes an inconceivably delightful impression on the imagination." After indulging in the usual refreshment of tea and bread and butter he climbed to the gallery to look down on the people promenading below. They were the usual cross section of London society. He could "easily distinguish several stars and orders of knighthood; French queues and bags contrasted with plain English heads of hair, or professional wigs; old age and youth, nobility and commonalty, all passing each other in a motley swarm. An Englishman who joined me during this my reverie pointed out to me on my inquiring princes and lords with their

[15]Grosley, op. cit., Vol. 1, p. 153.

[16]Kielmansegge, op. cit., p. 23.

dazzling stars, with which they eclipsed the less brilliant part of the company."[17] The thought occurrs that with its music, its little tables, and its tea and bread and butter it was more a fashionable rendezvous then a place of entertainment. The blunt sea captain Mirvan was contemptuous of its charms, exploding at the prospect of being dragged there by his womanfolk! "Your famous Ranelagh, that you make such a fuss about;—why what a dull place is that! it's the worst of all." Such downright sentiments promptly exposed him to the contempt of the company and to a long lecture by the precious Mr. Lovell, which is worth quoting to illustrate the snob values of the period. "As to Ranelagh," he said, "most indubitably, though the price is plebian, it is by no means adapted to the plebian taste. It requires a certain acquaintance with high life, and-and-and something of-of-something d'vrai gout, to be really sensible of its merits. Those whose-whose connections, and so forth, are not among les gens comme il faut, can feel nothing but ennui at such a place as Ranelagh."[18]

Nevertheless it provided a splendid setting for the gossiping and the parade of fashion so dear to the society of the day, who went there to be seen and gave to less distinguished Londoners the brief illusion that they too were part of "the ton." In April of 1749 it was graced by the presence of George II who, together with other members of the royal family, came to the celebration of the Grand Jubilee, which took place there at his command. On less impressive occasions the Rotunda was used for a ridotto, or dance, when the tickets were priced at a guinea. After a Regatta in June of 1775 a magnificent supper was provided for subscribers. This was to see Ranelagh at its gayest. Londoners dearly loved a spectacle, and such occasions provided it both for those whose boats crowded the Chelsea reach and for those who watched on the banks. Every kind of craft was filled with gay parties, all bent on enjoying themselves. One can imagine the laughter, the sudden bursts of music and song, the calling from boat to boat as friends and acquaintances caught passing glimpses of each other. At half past seven the Lord Mayor in his magnificent barge headed the irregular procession that moved

[17]Moritz, op. cit., pp. 22, 23.

[18]Burney, op. cit., Letter XXIII.

down the river to Ranelagh. In the Rotunda itself gigantic prepa-
rations had been made for a splendid supper; every kind of food
was laid out on three great, circular tables, and an orchestra,
reputed to be 240 strong, played to the assembled company.
Afterward there was dancing in a temporary structure in the
gardens, christened for the occasion the Temple of Neptune. The
crush must have been tremendous, for it was reported that more
than 2000 people were present.

The third of London's famous places of recreation was the
Pantheon. The shutting of Vauxhall and Ranelagh in the winter left
a gap in the social life of the town, and to fill this the Pantheon
was opened in Oxford Street in the January of 1772. The architect
was James Wyatt, and the scheme was largely prompted by his
brother. All London flocked to see it and to criticize or approve.
Horace Walpole thought it "the most beautiful edifice in England," but Johnson and Boswell, who visited it in March, were less
impressed, the latter declaring that there was not "half a guinea's
worth of pleasure in seeing the place." Then followed a characteristic conversation between the two men. Johnson: "But, Sir, there
is half a guinea's inferiority to other people in not having seen it."
Boswell: "I doubt, Sir, whether there are many happy people
here." Johnson: "Yes, Sir, there are many happy people here.
There are many people here who are watching hundreds, and
who think hundreds are watching them."[19] Their main criticism
seems to have been that Vauxhall on entering, made a less dramatic impact than did Ranelagh when one stepped out of the
dimly lit gardens into the great Rotunda. The modern reader is
apt to forget the sheer dramatic impact of massed lights and their
glinting on chandeliers on a public that had never experienced
the wonders of electric light, now so familiar as to be unnoticed.
Boswell also thought the form and majestic proportions of the
Rotunda more impressive than those of the Pantheon, which has
been described as a compressed version of St. Sophia in Istanbul.
James Wyatt, however, was not aiming so much at a brilliant
scene as at an exotic reconstruction of the mystery of the East.
Paintings decorating the walls gained a new mystery from the
flickering candlelight, while the great dome seemed to melt away

[19]Boswell, *op. cit.*, Vol. 2, p. 169.

into a misty twilight shot with the brighter reflections from gilded ornaments. Much of the illumination came from green and purple lights that added a touch of extravagance to the scene, though they can hardly have been kind to costumes and complexions. Evelina thought that "it has more the appearance of a chapel than of a place of diversion; and though I was quite charmed with the magnificence of the room, I felt I could not be as gay and thoughtless there as at Ranelagh; for there is something in it that rather inspires awe and solemnity than mirth and pleasure."[20]

On this occasion the formal entertainment was provided by a concert, although Evelina complained that everyone talked so much that she could hardly hear the music. No doubt the complaint was justified. People came because it was the fashion to do so and were apt to congregate in the large room below where tea was served rather than to give their undivided attention to the performers, who for many people did little more than provide the background to gossip and conversation. When Dr. Campbell spent an evening there while visiting London, he commented on the distinguished company present, among whom were the Prussian ambassador and the Duke of Cumberland. Not all the women met with his approval. Lady Grovernor was described as "a fine woman but lost to all sense of modesty" and Lady Archer as "painted like Doll, but handsome, her feathers nodded like the plumes of mambrinos helmets yet some of the whores had longer peacock feathers." When he wrote in 1776, the peak of fashion was to wear one's hair dressed high, surmounted by an elaborate arrangement of feathers. Perhaps the company had some excuse for the scant attention they paid to the orchestra, for Campbell thought that "all the orchestra seemed by no means of a piece and awkwardly disposed."[21] Certainly, the musicians failed to distract Johnson and Boswell from the pleasures of conversation; running into Sir Adam Ferguson, they engaged in a long argument on the British Constitution, the spirit of Liberty, and the impropriety or other acts of bishops sitting in the House of Lords, topics that neatly underline the impression of foreign visitors that politics was a subject of absorbing interest to Londoners.

[20]Burney, *op. cit.*, Letter XXIII.

[21]*Dr. Campbell's Diary, op. cit.*, p. 63.

Although the ridottos held at Ranelagh and the Pantheon were popular, there were some people who preferred more select company. Mrs. Cornley, a German by birth and a woman of great enterprise, realized that this was a demand to be exploited.[22] In 1760 she rented Carlisle House in Soho Square, furnished it elaborately, and attracted the fashionable world with a series of subscription concerts where, according to Dr. Burney, "the best performers and the best company were assembled."[23] She also organized balls and masquerades on a subscription basis. The latter in particular were always popular because of the freedom and opportunities for intrigue that wearing masks afforded and because the fact that they were not open to the general public was some guarantee that the more undesirable element would be excluded. Unfortunately for the success of her ventures, which at first did extremely well, she soon found herself in competition with serious rivals. When Bach and Abel also started weekly subscription concerts, many of her more musical patrons left her. She was unlucky too in that Almarck opened rival Assembly Rooms in King Street, St. James, in 1765. Dr. Campbell thought that they were the finest he had seen and that everything was in the most elegant style. The subscription was high, ten guineas for a series of twelve entertainments consisting of a ball and a supper that took place every week. Mrs. Cornley had failed to keep her assemblies select; Almarck made no such mistake. The decision about who should have the privilege of becoming a subscriber was entrusted to a committee of ladies whose position in society was beyond question, and assemblies at Almarck's were an exclusive affair. Mrs. Cornley could no longer compete and, to add to her misfortunes, she became involved in one of the perpetual squabbles about the merits of rival singers that periodically rent society. Some of her enemies then indicted her before a Grand Jury on the charge of keeping a disorderly house, and Carlisle House was closed. The popularity of the subscription ball was not limited to the West End; within the City similar functions took place. Kielmansegge went to one at Haberdashers' Hall,

[22]See *The Survey of London*, Vol. 33, *St. Anne, Soho* (Athlone Press for Greater London Council) for details of her enterprise.

[23]Charles Burney, *History of Music* (1776-1789), Vol. 4, p. 676.

where the privilege of subscribing was confined to City men and people from "the other end of the town" were excluded.

Music continued to play a major part in the amusements of London, sometimes as an additional attraction and sometimes in its own right, throughout the eighteenth century; but by the time that Samuel Johnson came there the great days of Italian opera were over. This had been very much the vogue in the first two decades of the century. In 1706 Bononcini's *Camilla* had been given with an all-English cast; the next year the experiment of a mixed company of English and Italian singers was tried, each singing in his or her tongue. In 1710 *Almahide* was sung completely in Italian. During the next year young Handel paid his first visit to England where his opera *Rinaldo* had a conspicuous success, which by 1712 had induced him to settle in that country. His well known *Water Music* was written in 1715 for George I, and in 1720 he became director of the first Royal Academy of Music. From this point Handel's career and the future of Italian opera in London became closely interlocked. It was not a happy connection. The presentation of Italian opera was fraught with difficulties. It was bound by a set of artificial conventions, its main masculine parts were by tradition written for the castrati; the practice of castrating choir boys to prevent their voices from breaking at puberty had long been an Italian practice, so that the greatest operatic male singers were all Italian. They demanded large salaries; almost as expensive were the leading female singers of the standing of Cuzzoni and Bordoni. The orchestra was inevitably costly, and the public expected lavish scenery and extravagant mechanical devices to charm the eye. They also expected constant variety. Handel wrote new operas regularly. In twenty-seven years he wrote thirty-four, and even his genius could not always produce a masterpiece. There were other difficulties of a political nature. Walpole's unpopularity reflected back on the Crown, and the fact that George I and even George II were known to be supporters of Handel flung a section of fashionable society against him. Thus for a time Handel's company played to empty houses, with only the royal box conspicuously full, while much of the town flocked to the so-called Opera of the Nobility, then playing at Lincoln's Inn Fields. By the late thirties society had had its fill of Italian opera; both companies were bankrupt, and by 1741 Handel's connection with Italian opera came to an end. In addition to producing this redoubtable output of operas, Handel had been a prolific composer in other directions. As early as 1720 he had written a masque for the Duke of Chandos, which later was to form the basis of the oratorio *Esther*. In the itervening years he had some successes in this field, notably *Esther* itself, as well as *Deborah* and *Athaliah*, and when it became clear that interest in Italian opera was waning, it was to this style of composition that Handel turned. Although his most popular work in England today is the *Messiah*, it was not then well received; he established a great reputation with *Judas Maccabaeus* in 1745. Works such as these appear to have had a wider appeal than Italian opera; they were something that sober citizens as well as the fashionable world could enjoy and approve.

Music and concerts were not enjoyed only in the West End or by society and substantial citizens. The East End, too, had its musical evenings. Spitalfields's enthusiasts used to gather at the Angel and Crown, where a convenient long room was set aside for them and where the presiding spirit was Peter Prelleur, who later became the parish organist at Christ Church. A madrigal society with a strong contingent of Spitalfields weavers started to meet at the Twelve Bells just off Fleet Street in 1741. Later they moved to more commodious quarters at the Queen's Arms. Its twenty-five members paid a quarterly subscription of five and six pence, some of which was spent on porter and tobacco. There were many less ambitious clubs patronized by craftsmen which, though they lacked the elegance of the concerts given for their betters, no doubt gave equal if not greater pleasure as the audience kept time with their pots of porter or joined in the chorus of popular songs, such as Dr. Arne's "Rule Britannia." This widespread love of music is one of the pleasanter aspects of eighteenth-century London. It was a pleasure that Dr. Johnson found difficult to share. As he once confessed to Boswell, he found himself very insensitive to the power of music.

Londoners have always had a great affection for the theatre, and the eighteenth century was no exception. The town was well provided with playhouses as well as concert halls and other places where theatrical performances took place. The oldest of these was Drury Lane, which opened in the reign of Charles II and was rebuilt after the Great Fire by Christopher Wren. It was to this theatre that the gallants of Restoration London had come and in it that Nell Gwyn is reputed to have sold her oranges. For most of Johnson's time it was substantially the same building, until in 1775-1776 it was remodelled with greater elegance by Robert Adam, the new side boxes being decorated with red-spotted paper and supported by pillars inlaid with glass. Next in seniority came the Queen's Theatre in the Haymarket, built in 1705, which after Queen Anne's death became known as the King's Opera House. It was the first theatre to be built in eighteenth-century London and, though designed by Sir John Vanbrugh, was not an unqualified success. The acoustics were poor, and its size precluded the lines of the actors being clearly heard. It was more suitable for opera and was in fact used for this purpose for most of the century. A third theatre was located in Lincoln's Inn Fields; this was built in 1714, and it was here that all London flocked when Rich put on Gay's *The Beggars' Opera,* previously rejected by Drury Lane. With his profits Rich planned to build a new playhouse further west; having arranged to transfer his license, he secured a site on Covent Garden, opposite Drury Lane, in what then was the heart of theatre land. On it he built a magnificent new theatre, designed by Edward Shepperd and financed very largely by subscriptions provided by the aristocracy. Henceforth there was intense rivalry between the two theatres. Each had its own company of players and endeavoured to secure for itself the most popular dramatic works by contemporary authors and to exploit them. Any monopoly could, however, only apply to new plays. Revivals of both Shakespeare and of Restoration comedies were frequent, and here clashes were possible. In the season 1750-1751 a clash was deliberately contrived as a challenge and test of strength. Among the favourite actors of Garrick's company at Drury Lane was Spranger Barry, whose romantic good looks had earned him high praise as Romeo but whose jealousy of Garrick had subsequently induced him to transfer to the rival company at Covent Garden under the management of John Rich. Determined to accept the challenge, Garrick, who had not played the part before, on September 28 cast himself as Romeo, with the beautiful young Bellamy as Juliet. Across the road Barry and Mrs. Cibber were featured in the same play. At first society was amused and flocked to both theatres to pass judgment, but after twelve nights of Romeo and Juliet in both houses boredom succeeded amusement. On the thirteenth night a diplomatic indisposition on the part of Mrs. Cibber brought the contest to a close.

The only other main playhouse that remained constant to theatrical performances, though there were other places where these occasionally took place, was the New or Little Theatre in the Haymarket, almost opposite the King's Opera House. Chronologically it comes between the building of the latter and the theatre in Lincoln's Inn Fields and that of Covent Garden, being opened in 1720. It was here that Henry Fielding tried his hand at management and Samuel Foote built a reputation on his savage caricatures. This concentration of theatres was inconvenient for the inhabitants of the City and even more for people living in the developing areas of the East End, when there were no buses or undergrounds (subways) to transport them with speed and safety to an evening's entertainment. The dimly lit and filthy streets, apart from the dangers of drunken revellers or casual robbers, were enough to make men, and particularly women, look for an evening's diversion nearer home, unless it could be had at the expense of a hackney coach or a sedan chair. To meet this situation enterprising managers set up playhouses in those parts of the town that were most likely to patronize such local entertainment. The theatrical centre for the East End of London was Goodman's Fields between the City and Whitechapel. Since 1729 there had been a small theatre, known as Odell's, in Ayliffe Street. In 1731 this was taken over and rebuilt by Giffard, who was to show himself to be one of the most enterprising of the eighteenth-century theatrical managers. As for most of the newer playhouses, funds were raised by subscription from interested people. Giffard collected twenty-three subscriptions of £100 each and with these funds employed Edward Shepperd, the designer of Covent Garden. It must have been an attractive little theatre, with a painted ceiling depicting in the middle of a large oval His Majesty, attended by Peace, Liberty, and Justice, trampling Tyranny and Oppression under his feet. Around it were medallions of famous theatrical personages—Shakespeare, Dryden, Congreve, and Betterton. In addition to Giffard's, the New Wells in Goodman's

Fields and the New Wells Clerkenwell both put on shows of a more varied type, including a good deal of pantomine.

When to the theatres and concert halls are added the booths set up at the great fairs, such as those held at St. Bartholomew's, Smithfield, at Southwark, and at the disorderly May Fair, it is clear that all parts of the town were well provided with dramatic entertainment. Authority considered this provision overlavish. The playhouse was thought to be a constant temptation for working folk to neglect their business and waste their time on what could benefit neither the community nor themselves. There was also some disquiet at the type of play so frequently performed: Restoration comedy, which remained popular, was hardly calculated to raise the moral tone of society, and the middling sort at least were becoming more and more straightlaced in their outlook. Politicians, too, and one politician in particular, Sir Robert Walpole, had their own reasons for disliking the contemporary theatre. Because Walpole was "the Great Man" who had held power for so long, it was perhaps inevitable that he should be the target for satire and that his enemies should be numerous. In addition he was not at home in the company of wits and men of letters, many of whom gravitated to the ranks of his opponents. Moreover, his methods of political manipulation and the more than substantial fortune that he acquired in office laid him particularly open to the charge of corruption. After the failure of the Excise Bill and his vengeful reaction the storm of abuse grew steadily stronger. Henry Fielding in particular, at the Little Theatre in the Haymarket, made him the butt of his wit in such plays as *The Historical Register* and *Pasquinade*. *Polly,* which followed the *Beggar's Opera,* was equally anti-Walpole. In consequence even by the mid-thirties Walpole was looking for some means of muzzling the stage. He found an unexpected, from the angle of politics, ally in Sir John Barnard, whose Quaker background made him particularly disapproving of the low moral tone of many plays and particularly fearful of their effect on the frugality and industry of London's poorer inhabitants. He was therefore anxious to limit the number of playhouses that they could frequent; Walpole was equally anxious to control the plays they saw. He played his cards skillfully, and in 1737 the licensing act was passed. This affected the London theatre in two ways. By its provisions only theatres, whether in London or the provinces, that received a royal licence were allowed to give public dramatic performances, and new plays and alterations to old ones had to be submitted to the Lord Chamberlain before they could be presented.

This denial of freedom had a stultifying effect on the London theatre, for, apart from the King's Opera House, only Drury Lane and Covent Garden had an uncontested legal right to present plays. The immediate result was that Fielding gave up the Little Theatre and Giffard was driven to contemplating disposing of his properties and effects. Walpole, however, was not wholly successful: enterprising managers found ingenious ways of circumventing the new act. One was the so-called concert formula—a playhouse sold tickets to a concert, for which no licence was required, and between the two parts of the concert a full-length play was sandwiched gratis. By 1740 Giffard's was again in production, and in that decade the Little Theatre, after some vissicitudes, came under the management of Samuel Footc. Nevertheless their position remained precarious. It was dangerous to score too great a success, which threatened the profits of the two royal theatres. This happened when David Garrick made his debut at Giffard's in the autumn of 1741. Though still nominally engaged in the wine trade in Durham Yard, just off the Strand and conveniently near both Covent Garden and Drury Lane, young Garrick had long been haunting them both and cultivating the society of actors rather than mixing with more solid citizens. When Yates, who was playing at Goodman's Fields, fell ill, Garrick took his part at a moment's notice, and his success confirmed him in his desire to become a professional actor. Accordingly when Giffard sent his company to Ipswich after his London theatre closed for the summer Garrick, under an assumed name, went with it and did so well that when the company opened for the autumn season in London, Garrick played Richard III. It was a wise choice that suited both his stature—he was only five foot four inches tall, and his dramatic genius. His performance was an instant success. All the town flocked to see him, and it is reported that the road from Temple Bar was blocked with coaches. For Garrick it was the beginning of a triumphal career, but it focused the rivalry and pressure of the two licensed theatres on Giffard, who next year lost his star to Drury Lane. Such was the hazard of running an unlicenced theatre: it must never become too successful and popular with the people who counted.

That Giffard should have fallen a victim to the licensing act was a misfortune for the London theatre, partly because he was always ready to try out new plays and partly because he took great pains to train his company in the technique of acting, thus providing a reservoir of talent for the stage. Samuel Foote at the Haymarket proved more successful in surviving the hazards of the licensing law. One of his ingenious devices for getting around its provisions was to invite his friends to take a cup of chocolate with him, selling the tickets beforehand at George's Coffee House at Temple Bar, and, the refreshment having been paid for, the entertainment was in theory free. Because his shows started at noon, so avoiding any clash with those put on by the licensed theatres at the conventional hours, they were less inclined to invoke the law against Foote. Perhaps, too, and with reason, they thought him a dangerous man to provoke. His talent lay in mimicry and in cruel personal caricature, and nobody cared to be his victim. Johnson, having heard that Foote had resolved to apply this treatment to him, took characteristic steps to deal with the situation. At a dinner with Mr. Thomas Davies, the bookseller, he asked his host what was the usual price of an oak stick and, on being told that it was sixpence, replied: "Why then, Sir, give me leave to send your servant to purchase me a shilling one. I'll have a double quantity; for I am told that Foote means to *take me off*, as he calls it, and I am determined the fellow shall not do it with impunity."[24] The information was duly passed on, and the performance did not take place! Apart from his mimicry Foote put on many comedies and a good deal of pantomine, which was very popular with eighteenth-century audiences. In 1766 he finally secured a patent for his theatre and so entered the select group of royal theatres.

The original rhythm of the theatrical season had been geared to the habits of the nobility and gentry rather than to those of London's less influential population. Because the nobility avoided the town in the summer months, returning only when Parliament

[24]Boswell, *Life of Samuel Johnson*, Vol. 2, p. 299.

resumed its sittings in the pleasanter autumn, Drury Lane and
Covent Garden closed in mid-May and opened again in mid-
September, playing even then only every other night until the full
season started in early October. Originally no performances were
given on December 24 and 25 and on January 30, which was still
kept as a fast day in memory of the execution of Charles I. Lent
brought further closures. There were no performances on the
traditional fast days of Wednesday and Friday, and in Holy Week
all the theatres were shut. So avid were Londoners for the theatre,
however, that early inroads were made on these sacred holidays.
Oratorios, though not plays, were allowed at Drury Lane and
Covent Garden on the Wednesdays and Fridays in Lent, but the
prohibition against opening in Holy Week continued. To meet
the needs of genuine Londoners who resided there throughout the
year, the smaller theatres began to provide entertainment of a less
serious kind during the summer months. Foote kept the Haymarket open, which meant that after 1766 London had at least one
theatre where plays could be legally given. Nevertheless, this was
scanty fare for any place as big as London, particularly after two
acts of Parliament in 1752 and 1755 cut the supply of popular
amusement still further, and even performances of singing, dancing, and acrobatics had to be licensed by a magistrate.

London theatres were built roughly on a common plan. The
stage itself had not yet become a magic box with one side removed. Instead an apron stage or platform extended well into the
auditorium. This suited the style of acting in vogue in the earlier
part of the century, before the more natural technique favoured
by players like Peg Woffington and Garrick became fashionable.
In tragedy dramatic declamation rather than acting was required,
and while the leading actor or actress was confiding his or her
villainies or tribulations to the audience, the other players relaxed
their attention and stared around. Kitty Clive was apt to nod or
curtsey to friends in the house, and in the course of one particularly long speech the supporting player is reported to have dozed
off! Until the middle of the century the scenery remained simple
because of the construction of the stage. At either side was the
proscenium door through which all exits and entrances were
made. This was a permanent feature and remained even when
more elaborate scenery allowed of a back entrance. The second

restricting feature was the stage boxes which, being located along each side, completely destroyed the illusion of the stage as a place apart, though they were useful for the balcony scene in *Romeo and Juliet*. With the Quality intent on displaying their finery, chattering with their friends, and commenting on the play and its players, it must have been difficult for any producer to build up the necessary atmosphere for the drama. If the demand for places was great, additional chairs were often provided against the side of the stage itself, making the spectator almost a part of the scene that he was supposed to be watching. Only favoured patrons were obliged in this way, but a line of elegant quizzing beaux was little likely to contribute to the realism of the set. When Garrick became co-manager of Drury Lane he struggled to put a stop to the practice, but it was too deeply rooted to disappear overnight and lingered on into the early sixties. The difficulties connected with elaborate scenic effects were further enlarged by the fact that until the mid-century the curtain was never lowered between acts, and any changes in scenery had to take place in full view of the audience. This tended to limit them to carrying on and off a few stage properties and to the minimum of furniture for a scene. Of late there has been a revival of this practice in order not to hold up the action by a series of changes between short scenes, although, unlike his Georgian counterpart, the modern producer has all the advantages of a revolving stage and similar devices to maintain illusion and secure speed. Throughout the century the scenery and effects tended to become more and more elaborate. The public loved a spectacle, whether in the theatre or in the streets of London, and managers found it profitable to cater to this taste. As a result displays grew more lavish, and most managers spent considerably on costumes, effects, and properties. They recouped the costs of an especially expensive production by charging an additional price. This new concentration on scenery demanded the elimination of spectators from the stage itself: their presence made it difficult to create the necessary illusion, and in the more complicated arrangement of the set there was no place for their chairs. There was also some physical danger from the various contrivances and machines used, particularly in pantomine when dragons appeared, breathing fire. When John Yeoman went to Drury Lane during his visit to Lon-

don in 1774, he was almost overwhelmed by what he saw and
wrote with awe in his diary: "There not That Man Living who
can form any Idea of Unless they See it. Some of the Scines I've
heard say they Represent Street as Real as any in London . . . and
all the Streets as Natural as If you was out in Town and it is so
much Impossible for any Person to form any Idea of the Town
as of the play unless they have."[25] Yeoman's own description
certainly leaves confusion worse confounded.

Modern audiences would think the eighteenth-century auditorium uncomfortable and noisy. Instead of well-upholstered
seats only backless benches were provided. Apart from the boxes,
the theatre, which was either rectangular or horseshoe in shape,
was divided into the pit and the first and second galleries. The
seats cost 4/6 in the boxes, 2/6 in the pit, 1/6 in the first gallery,
and 1/- in the second. If the production had been newly and
elaborately dressed, or if the Afterpiece were a pantomine, advanced prices were charged, namely 5/- in the boxes, 3/- in the
pit, and 2/- or 1/- in the galleries. For these prices the audience
was given a very full measure of entertainment. After the First,
Second, and Third Music, which took place between the opening
of the doors at five and the raising of the curtain at six, came the
main production of the evening, usually a five-act tragedy or a
comedy. Between the acts some lighter fare was provided by
either singers, dancers, or instrumentalists. Following the main
piece there was an Afterpiece, usually a farce, a ballad opera, a
pantomine, or a burletta. This double bill was the result of the
practice, which had grown up in the late seventeenth century, of
letting people in at half price after the end of the third act. Six
o'clock was inconveniently early for people whose work or business absorbed them for most of the day, and the reduced price
was to lure them in. Because there was little inducement to pay
even these reduced prices to see only the last two acts of the
current play, managers added the Afterpiece. Until 1747 it was
not usual to provide this added attraction after a new piece,
which presumably was capable of filling the house without resort-
ing to packing it with a half-price audience, but by the second
half of the century the Afterpiece had become customary. As a

25Yeoman, *op. cit.*, p. 30.

result elaborate and expensive Afterpieces also were used to justify advanced prices, and on these occasions the Afterpiece was sometimes suspended, though if a member of the audience left after the main piece and before the Afterpiece, he had the difference between the ordinary and advanced price refunded as he left the theatre.

The fashionable world filled the boxes. The main part of the respectable audience congregated in the pit. Here sat the solid citizens and their wives, the critics, writers, and wits, and the young men about town like James Boswell. The first gallery was occupied by the less affluent of the middling sort, and in the second sat the poorer shopkeepers, journeymen, apprentices, and, above all, the footmen. They were always in evidence, having by tradition established their right to a free seat for the second half of the performance. This was because there was no system of booking a particular seat in advance, though tickets could be bought beforehand. Footmen were therefore sent to keep places until their masters and mistresses arrived. It was, however, possible to buy or subscribe for an entire box, and to make this easier for patrons the office of box-book keeper was instituted. Today the ticket office of a modern London theatre is still "the box office," though in many it is now possible to reserve a seat even in the gallery. People who had no servants to send had to arrive early. In the second half of the century the doors at Drury Lane opened at four, though the performance did not start until six thirty; when Garrick played Lear on May 12, 1763, Boswell reported that the house was packed by ten minutes past. Garrick's Lear was of course a great draw, but even on less popular nights keeping seats for friends could be difficult. When Boswell went with Dempster and Erskine to the first night of Mrs. Sheridan's comedy *The Discovery*, his companions put their hats on either side of him and went off to dine; Boswell wrote ruefully in his diary: "I had but a troublesome occupation keeping the two seats while my companions were enjoying themselves over a bottle and lolling at their ease, in no hurry to come in."[26] On popular nights the audience must have been packed like sardines: Garrick calculated only 21 inches per person. They would also have to face the

[26] J. Boswell, *London Journal*, (1950), p. 177.

struggle to get in with the first rush when the doors opened, for Londoners had not yet been broken in to the discipline of the queue; people hustled and shoved, clothes were torn, and limbs were bruised. A final discomfort might well be caused by extremes of weather. Facilities for either heating or cooling the theatre were scanty, and audiences either shivered or half-suffocated. Enterprising managers sometimes tried to combat a sudden heat wave by advertising that the performance would commence later than the conventional hour to take advantage of the evening cool. Audiences took their own measures against the rigours of winter by dressing in quilted skirts, capes, and coats. Boswell on one occasion even wore two shirts. The stage itself must have been a chilly place, in spite of a trickle of warmth from the oil lamps that furnished the footlights and from the chandeliers of wax candles overhead. Indeed it has been suggested that one very practical reason why so many historical plays were given in contemporary rather than in historically correct costume was the matter of warmth. Roman tunics and bare legs were not well adapted to a draughty stage. Sometimes the severity of the cold forced the theatre to close.

If eighteenth-century audiences were more uncomfortable than their modern counterparts, they were also less inhibited in expressing disapproval of any play that failed to please them. They thumped with oak sticks on the floor, blew on a devastating whistle, known as a catcall, and generally created an appalling din. When a new play was to be performed, an author exerted every effort to get his friends and supporters to attend, so that their cheers and applause might drown the jeers and catcalls of his enemies. When Robert Dodsley's tragedy *Cleone* was presented, Johnson went along, for as he wrote to Bennet Langton, "Doddy, you know, is my patron and I would not desert him. The play was very well received. Doddy, after the danger was over, went every night to the stage-side, and cryed at the distress of poor Cleone."[27] When Kelly's *A Word to the Wise* was given at Drury Lane in 1770, it got a very different reception. Kelly had been rash enough to write against Wilkes, and in revenge that gentleman's friends created such an uproar that it was impossible

---

[27]Boswell, *Life of Samuel Johnson*, Vol. 1, p. 326.

to announce even a second performance of the howled down play. When this happened the unfortunate author received nothing, because for most of the century the usual system of payment was for the playwright to receive the profits of the house for the third, sixth, and ninth nights instead of fees or royalties on each performance. At the best of times the occupants in the gallery showed themselves to be no respecters of persons. Pastor Moritz, when he visited the Haymarket, was shocked by their behaviour: "It is the tenants in the upper gallery who, for their shilling make all the noise and uproar, for which the English playhouses are so famous. I was in the pit, which gradually rises amphi-theatre wise from the orchestra, and is furnished with benches one above the other from the top to the bottom. Often and often as I sat there did a rotten orange, or pieces of the peel of an orange, fly past me, or past some of my neighbours, and once one of them actually hit my hat, without my daring to look around, for fear another might come plump in my face. Besides the perpetual pelting from the gallery which renders any English playhouse so uncomfortable there is no end to them calling out, knocking with their sticks, till the curtain is drawn up. I saw a miller's, or a baker's boy, thus, like a huge booby, leaning over the rails, and knocking again and again on the outside, with all his might, without being ashamed or abashed."[28] Oranges, which were on sale in the theatre, seem to have been the usual ammunition of the gallery, and since theatres were small, the stage itself was within range. Even popular actresses might sometimes find themselves in a hail of flying peel. When, owing to a backstage feud, Peg Woffington failed to appear in *The Constant Couple*, her disappointed fans treated her to this display of their displeasure at her next appearance. Indeed the public regarded the players as very much their servants. In the oft quoted words of Johnson's prologue to *The Merchant of Venice*, given on September 15, 1747, lies the bitter truth of their profession:

> The drama's laws, the drama's patrons give,
> For we that live to please, must please to live.

Sometimes an affronted audience showed its disapproval by

---

[28]Moritz, *op. cit.*, p. 38.

methods more violent than a shower of oranges and an uproar of
stick thumping and catcalls. Occasionally serious riots occurred,
not necessarily incited by the rough crowds in the gallery. When
on January 23, 1740, at Drury Lane two of the principal dancers
failed to appear, "several gentlemen in the Boxes and Pit pulled
up the Seats and Flooring of the Same, tore down the Hangings,
broke down the Partitions, and all the Glasses and Scones; the
King's Arms over the middle Front Box was pulled down and
broke to Pieces; they also destroyed the Harpsicord, Bass Viol, and
other Instruments in the Orchestra and the Curtain they cut to
pieces with their Swords, forced their Way into the lesser Green-
Room, where they broke the Glasses etc. and also destroyed every
Thing they could get asunder."[29] On another occasion, when
Garrick had been so unwise as to engage a troop of French dancers in 1755 when the two countries were on the verge of war, the
ensuing riot did £4000 worth of damage. The most frequent cause
of trouble was any attempt of the management to raise prices or
withdraw privileges. In 1737, when Drury Lane management
decided no longer to allow footmen who had been keeping places
to sit in the second gallery without payment, the result was a riot
in which, according to the *Gentleman's Magazine,* some 300
footmen broke into the theatre and got as far as the door leading
to the stage before they were stopped, but not before twenty five
people had been seriously injured. They then sent Fleetwood, the
manager, an ultimatum that unless their rights were restored to
them, they would reduce "the playhouse to the ground." Next day
fifty soldiers were on guard at Drury Lane, but though there was
no further trouble, Fleetwood made no subsequent attempt to
curtail their privileges. It was not until after particularly noisy
demonstrations from the servants in the second gallery on the
presentation of the play *High Life Below Stairs* in 1759 that
Garrick took a strong line and so rid the theatre of what had often
been a disorderly nuisance. He was not always so lucky and had
to face fresh rioting in 1766 when he tried to abolish the second
price for patrons arriving after the third act. With such turbulent
audiences it is not surprising to read that a row of formidable
spikes divided the orchestra from the auditorium or that it was
usual to station a soldier behind the proscenium door!

[29]Maitland, *The History of London* (1756), Vol. 1, p. 605.

If contemporary accounts are to be accepted, the century seems to have been an age of great acting rather than of great plays. Indeed the habit of coming to the theatre when the play was half over hardly suggests that the plays were of surpassing interest. During the first half of the century theatrical taste was being more and more moulded by the theatregoing public. The playhouse was popular and had to cater to every shade of social outlook. The Quality enjoyed the witty, amoral comedies of the Restoration period when intrigue, the pursuit of the fair, and the stratagems of lovers filled the greater part of the gallant's life. Such plays were often revived and could be counted upon to draw good audiences. But just because among some sections of society loose morals were condoned, it is a mistake to regard this as universal. Charity Schools and the Society for the Propagation of the Gospel are as much a part of Georgian England as gambling and gin. The middling sort and the sober citizens and their wives enjoyed lofty sentiments and the pathos of the sufferings endured by the virtuous. Perhaps as a reaction from the scenes of brutality and squalor around them they liked to escape into a world of refinement and sensitivity, away from the harsh realities into a world of sentimental drama. Perhaps they were sensitive also to the social scorn that "the ton" displayed toward the citizen, making fun of his manners and stuffy morals alike. Certainly this section of the theatregoing public shrank in genuine or simulated disgust from any speech or action that could be described as coarse or crude. There would have been no place in the London theatre for "kitchen sink" plays of the kind that have had so great a vogue in the postwar period. Tragedy, too, was intended to appeal to the nobler instincts of mankind: written in blank verse or rhymed couplets and dealing with the heroic character of some heroic age and distant country, it made its stately progress through five acts of noble sentiments.

Even Dr. Johnson was not exempt from the urge to have a tragedy performed at Drury Lane. Since his Edial days he had been working on a piece entitled *Irene*, which Garrick arranged to put on. There were stormy scenes during the rehearsals, for the Doctor, with the tenderness of an author for his work, could not bear to see it altered, and Garrick was convinced that unless its more dramatic elements could be brought out it would have little audience appeal. Johnson accused him of merely wanting a fat part for himself grumbling that "the fellow wants me to make Mahomet run mad, that he may have an opportunity of tossing his hands and kicking his heels."[30] Finally the actor-manager was allowed to make some changes, and the play ran for nine nights. It was not, however, revived at intervals, as more successful tragedies were. Boswell thought that this was because it was "deficient in pathos, in that delicate power of touching human feelings, which is the principal end of drama." Johnson was more successful with his prologues, then an essential part of the play.

Genteel or High Comedies, in which nothing gross was allowed to appear, or the artificial tragedies that contemporary taste demanded, could not be turned out in sufficient quantities when new plays were given such short runs, yet the paucity of theatres and the limited clientele on which they could draw forced this policy on the management. To secure a frequent change of play, therefore, they had to fall back on revivals of late-seventeenth-century comedies, or the tragedies of Otway and Dryden. Shakespeare was always popular, but even he was altered to fit eighteenth-century taste. Garrick was not the first man to do so, but he was certainly a great practitioner of this art. He might perhaps be forgiven for providing a happy ending to *Romeo and Juliet* or for producing his own version of the *Taming of the Shrew*, but the liberties that he took with the text of *Hamlet* were such that Shakespeare would hardly have recognized the play. It was in accordance with the high-flown moral sentiment of the contemporary theatre that he made Gertrude go mad with remorse and removed the gravediggers completely as too jarring and common an element quite unsuited for a high tragedy. He tidied up *Lear* in the same way. When Count Kielmansegge went to see it in 1761, he wrote that "the play is very much in the style of the old English plays in fashion when the author wrote it, in which most of the characters go mad, or get blind or die; but as the English taste has changed latterly, many alterations have been made in this tragedy; amongst others the omission of the court jester, who in the original brings his tomfooleries in everywhere, even in the most tragic scenes."[31] Alas poor fool: it is clear that Count Kielmansegge thought his elimination an improve-

[30]Boswell, *Life of Samuel Johnson*, Vol. 1, p. 196.

[31]Kielmansegge, *op. cit.*, p. 214.

ment! Though mangled versions of Shakespeare continued to be popular and good new tragedies were rare, in the field of comedy new ground was broken by such plays as Goldsmith's *She Stoops to Conquer* and Sheridan's *The Rivals*. In addition to the numerous and varied attractions that London had to offer after dark there was much to interest the visitor during the daylight hours. Then as now two of the notable sights were the Tower of London and the British Museum. At the former the Crown Jewels were kept and there was also a small menagerie that was very popular; at Montague House, bought for this purpose, Sir Hans Sloane's bequest, the Cottonian Library and the Harleian MSS. were on view to those who secured the necessary ticket of admission.

Not all the amusements to which Londoners were prone were so decorous. Every strata of society was streaked with recklessness, with drunkenness, and with brutality. Gambling was a mania from which no class and no sex was exempt. Kielsmansegge noted that at the Duke of Ancaster's ball the Duke of Cumberland "again played a game of quinze for just as high stakes as he had played some time before at Lord Walgrave's; but what he won or lost this time I cannot say. On a previous occasion he had lost 1000 guineas by twelve o'clock."[32] Almarck's and White's were notorious for high play. In 1770 Horace Walpole wrote that "The young men of the age lose ten, fifteen, twenty thousand pounds in an evening there. Lord Stavordale, not one and twenty, lost £1,000 there last Thursday but recovered it by one great hand at hazard."[33] Gossip writers are given to exaggeration, but losses less considerable than these could soon cripple even the wealthiest players, though in many cases their embarrassment may have been temporary. Most of them belonged to the same social set and played regularly with one another: large sums might change hands each evening, but the man who lost on Tuesday might well win on Wednesday. If a run of bad luck went on too long, tragedy sometimes intervened. In 1755 Sir John Bland lost all his estates playing hazard at White's and shot himself. Lord Mountford was another man who committed suicide as a result of his gaming losses. In taverns and less salubrious gaming dens throughout London night after night the same scenes were being

[32]*Ibid.*, p. 282.

[33]J. Timbs, *Clubs & Club Life in London*, (1872), p. 72.

enacted. Even in the prisons men would stake the very coat off
their back.

Recklessness went hand in hand with brutality. Men were
prepared to gamble on cocks, on horses, and on men, whether
they fought with cudgels or fists. Cockfighting appealed to all
classes. Hogarth's print "The Cock Pit" depicts a nobleman wearing his star nearly smothered by the artisan who is leaning over
him. The regular cockpit, built in the late seventeenth century,
was situated in Dartmouth Street, near both St. James's park and
Westminster. Kielmansegge painted in words the scene that
Hogarth painted with his brush. "In the middle of a circle and a
gallery surrounded by benches, a slightly raised theatre is erected, upon which the cocks fight. They are a small kind of cock to
the legs of which a long spur, like a long needle is fixed, with
which they know how to inflict damage on their adversaries very
cleverly during the fight, but on which also they are frequently
caught themselves, so breaking their legs. One bird of each of the
couples we saw fighting met with this misfortune, so that he was
down in a moment and unable to rise or help himself, consequently his adversary had at once an enormous advantage. Notwithstanding this he fought with his beak for half an hour, but the
other bird had the best of it, and both were carried off with
bleeding heads. No one who has not seen such a sight can con-
ceive the uproar by which it is accompanied, as everybody at the
same time offers and accepts bets. You cannot hear yourself
speak."[34] Defaulters who failed to pay their debts risked the
ignominity of being placed in a large basket and slung from the
roof over the cockpit as a warning to others. When Boswell visited the cockpit in 1762, he was shocked by the mixture of cruelty
and avarice of the crowd: "I was sorry for the poor cocks. I looked
round to see if any of the spectators pitied them when mangled
and torn in a most cruel manner, but I could not observe the
smallest relenting sign in any countenance. I was therefore not
ill pleased to see them endure mental torments."[35] Few people
shared Boswell's concern, though one writer in the *Gentleman's
Magazine* in January 1753 condemned what he called "the
wretched custom of throwing at cocks" as initiating the youth of

[34]Kielmansegge, *op. cit.,* p. 241.

[35]Boswell, *London Journal, op. cit.,* p. 87.

the country "into cruelty and vice". Indeed most of the rougher
amusements of the age involved the infliction of cruelty on animals. Dogs, like cocks, were trained to fight while the spectators
backed their fancy and their masters hallooed them on. Dogs, too,
were pitted against baited bulls and bears. Often the tea gardens
that lay beyond the confines of the town had ponds where patrons
could set their dogs on the ducks provided for that sport.

Contests between men were equally popular and equally
brutal. James Figg, a skilled swordsman who gave lessons in
swordsmanship to the gentry and nobility at his house in Oxford
Street, in 1725 opened an arena behind it where he promoted
fights. Unlike in modern fencing contests, bare blades were used,
though the points were fashioned in such a way that the maximum of blood appeared to flow for the minimum amount of
serious injury. Nevertheless it was a dangerous sport. Fighting
with long staffs was also common, since the first man to draw
blood on such encounters could cause serious injuries. But from
the twenties on boxing grew in popularity. Here again the appetite of the spectators was stimulated by the spectacle of physical
violence. Men fought with their bare fists, they could seize their
opponent by the throat, hurl him to the ground, and employ
tactics that today would be reserved for wrestling. Booths for
boxing contests were set up in most fairs, but the permanent
centre of the sport was in the area of Oxford Street and Tottenham Court Road. John Broughton, a former Thames waterman,
had his new Amphitheatre there in 1743, and in 1747 he set up a
Boxing Academy in the Haymarket to teach the art to men of
fashion. Because the gentry and nobility would obviously be
disinclined to face the disfigurement of broken noses and other
facial injuries, his advertisement assured them that this hazard
would be avoided by the use of "mufflers" or boxing gloves. For a
time Broughton dominated the boxing world and became the
protégé of the Duke of Cumberland until in a notable fight Slack,
the Norfolk butcher, by concentrating his blows on Broughton's
face so blinded him with his own blood that he was defeated, to
the great mortification of the Duke, who had backed him heavily.
In 1752 Broughton retired from the ring with a fortune of £7000.
Though there was an attempt in the middle of the century to
have such contests suppressed by the justices as disorderly gath-

erings, they continued to be patronized by all classes of the community from the duke to the craftsman.

The range of London's amusements underlines the fact that the eighteenth century was above all a century of contrasts. The polite world supported subscription concerts and drank tea at Ranelagh, the middling sort and even the craftsmen and their families flocked out to the tea gardens that surrounded London, both patronized the theatre, and yet underneath it all ran the streak of violence and cruelty. Well-bred and respectable women were almost ostentatiously protected from this undercurrent, but the common people and the men of fashion alike were fascinated and drawn by it, flocking to see women whipped at Bridewell, men, women, and even children hanged at Tyburn, cocks mangling each other at the cockpit, and men maiming each other in the Ring. In London every taste, from the most civilised and sophisticated to the crudest and most barbarous, could find the amusement that it sought.

SIX

Learned and Artistic London

The very words "Johnson's London" conjure up a picture of the burly Doctor, leaning forward slightly in his chair as he scores a point in the argument; of Sir Joshua Reynolds with his ear trumpet, ruminating over it and minutes later coming out with some surprising contribution of his own; of Goldsmith focusing the attention of the group on himself by some extreme statement or antic gesture; and of Boswell storing up every word and gesture as a tribute to lay at the feet of History. It is difficult indeed to escape from the magic circle known as the Literary Club and to present a sober account of the intellectual and artistic life of London of which it was so brilliant a part. In both spheres London was very much alive. The Club itself was a microcosm of this activity. Apart from Johnson, Goldsmith represented the world of letters and made a link between it and the stage with his comedies *The Good Natured Man* and *She Stoops to Conquer*. Sheridan, with his satirical comedies *The Rivals, The Critics*, and *School for Scandal*, and his popular light opera *The Duenna*, was a dramatist par excellence who helped to save the contemporary theatre from the tedious moral sentimental plays that threatened to engulf it. Garrick, Steevens, and Malone were linked by the common bond of Shakespeare—the first as one of the great actors of the day, the last two as editors of his work. Politics and philosophy were represented by Charles James Fox and Edmund Burke and economics by Adam Smith when he visited London. Dr. Burney and Sir John Hawkins spoke for music, but Johnson found the latter "unclubbable," and he was soon excluded. Science had as its spokesman no less a person than Sir Joseph Banks, the President of the Royal Society, who was later one of the pallbearers at Johnson's funeral. Gibbon the historian was a member. It is a galaxy of famous men. Not all the members have had their names so widely splashed across the pages of history; the Doctor's close friends Bennet Langton and Topham Beauclerk are less well known, though they were men of wide reading and cultivated minds, capable of appreciating and contributing to the charmed circle.

The eighteenth century was a period of achievement after the frustration of the Commonwealth and the hectic flowering of Restoration England. When Johnson first came to London, society had already learned to appreciate the elegance of Addison and Steele, to wince or delight in the satire of Pope, and to enjoy the bawdy comedy of the *Beggars' Opera*. Hogarth had created a new style of portrait painting with his conversation pieces and a new field of dramatic moralizing on canvas with such series as "The Rake's Progress" and "Marriage a la Mode." The world of fashion was very much aware of the world of intellectual and artistic achievement, which it encouraged by its patronage; where the nobility led, the solid citizens of London followed. Booksellers and authors, whether of poems, plays, novels, or belles lettres, could all find a market for their talents, though the search at times was heartbreaking and humiliating. The fashionable painter had the easier task. All society came to Sir Joshua's house in Leicester Fields; in one year he painted 170 portraits, but his sitter's books showed that seventy was the average for his established years. There was a bustle about London in the mid-century. After 1756 there was the excitement of war, which from 1759 Pitt was making glorious. Population was growing, not so much in London as in the provinces, and with its growth combined with the increase in trade came a mounting demand for goods. Men were aware of the new resources that Science was making, or might make, available. Endless experiments were being conducted, endless questions, both practical and theoretical, material and moral, were being asked. Even the world of politics felt the restless wind of change. Of all this excitement London was the hub. No wonder that it teemed with brilliant men and some brilliant women. In many ways it was a curiously unorganized world, a world of coteries and groups and individuals rather than of institutions. Its members were scattered throughout London—some in garrets, some in mansions, some in danger of debtors' prisons and the bailiffs, others hedged around with the security of success. Their centres were taverns, coffeehouses, and the dining rooms of their more affluent friends. Mrs. Thrale, who rather disliked Sir Joshua, spoke disparagingly of his habit of issuing invitations to any new author whose latest work had captured the limelight. Whatever his motives, many types met around his table: most of the people in London worth knowing came there at one time or another. It was this intermingling of different disciplines that gave its particular flavour to the intelligentsia of the town. Factual knowledge was not so great that a man needed a lifetime to absorb one tiny field of specialization. The educated man was still the man of wide interests, aware of what was happening in branches other than his own, and able to discuss it. The framework of thought and of education was still classical and moral, and men, whatever their interests, spoke a common language. Sir Joshua was not content to be a painter; he felt the driving necessity to cultivate the polished style of a professional writer. Though his spelling was decidedly erratic, even for the eighteenth century, the *Discourses*, which he delivered to the Academy and afterwards printed, were so excellently expressed that many people thought that Dr. Johnson must have written the major part of them.

By the mid-century the booksellers had already become the main channel by which men of literary ambitions hoped to achieve fame, if not fortune and a respectable competency. Earlier in the century the wealthy patron had still been the main hope of a struggling author, who had been paid for his dedication in guineas, generous or niggardly as his patron's liberality and means had dictated, but depending on the whim and taste of an individual. To a man of independent spirit, even though the code of the age recognized as respectable the relation of client and patron, it represented a gilded bondage. By the time George II became king it was no longer an economic necessity. In London the reading public was growing yearly, and though the favour of a great man was socially useful, there were enough solid citizens and people of the middling rank to provide a market for novels, poems, essays, pamphlets, and a growing number of newspapers. To supply this market, with the exception of the newspapers, was the function of the bookseller. Patronage still had its attractions: the patron asked only for fame, the bookseller needed profit as well. Johnson himself sought the sponsorship of Lord Chesterfield for his *Dictionary*, and when this was not forthcoming until the success of the work made it unnecessary, he penned his famous letter to the noble lord,[1] which is one of the most scornfully biting letters in the English language. In contrast, elsewhere he described the booksellers as generous liberal-minded men. Not all contemporary writers would have agreed with this assessment!

In the eighteenth century the term "bookseller" carried with it a much wider connotation that it does today. In Johnson's London he was no mere retailer of books; rather, he was the pivot of the whole book trade. It was he who made contracts with authors, arranged for the printing, organized the puffs and publicity, and assumed many of the functions of the modern publisher. He could make his own contracts with the printers and arrange for subsequent distribution through other booksellers and through his friends, even though a bookseller who merely collected the profits of retailing, not those of promoting, could hardly be expected to push energetically the sales of a volume so launched. Popular, too, was publication by subscription, particularly if the would-be author had a large circle of influential friends. In such cases the usual practice was to collect from the subscriber half the price of the proposed volume, which on completion was handed over to the subscriber on his handing over the other half of the agreed price. This method was often employed when works were too expensive or too limited in appeal for a single bookseller to risk his capital. The *Dictionary* itself was financed in this way. Boswell listed its promoters as Mr. Robert Dodsley, Mr. Charles Hitch, Mr. Andrew Millar, the two Messieurs Longman, and the two Messieurs Knapton. Johnson himself thought that the best way to place a manuscript was to negotiate with a likely bookseller. When he had completed his famous poem *London*, he wrote to Mr. Cave, the proprietor of the *Gentleman's Magazine*, to which

[1] J. Boswell, Vol. 1, p. 361.

he was already a contributor, on behalf of an imaginary author: "I believed I could not obtain more advantageous terms from any person than from you who have so much distinguished yourself by your generous encouragement of poetry."[2]

To attempt to live by writing was then, as now, a precarious way of life, involving both drudgery and luck if any measure of reputation was to be gained. Since 1710 the law had recognized the right of an author to the property of his writings in that he was given a copyright for an initial fourteen years, renewable for a similar period, unless he had died in the meantime. In 1739 this protection was extended to prohibiting the sale in England of editions printed abroad. Notwithstanding this improvement in the legal position, because of the inefficiency of the administration and the expense of securing a conviction, pirating of popular books did occur, but normally it did not cause a disastrous leak in the writer's remuneration. Much more hampering was the poverty of the unknown writer whose lack of reputation weakened him in his bargains with the booksellers. With rent unpaid, larder empty, and the last remaining coat woefully threadbare, half a loaf was indeed better than starvation. Today the payment of royalties on the sales of a book insures that even the most obscure author will benefit if the book scores a success, not only in future reputation but in present cash. In the eighteenth century such windfalls chiefly went to the bookseller, who in most cases bought the copyright before printing. This was not always done. The author might sell the copyright of the first edition only, retaining the rights to a half or a third of the profits on subsequent ones. It depended on the strength of his bargaining position. When Johnson sold his poem *London*, he received 10 guineas for it. As his reputation grew, so did his remuneration; in 1759 he received £100 for the first edition of *Rasselas*. Even so Boswell thought this a low price for a work that "though he had written nothing else, would have rendered his name immortal in the world of literature."[3] Nevertheless, for one week's work, which, he told Sir Joshua, had been the time he had spent on its composition, it was not ungenerous pay. In calculating the minimum sum necessary

[2]*Ibid.*, Vol. 1, p. 120.

[3]*Ibid.*, Vol. 1, p. 431.

for a frugal existence, an Irish friend informed Johnson that he could live in London "without being contemptible" for £30 a year, but Boswell's comment at the time of writing his *Life* was that "double the money might now with difficulty be sufficient."[4] Modern readers sometimes forget that the erosion of rising prices is not confined to their own day and age. But, as no man can write a *Rasselas* every week, it must have been an enormous relief from financial strain when in 1762 George III was graciously pleased to grant Johnson an annual pension of £300. The booksellers cannot fairly be blamed for the modest rewards that authors received. The reading public was limited, paper was expensive, and the bookseller, like the modern publisher, had to depend on his judgment. When he erred, he lost his money, and he felt that he should have his occasional scope, even at the expense of men like Johnson and Goldsmith.

Though the reading public was limited, its taste was remarkably varied; history, translations from the classics and from modern languages, poetry, essays, novels, were all in demand. The education of the educated part of society was based on the classics, which gave an inescapable flavour to the literary products of the age. When Johnson sought to attract the favour of Cave, he sent him an ode in Latin, which is hardly the method that a modern author would employ when approaching the editor of a popular magazine. His *London* was an imitation of the *Third Satire* of Juvenal. Goldsmith, struggling with poverty and gambling debts, drove himself to compile a *History of Rome*. It was an age in which readers were familiar with the language and style of philosophy, an age at once moralizing and sentimental. Boswell writes of "the philosophick dignity" of Johnson's *Vanity of Human Wishes*, an imitation of the *Tenth Satire* of Juvenal. Of *Rasselas* he wrote: "They who think justly and feel with strong sensibility will listen with eagerness and admiration to its truth and wisdom."[5] It was this market that enabled the struggling author to survive. By mid-century London was flooded with newssheets and periodicals. Though the purveying of hot political or foreign intelligence was specialized work, most publications carried what

[4]*Ibid.*, Vol. 1, pp. 105-106.

[5]*Ibid.*, Vol. 1, p. 342.

today would be described as features, calculated to appeal to the taste of their regular readers. During the days of his early struggles Johnson was a regular contributor to the *Gentleman's Magazine,* supplying, among other articles, an account of the "Debates in the Senate of Magna Lilliputia," which was based on such scanty information as he could glean of the sense of the debates in Parliament. In 1758 he started a regular Saturday feature entitled *The Idler* in the *Universal Chronicle.* The previous year he had helped Dodsley to frame a policy for his new evening newspaper, *The London Chronicle,* which was to appear three times a week and was to include regular book reviews. Most writers did some hackwork of this kind. Goldsmith wrote for *The British Magazine,* and his *Chinese Letters* were first published in *The Public Ledger,* a daily paper largely devoted to items of commercial interest; he commented bitterly on the writer's lot when "the author bids adieu to fame, writes for bread and that only. Imagination is seldom called in; he sits down to address the venal muse with the most phlegmatic apathy."[6]

Doubtless many eighteenth-century pieces were produced as a result of the writer's discipline rather than the writer's joy, but in that they were hardly unique! Johnson confessed that he had not always time to reread his *Rambler* articles or his *Idler* essays when proof had to be rushed to the printer. No doubt a mass of turgid and second-rate work, then as now, was turned out in response to economic necessity. To concentrate on the writings of a Johnson or a Goldsmith is to overestimate the quality of the literary outpourings of the London in which they lived. Much of it was ephemeral and had no claim to be remembered either for its philosophy or its style. Goldsmith had some right to feel bitter, for to him the compilation of Roman or English history was a breadwinning, not a literary, activity. The Doctor himself had little appreciation of the historian's skill; to him the writing of history was the mere collecting of facts that any hack could do, though one member of his circle was to disprove this judgment for all time. Edward Gibbon settled in London in 1772 and two years later became a member of the Club, though it was not until 1776 that the first volume of the *Decline and Fall of the Roman*

[6]Oliver Goldsmith, *The Present State of Polite Learning* (1759), Chapter X.

Empire was published. By then Goldsmith had been dead two years. In addition to the demand for history and belles lettres there was a steady market for both classical and contemporary poetry. Goldsmith made his reputation with *The Traveller or a Prospect of Society in 1764* and enhanced it four years later with *The Deserted Village.* Johnson's reputation also had first been established by his poetry: *London* had appeared in 1731 and the *Vanity of Human Wishes* in 1749. Chatterton, dying in his garret off Holborn in 1770 at the age of nineteen, was less fortunate. Classical verse, or translations from it, were nearly as popular. Mrs. Elizabeth Carter, the bluestocking, made her reputation when her translation of *Epictetus* was published by subscription in 1758. One has only to turn the pages of the *Gentleman's Magazine* to be aware of the mass of verse, English and classical, good, indifferent, and frankly bad, that was churned out month after month for the amusement of London's reading public. Most of the so-called bluestockings contributed their quota to this flood. Mrs. Thrale wrote verse, Mrs. Carter published a volume of poems in 1762, Hannah More made her name with *Sir Eldred of the Bower* and *The Bleeding Rock.* Mrs. Barbauld produced poems as well as a treatise on education. Understandably criticism of poetry was a major activity in London intellectual circles. Johnson's last great work, the prefaces to *The Lives of the Poets,* published in 1781, was a major contribution in this field. Though not all the best known eighteenth-century poets were Londoners, most of them, either in their search for fame or because they had already achieved it, visited the capital for longer or shorter periods, and no description of London's literary life can ignore its poetic interests.

Playwriting was another field in which literary men might hope to make money. Playwriting could be profitable; though runs were short, a successful play was constantly revived, and the very shortness of the average run meant that managers were constantly on the lookout for new authors and new plays. Eighteenth-century writers tended to specialize less than their modern counterparts: most leading literary figures tried their hand at a play. Johnson's attempt, as we have seen, was his tragedy *Irene.* Its reception was respectable but its run limited. Mrs. Sheridan, the mother of the more famous Richard Brinsley Sheridan, turned to playwriting to augment the family income and scored a success with her comedy *The Discovery,* which Garrick acted in 1763, though her second attempt, *The Dupe,* was less successful. Of the bluestockings, Hannah More scored a hit with her drama *Percy,* produced in 1777, but of all the Johnson circle the two outstanding dramatists were Oliver Goldsmith and Richard Brinsley Sheridan. Goldsmith's first comedy, *The Good Natured Man,* produced in 1767, had only a moderate success, its scenes of low life being at odds with the moralistic, sentimental comedy of the day, but *She Stoops to Conquer* established his reputation as a writer of comedy for all time. Even more successful was Sheridan. The reception of his first play, *The Rivals,* which was produced in 1775, encouraged him to collaborate with his musician father-in-law, with whom he was now reconciled after his romantic marriage with the latter's daughter, the Nightingale of the Bath, and to write the comic opera *The Duenna.* This was the theatrical hit of the 1775-1776 season; stimulated by the profits that it brought him, young Sheridan (he was twenty-five at the time) decided to go into management and bought a share in Drury Lane from Garrick. In 1777 he scored another triumph with *School for Scandal;* the famous Mrs. Abington played the lead. In 1779 he staged the last of his outstanding comedies, *The Critics,* a commentary on the pretentious and pedantic criticism that, like the tares with the wheat, had grown alongside the massive literary and dramatic output of the age. Fanny Burney, who met him at the height of his success in 1779, was charmed with him. "Mr. Sheridan," she wrote, "has a very fine figure, and a good, though I don't think handsome face. He is tall and very upright, and his appearance and dress are at once manly and fashionable, without the smallest tincture of foppery or modish grace."[7]

For most modern readers the novel is the century's most important literary product. At least two of the great fathers of the English novel were Londoners—Henry Fielding and Samuel Richardson. Smollett was a Scot and only intermittently a not very successful London journalist. Fielding and Richardson were very different persons, both in character and in achievement. Fielding's novels might almost be described as the by-product of

[7]F. Burney, *Diary,* Vol. I, p.155.

his zest for life and of his involvement in the human predicament
and the social scene. Fielding, the playwright of the Haymarket
and the Bow Street magistrate, wrote some thirty plays, now mostly forgotten and unread, as well as *Joseph Andrews, Tom Jones,*
and *Amelia.* With all his commitments and his struggles with ill
health toward the end of his life, Henry Fielding had little time
for literary parties and lionizing. Also, when *Tom Jones* was published in 1749, neither the Literary Club nor the bluestocking
circles had yet come to full flower. Samuel Richardson, in contrast, enjoyed being a literary lion. His early connection with this
world had been on the technical side: he was a master printer
who, half by accident, turned to the writing of novels. *Pamela,*
published in 1740, was an outstanding success, and though Fielding parodied it in *Joseph Andrews* (1742), the literary ladies of
London took it to their hearts. To have read *Pamela* was a must,
just as later to have read *Evelina* was a must, and to be unable to
express an opinion on its merits was to be excluded from the
conversation of the cultivated. In its mixture of sentimentality
and materialism, the reward of virtue being an affluent marriage,
it caught the approval of an age that rated women's virtue highly
just because the odds were so heavily weighted against a woman
in an inferior station preserving it when tempted by a man of rank
and fashion. Campbell, in the *London Tradesman,* declared that
for a poor but pretty girl to be apprenticed to a fashionable milliner was tantamount to condemning her to a life of prostitution.
To the ogling fop she was fair game; her mistress dared not inter-
fere with his attentions, however distasteful they might be, for
fear of alienating a valued customer, while the poor wages such
girls received, perhaps 5 or 6 shillings a week out of which she
had to find bed and board, made the temptation of easy money
very great. In consequence, declared Campbell, "Take a survey of
all the Commen Women of the Town, who take their Walks
between Charing Cross and Fleet Ditch, and, I am persuaded,
more than Half of them have been bred Milliners, have been
debauched from their Houses, and are obliged to throw themselves upon the Town for Want of Bread."[8] *Pamela* was followed
by *Clarissa Harlowe* who, though betrayed, remained essentially a

[8]R. Campbell, *The London Tradesman* (1747), p. 203.

virtuous woman until death released her from her miseries. Finally, to redress the balance Richardson invented *Sir Charles Gran-
dison,* a character with so little spot or blemish that all his female
readers could succumb to his charms without the least reproach
of their consciences. No wonder that Mrs. Chapone and Mrs.
Carter, whom Fanny Burney later described as being as ignorant
of life as any nun, were among his admirers, and no wonder that
he became a prominent figure in their literary circles. Women not
only read novels; they wrote them. Sometimes it was for occupation, sometimes for reputation, and sometimes for cash. Mrs.
Sheridan, who had written a novel *Eugenia and Adelina* at the
age of fifteen because the writer's urge was on her, turned again
to writing to relieve the family finances and produced *The Memoirs of Mrs. Sidney Biddulph,* which was published by Dodsley in
1761 and won her instantaneous recognition. But the success story
of the century was Fanny Burney's *Evelina.* From girlhood she
had had the stimulation of a literary circle: her father Dr. Burney
was not only one of the most fashionable music masters in London, but also a friend of Johnson and Garrick. The novel was
published anonymously and at first made no great stir, but within
six months everyone was reading it. Fanny tried to keep its authorship a secret, confiding to her diary her embarrassment, her
palpitations, and her pride on hearing it discussed on every hand.
When she heard that it had won Johnson's approval, she wrote:
"But Dr. Johnson's approbation!—it almost crazed me with agreeable surprise—it gave me such a flight of spirit that I danced a jig
to Mr. Crisp, without any preparation, music or explanation."[9]
Inevitably the secret leaked out, and Fanny became a literary
figure almost overnight. When she was invited to one of Mrs.
Montagu's parties, she felt that the measure of her literary recognition was indeed complete.

    Other people when first invited to her famous parties felt
equally flattered, for Mrs. Montagu was the acknowledged leader
of London's literary women, the so-called bluestockings. There is
some uncertainty as to how the nickname arose, but when Hannah More wrote her poem *Bas Bleu,* which was circulated privately and published in 1786, it had become the accepted term.
Though in general women's education was much neglected,

[9]Burney, *Diary, op. cit.,* Vol. 1, p. 45.

ability and favourable circumstances had combined to produce a small group of highly educated and intelligent women who, because they wrote poems, novels, or plays or were well read or proficient in languages, tended to gravitate into one another's society. Most of them owed their intellectual interests and education to a well read father, or friend, or family connection. Mrs. Barbauld indeed argued that "The best way for women to acquire knowledge is from conversation with a father, a brother or a friend, in the way of family intercourse and easy conversation, and by such a course of reading as they may recommend." According to her, young ladies "ought only to have such a general tincture of knowledge as to make them agreeable companions to a man of sense, and to enable them to find rational entertainment for a solitary hour."[10] One feels that Jane Austen would have agreed with her sentiments. Many of the bluestockings went far beyond this and were scholars in their own right. Mrs. Carter was a linguist; she knew Latin and Greek and a little Hebrew, she spoke French well, and was familiar with Italian, Spanish, and German, even acquiring some knowledge of Portuguese late in life. The urge that drove her to acquire this wide facility with both classical and modern languages was purely intellectual. As a parson's daughter and a spinster of limited means, the "Mrs." being merely a formal mode of address, she had little hope of ever being able to travel abroad and put her accomplishments to practical use. Another member of the circle, Mrs. Delany, was a fine botanist. At the age of seventy-four she started a collection of flower studies, using for this purpose paper of every texture and colour, cut out with exquisite fineness and pasted onto a black background. This was no pretty pretty work. No less an authority than Sir Joseph Banks declared them to be so accurate that he could venture to describe a plant botanically from them without having seen the original and without any fear of making a mistake in so doing. Fanny Burney, as we have seen, was a novelist, Hannah More wrote plays and poems, Mrs. Barbauld, whose views on female education have already been quoted, wrote a famous treatise *Lessons for Children,* and Mrs. Chapone contributed *Letters on the Improvement of the Mind.*

[10]A. L. Barbauld, *A Memoir of Mrs. Anna Laetitia Barbauld,* edited by Grace A. Ellis, (Boston, 1874), p. 57.

To such women conversation was both an art and a social duty. Through its medium they hoped to deepen their understanding not only of literature, but of the moral and philosophical truths that lay behind all human action. To some extent this was a reaction against the emptiness and frivolity of ordinary female social life. To the bluestockings, both male and female, cards were the great enemy and gambling the great sin. Mr. Delany considered its bite more dangerous than that of a mad dog. Dr. Johnson, in *The Rambler,* called it "a fatal passion for cards and dice, which seems to have overturned not only the ambition of excellence, but the desire of pleasure; to have extinguished the flames of the lover as well as of the patriot; and threatens in its further progress, to destroy all distinctions of rank and sex, to crush all emulation but that of fraud, to corrupt all those classes of our people . . . and to leave them without knowledge, but of modish ganes, and without wishes, but for lucky hands."[11] Neither Mrs. Montagu, Mrs. Vesey, Mrs. Chapone, Hannah More, nor Mrs. Thrale tolerated cards at their assemblies, though the Doctor did advise the latter to provide interesting sweetmeats in their place when she gave a dinner party. This was realistic advice in the early days of the Streatham circle, when she was still climbing the ladder of intellectual recognition. Not until she had been taken up by Mrs. Montagu did she, like Fanny Burney, feel that she had "arrived." Even the Doctor was inclined to share her feelings with regard to that redoubtable lady, declaring that one would much prefer to drop Mrs. Montagu than to be dropped by her, which happened after they had quarrelled over the merits of *The Dialogues of the Dead,* written by her friend Lord Lyttleton.

High though their intellectual and moral aims might be, all was not sweetness and light among these learned ladies. Rivalries, ambitions, and vanities played their part. To the outside world they might show a solid front, but there was competition among them as each tried to make her assembly preeminent, though this rivalry was the rivalry of friends. Mrs. Montagu had the advantage of great wealth and few emotional ties. Her intellectual interests, and perhaps her intellectual vanity, had been stimulated by the praise of Cambridge dons when she was a child of eight,

[11]S. Johnson, *The Rambler,* No. 15, May 1750.

and the desire to shine never left her. Her marriage to wealthy
Edward Montagu gave her a secure base. It was a harmonious
partnership, grounded on affection and respect, but in no way
emotionally disturbing. He had his scientific interests, she her
literary ones, and each followed his or her own bent untouched
by any breath of scandal. Both socially and financially she was
secure. Loving space, she had the means to indulge that love,
which in turn gave her the right milieu to entertain with distinction. Because of her taste, both innate and cultivated, this just
escaped ostentation, but she was the great lady entertaining in
the grand manner. That she should collect a large circle around
her was inevitable. Her friends ranged from wits like Lord Lyttleton and men of letters like the Earl of Bath to single ladies of
straitened means like Elizabeth Carter of whom Hannah More
wrote that "Mrs. Carter has in her person a great deal of what
gentlemen mean when they say such a one is a poetical lady,
however independently of her great talents and learning, I like
her very much, she has affability, kindness and goodness."[12] With
characteristic generosity Mrs. Montagu, after her husband's
death, settled £100 a year on her impecunious friend. When
Johnson became a recognized lion in literary London, he too was
sucked in and with him, because of his close connection with
them, the Thrales. She also took up Fanny Burney and Hannah
More, who declared that "she was not only the finest genius, but
the finest lady I ever saw; she lives in the highest state of magnificence; her apartments and table are in the most splendid taste;
but what baubles are these when speaking of a Montagu! Her
form, (for she has no body) is delicate even to fragility: her countenance the most animated in the world; the sprightly vivacity of
fifteen, with the judgement and experience of Nestor." Lack of
birth and background were no barriers to the entry into her circle;
intelligence, some literary success, and a proper appreciation of
Mrs. Montagu, which judging by Hannah More's rhapsodies her
friends found easy to accord, were the necessary qualifications.
Mrs. Montagu's own claims to literary eminence were surprisingly
slight. Her forte was her conversation and the then-fashionable

[12]Hannah More, *Life of Hannah More with Selections from Her Own Correspondence* (London, 1856), p. 17.

accomplishment of letter writing. For this posterity may well be grateful. Today few read Mrs. Carter's poems or Mrs. Sheridan's novel or Mrs. Barbauld's works on education, but the letter writers of the group—Mrs. Montagu, the gentle Mrs. Delany, and the indefatigable scribe Horace Walpole—have left for all time a chronicle of their day and generation.

Very different were the other two contenders for the leadership. Mrs. Boscawen, the Admiral's wife, had a warmheartedness that Mrs. Montagu sometimes lacked. Though the two women had been friendly, it was not until after the Admiral's death in 1761 that his widow really became one of the small intellectual coterie. In 1774 Hannah More wrote that "I have been at Mrs. Boscawen's, Mrs. Montagu, Mrs. Carter, Mrs. Chapone, and myself only were admitted. We spent the time, not as wits, but as reasonable creatures; better characters I trow. The conversation was sprightly but serious."[13] The third of the trio, Mrs. Vesey, had the indefinable gift of sympathy. Irish by birth (her father was Bishop of Ossoy), she was a dreamer at heart, impractical and romantic, with a fey quality that marked her off from the rest of her learned friends. Mr. Vesey, her second husband, was neither particularly faithful nor particularly considerate, and, in addition, money was not too plentiful. Moreover, she was hampered by deafness, causing affectionate amusement among her friends by the way she hurried from guest to guest, ear trumpet in hand, in an attempt to catch the latest bon mot. As a hostess she was markedly successful, not so much because of her own brilliance as because of her capacity to bring out that of her friends. This was certainly the impression of Fanny Burney who described her in 1779: "She has the most wrinkled, sallow, time-beaten face I ever saw. She is an exceedingly well bred woman, and of agreeable manners; but all her name in the world must, I think, have been acquired by her skill and dexterity in selecting parties, and by her address in rendering them easy with one another, an art, however, that seems to imply no mean understanding."[14] A possible fourth contender for attracting the most brilliant contemporary conversationalists to her house was Mrs. Thrale, at whose home Johnson

[13]*Ibid.*, p. 19.

[14]Burney, *Diary*, Vol. 1, p. 205.

was a constant visitor. Though not beautiful—she was short, inclined to be plump, with large hands and a prominent nose— she had expressive grey eyes and her manner was animated. Like Mrs. Vesey, she was a good hostess, ready to talk herself, but clever at stimulating the Doctor and drawing him out of his moods of black depression. Unlike those of the other learned ladies, her husband Henry Thrale was a competent and pleasant host, except when his business worries pressed heavily on his spirits and his health. Of all the learned circles this most represented a family unit. Until Henry Thrale's death in 1781 Streatham was a place where friends gathered for the sake of each other's company, as well as to enjoy the pleasures of intelligent conversation.

The technique of holding an assembly varied almost as much as the character of the hostesses, which perhaps was to be expected. Mrs. Montagu's gatherings were organized with almost undeviating formality. A semicircle was formed round the fire; at one end of this crescent sat Mrs. Montagu. Beside her was placed the person of highest rank, for even in a society so avowedly intellectual due reverence was, in practice, still paid to rank. On her other side sat the most distinguished of her guests—a practice that must have caused much heartburning at times. Such an arrangement favoured the set conversation pattern: the guests came to hear Mrs. Montagu converse with a few choice spirits; the majority were there not so much to contribute as to provide an intelligent and appreciative audience. It could be a rewarding experience when she and her principal guests were in form, for the placing of the chairs lent itself to the exchange of dazzling repartee and well-phrased criticism or to the thorough exploration of some philosophical concept. Nevertheless it had its hazards. Not even a Mrs. Montagu was always equal to sustaining her role, and a prosy talker or a bore, who managed to seize the conversational initiative, was difficult to silence while the company sat in a formal semicircle from which there was no escape. Some hostesses ranged their chairs against the walls, which, in most eighteenth-century rooms, meant that the company sat in a square or rectangle. Others grouped them around a table, which, though it had the merit of bringing the members of the group into closer contact, seemed to overemphasize the fact that mental, not physi-

cal, food was the object of the gathering. Mrs. Vesey would have
none of these arrangements and indeed went to the other extreme, placing her chairs and tables in such small and unrelated
groups that no general conversation was possible. Everything was
to be easy and relaxed, and each individual was to have the
opportunity to take a share in the conversation. Mrs. Vesey,
hovering between the groups, waving her ear trumpet, and stimulating the talkers by her sympathetic personality, was the only
connecting link between them. Not all her guests appreciated her
endeavours in this direction, Lord Harcourt saying ruefully that
"Mrs. Vesey is vastly agreeable, but her fear of ceremony is really
troublesome, for her eagerness to break a circle is such, that she
insists upon everybody's sitting with their backs to one another;
that is the chairs are drawn into little parties of three together in
a confused manner all over the room."[15] Of all these learned
women perhaps the most lovable was Mrs. Delany. Her husband
adored her, Edmund Burke thought her the highest-bred woman
in the world, and Fanny Burney, when she met her at the age of
eighty-three, still found benevolence, softness, piety, and gentle-
ness in her countenance, though her beauty had long faded.
There is a charming portrait of her as an old lady in the National
Portrait Gallery in London. Unlike Mrs. Montagu, she had no
desire to dominate; she was content to have many friends.

Such exclusive circles represented only a small segment of
London life. They were singular in that there women met men on
equal terms, and among their members, male and female, were
some of the most cultivated minds of the metropolis and indeed
of Europe. In the scope of their interests—classical, literary, and
moral—they represented the essence of the intellectual life of
Johnson's beloved city, where wit, breeding, and formality combined to mirror the standards of the age. But to suppose that they
alone were the centre of such interests would be to ignore the role
of the coffeeshop and even that of the tavern. By the time Johnson came to London, the coffeehouse was an institution whose
sudden disappearance would have disrupted the normal routine
of most London males. Although ostensibly their function was to
provide refreshment, for food and liquor were served as well as

---

[15]Burney, *Diary*, Vol. 1, p. 154.

the ubiquitous coffee, they were in fact places of rendezvous where men could be sure of finding others of their own tastes and interests and where, even if they found no friends, they could be sure of finding the latest newssheets and journals. Archenholtz explained that "An English coffee house is quite different from a French or German one. In the former there are neither billiards or gaming tables; no noise is made, everybody speaks low, that he may not disturb his neighbour. People go to them chiefly for reading the papers, an occupation which in England is one of the necessaries of life. The most frequented houses take in ten or twelve copies of the same paper not to make people wait, together with the best periodical publications."[16] In the coffeehouse world it was very much a matter of "birds of a feather flocking together," and the atmosphere varied according to the patrons of the house. The coffeehouses of the City that served the needs of the merchants—collecting information of a commercial character and providing a place where business could be transacted—were unlikely to attract the writer and the actor. But around Covent Garden and in the neighbourhood of Fleet Street conversation and relaxation, not business, was the magnet. For the struggling author, playwright, or painter having a regular coffeehouse was a matter of necessity. As Dr. Johnson pointed out, few people cared to reveal their poverty by acknowledging that the best lodgings they could afford was a dingy garret in some malodourous alley. It was much more dignified to say that one could always be found at such and such a coffeehouse. For regular patrons the host provided more services than a dish of coffee and the newspapers. Messages could be left there, letters directed, and appointments made. Here the poorest man who could afford clean linen and a decent coat could forgather with his friends and talk the hours away. Useful contacts, too, could be made and commissions secured. When Mrs. Lennox, one of Johnson's bluestocking friends, decided to learn Italian, her husband promptly went to the Orange Coffee House in the Haymarket, because he knew it was the haunt of foreigners and therefore a likely place in which to find an Italian master. There he met and engaged Guiseppe Baretti who, underemployed at the King's Opera House, was only

[16]Archenholtz, op. cit., p. 311.

too anxious to eke out his resources by giving lessons. It proved a fortunate meeting for him. Through Mrs. Lennox he later met Johnson and the Streatham set, and from 1773 he accepted the position of resident tutor to Mrs. Thrale's oldest daughter.

There was a fashion in coffeehouses as in everything else. The Cocoa Tree was popular with men of fashion. Edward Gibbon visited it in 1762, declaring that it afforded "every evening a sight truly English. Twenty perhaps of the first men in the kingdom in point of fashion and fortune, supping at little tables covered with a napkin, in the middle of a coffee room, upon a bit of cold meat or a sandwich, and drinking a glass of punch."[17] Earlier in the century it had been very Jacobite in its sympathies, so that good Whigs eschewed it and patronized St. James's. The coffeehouses in the vicinity of Drury Lane and Covent Garden were the haunt of actors and writers. Quin, Foote, and Garrick had their letters addressed to the Bedford, and men of letters such as Henry Fielding, who lived around the corner, Sheridan, Churchill, and Horace Walpole all frequented it. Violent episodes were by no means rare in its history. In 1776 Lord Malton's son, having supped there with four common women of the town, shot himself at 3 A.M. one morning. On April 9 three years later it was the scene of another tragedy when the Rev. Mr. Hackman, once of the 66th Regiment, sat there quietly drinking until the performance was over and then, taking his pistol, shot Miss Ray the singer, Lord Sandwich's mistress, out of jealousy. His subsequent attempt to shoot himself failed; so did his wild endeavour to brain himself with the butt of his own pistol. Next week he was hanged at Tyburn. Another popular coffeehouse was Tom's, situated in Russell Street, which ran from the east side of Covent Garden to Drury Lane. The subscription room upstairs was reserved for members, among whom Garrick and John Beard represented the stage, Dance and Samuel Scott the artists, and Dr. Schomberg medicine. Old Slaughter's was another artists' rendezvous. At one time or another Hogarth, Thomas Hudson, Roubillac, Richard Wilson, and Gainsborough were all to be found there. The Chapter House near St. Paul's was a favourite haunt for booksellers and printers, to whose needs it catered generously. Dr. Campbell

[17] J. Timbs, p. 69.

described how he "strolled into the Chapter Coffee House Ave Mary lane, which I had heard was remarkable for a large collection of books & a reading society &. I subscribed a shilling for the right of a year's reading, & found all the new publications I sought, & I believe what I am told that all the new books are laid-in some of which to be sure may be lost or mislayed—." That such places were not the resort of the learned only but that artisans also appreciated their amenities surprised him somewhat. He continued: "Here I saw a specimen of English freedom viz. a whitesmith in his apron & some of his saws under his arm, came in, sat down & called for his glass of punch & the paper, both which he used with as much ease as a Lord. Such a man in Ireland (& I suppose France too or almost any other country) wd not have shown himself with his hat on or in any other way unless sent for by some gentleman. Now nearly every other person in the room was well dressed."[18] At such a house the level of conversation could well be as erudite, if less self-consciously so, as in Mrs. Montagu's drawing room. Any appreciation of the literary and artistic life of eighteenth-century London must take account of the coffeehouse no less than of the saloon.

An important link between these two worlds was provided by Sir Joshua Reynolds. Undoubtedly Sir Joshua was more interested in literature than Dr. Johnson was in painting. Even before the two men meet Reynolds had been fascinated by Johnson's *Life of Savage*, and at their first meeting the two were attracted to each other. Sir Joshua's passionate desire to figure as a man of letters made him a little prone to lion hunting in that field. It was Sir Joshua who first collected the Literary Club around Johnson so that he should have a suitable group in which to display and by practice bring his conversational talents to their full power. Johnson for his part admired Reynolds' balanced judgment. When Boswell published his famous *Life*, it was to Sir Joshua that he dedicated it, calling him "the intimate and beloved friend of that great man." Today Reynolds is chiefly remembered as a great portrait painter; his contributions to literature concern only the historian of art. Just as London was the Mecca for men who hoped to live by their pen, so it was the lodestone of those who

18*Dr. Campbell's Diary, op. cit.,* p. 58.

hoped to live by their brush. Though artists of genius will paint with scant regard for the market, to men of competence and talent contemporary fashion and taste are of vital importance. Even genius is not necessarily unallied to a desire for recognition and worldly success. A William Blake might defy the contemporary demand; men like Reynolds, whom Blake blisteringly described as a man "Hired to depress Art," and Gainsborough fitted their genius to contemporary demand and in so doing transcended it.

The aristocracy was the only class with artistic traditions rooted in the culture of Europe and nurtured by the experience of the Grand Tour. In the eighteenth century aristocrats had the wealth to indulge their taste allied to the opportunity that their passion for rebuilding or extending their mansions gave them. Their taste, particularly in decoration, tended toward the Baroque, and Italian painters such as Tiepolo were popular. To buy Italian pictures was fashionable: Sir Robert Walpole demonstrated his eminence by the magnificent collection that he built up at Houghton. But though they might buy old masters abroad, the nobility were equally anxious to adorn their walls with portraits of themselves and their families. Here was a rich field for the English artist, and it is in portrait painting that they excelled in the eighteenth century. Almost inevitably the artists who served this market were drawn to London. Country mansions were scattered throughout the length and breadth of the land, but during parliamentary sessions anyone with social pretensions came at one time or another to the capital. The studio of a well known painter during the season was likely to be patronized by a string of fashionable visitors, both male and female, so that the sitters' book of a man such as Reynolds or Gainsborough reads like a Court circular. Just as today one fashion house or hairdresser is a "must" for people of fashion, so in eighteenth-century London it was a "must" to be painted by the artist of the hour. In terms of purchasing power, their prices were high. When Reynolds first set up in Great Newport Street, he charged roughly what his master Hudson had charged—12 guineas for a head, 24 for a half-length, and 48 for a full-length portrait—a sum that would have kept Johnson for twelve months in his first penurious London days. By 1777 Reynolds was getting 35 guineas for a head, 75 for a half-length, and 150 guineas for a full-length portrait. Some people thought the charge monstrous. One irate gentleman told Fanny Burney: "I knew him many years ago in Minorca; he drew my picture then, and then he knew how to take a moderate price; but now, I vow, ma'am, 'tis scandalous-scandalous indeed! to pay a fellow here seventy guineas for scratching out a head."[19] Even so, the head possibly represented the best value because by now Reynolds had adopted the expedient used by foreign painters of employing less well known artists to paint in the furniture, the curtains, and other properties, though the composition was his and he touched up his henchmen's contributions. Indeed, without some such arrangement it would have been almost impossible for Reynolds to undertake the number of commissions that he accepted each year.

The other great portrait painter of the century, Thomas Gainsborough, having failed as a young man to establish himself in London, had chosen Bath as his headquarters—another illustration of the necessity of having one's studio where the nobility and gentry were in the habit of congregating. It was not until 1774 that he returned to London, where, until his death in 1788, he remained a serious rival to Sir Joshua. As such he was part of Johnson's London rather than part of the Doctor's own circle, which the constant presence of Reynolds would have made unattractive to Gainsborough. Even apart from professional rivalry the two men were not sympathetic to each other. Johnson described Reynolds as the "most invulnerable man he knew, whom, if he should quarrel with him, he should find the most difficulty how to abuse."[20] In spite of being a most successful and charming painter of lovely women and beguiling children, he had remained a bachelor, shrinking from the risks of emotional attachment. He was fond of the bottle, of gaiety and good company, fond too of pretty women, but he appears to have given himself completely to no one person. Even toward his sitters he preserved a certain detachment: his canvases present the outward form rather than the inner personality. Gainsborough was a warmer person. He married when he was only nineteen, and his bride was three years

[19]F. Burney, *Diary, op. cit.,* Vol. 1, p. 241.

[20]J. Boswell, *Life of Samuel Johnson,* Vol. 1, p. 2.

his junior; in spite of Gainsborough's hot temper, the marriage seems to have been a happy one. His quick and instinctive sympathy with his sitters, unless he happened to dislike them personally, as occasionally he did, enabled him to catch a likeness that revealed something of the inner person. Yet at times he declared himself weary of portrait painting and resentful of the demands of the fashionable world that prevented his devoting himself to landscapes. At heart he was never a Londoner.

Throughout the century a host of lesser artists continued to meet the almost insatiable demand for portraits. A painter who had a reasonable amount of talent and a trick of flattery to make a patron feel that his guineas were well spent on the pictorial record that he wished to leave to his descendants could make a good living. Thomas Hudson, for example, with whom Reynolds studied when he first came to London, produced between 1745 and 1760 a stream of rather colourless likenesses. Joseph Highmore, whose patrons were largely drawn from the wealthy citizens, belonged to much the same category. Foreign artists also cashed in on the London portrait market. Zoffany came from Germany around 1761, and the charming Angelica Kauffmann from Switzerland in 1766. Even Sir Joshua appeared to be not unmoved by her, and for a time it almost looked as if a mutual attraction would ripen into something warmer. But success in this market required a complaisant as well as a skillful brush, and the former one great London painter lacked. Hogarth was at the height of his powers when Johnson first came to London, but life treated him harshly, not without some assistance from his own character, and his fortunes were on the downgrade when Reynolds' were soaring. Hogarth[21] coveted a reputation as a portrait painter, and such pictures as "The Shrimp Girl" showed how charming and individual his work could be when he had a subject who pleased him. But his brush was too unruly to flatter. Conventional sitters preferred the more stereotyped style of Hudson and Highmore, and Hogarth never achieved much commercial success, though he has some notable portraits to his credit. He did better with his conversation pieces. It was not only the aristocracy

---

[21]See F. Antal, *Hogarth and His Place in European Art* (Routledge and Kegan Paul, 1961).

who wanted to leave their features to posterity. The lesser gentry and wealthy citizens shared this ambition, but lacking picture galleries and magnificent apartments they had fewer suitable places in which to display a full-length or even a half-length portrait. Hogarth's solution, adapted from the Dutch, was the conversation piece. By this device a family group, painted in the surroundings of their everyday life rather than against draperies or imaginary landscapes, could be presented on a canvas of between twelve and fifteen inches high. In meeting this bourgeois demand, Hogarth found employment for his skill.

He is chiefly remembered today neither for his portraits nor his conversation pieces, charming though some of these are, but for the dramatic, satirical, moralistic canvases on which he presented such episodes as "Marriage a la Mode," "Industry and Idleness," and "The Four Stages of Cruelty" or for his contrasting social comment on "Gin Lane" and "Beer Lane." Taken as a whole these series provide a valuable pictorial record of the squalor, vice and misery of the capital. They are the counterpart in paint of Henry Fielding's word pictures. But they are more than a pictorical representation; they are also a revealing expression of the morality of the generality of sober, worthy Londoners. The middle-class virtues of sobriety, thrift, and industry lead to success and happiness; their absence to disaster, poverty, and a squalid or shameful death. Marriage without affection and respect, based only on false values, young girls tricked into harlotry, youths tempted into cruelty and theft, all mean social and moral ruin, whether the cause of misdoing be the vicissitudes of fate or weakness of character. This comment on the London of his day was often just, but a further question is raised, namely, why did Hogarth paint these aspects? His motives have been interpreted in different ways. To some critics their message is a moral one in the same way that the outlook of the middling sort was moral: their own cherished virtues are the only way to success and happiness. Neither the licentiousness of the rich nor the brutality and dishonesty of the poor hold out any hope for the future. In this sense the pictures are a tract in support of "middle-class morality" and the Puritan virtues. Another school of thought believes them to be the purveyors of a still more bitter and satirical message. "This," say Hogarth's canvases, "is the age in which we live. Here is the immorality, the brutality, the corruption in politics, that we all accept as part of our ordinary world. Is it nothing to you, all ye that pass by?" Perhaps the commentators on Hogarth's art read too much into these vivid series. All that he claimed himself was that he tried to treat his subject as a dramatic writer, that his canvas was his stage and the characters with which he filled it his players, whose actions and gestures, captured in dumb show, told a story. Whatever his motive, financially these series were profitable. The reason for this is interesting. There was no great demand for the originals, which did not appeal to wealthy patrons, and Hogarth had difficulty in disposing of some of them. Their success lay in their appeal to the popular market as engravings. In his youth he had been an engraver and realized that among the semiliterate, the respectable artisans, the small shopkeepers, and the tradesmen there was a steady market for dramatic engravings, which sold for about the price of the average book, namely, for a shilling or so. The same citizens who supported a popular candidate for office in Common Hall would buy such engravings to hang on the parlour walls. Therefore, when he had no commissions for portraits or conversation pieces or when the large historical subject after which he hankered failed to materialize or dropped away he could always fall back on another dramatic series, whose bustling, crowded, comic scenes would commend it to the wider public, even though the cheaper engravings were often of indifferent quality.

Closely allied to the art of portrait painter was the skill of the sculptor who could give to his busts a solidity and gravity that many sitters found attractive; so it is not surprising that like those of the portrait painter the sculptor's services were in demand. Campbell in his *London Tradesman* called it "a genteel and profitable Art" that was coming into much repute in England. It was used to commemorate both the living and the dead—the living in the shape of busts, the dead in elaborate memorials erected over tombs. Louis François Roubillac excelled in both. It was he who was commissioned to provide a statue for Vauxhall Gardens. Convention would have suggested that in a place dedicated to music the sculptor would have produced some fanciful interpretation of the Muse. Instead he provided a charming, full-length figure of a living composer, Handel, whose harmonies so often sounded there in the night air. Plump, solid, relaxed, there he sits, a soft cap on his head, playing a lyre, this last a concession to poetic licence. As Roubillac's reputation grew he took a house in St. Martin's Lane in 1740 and later taught in the academy with which Hogarth was connected. Among his many busts is one of his painter friend, which is clearly the fruit of his affection for him. His "Garrick" is less attractive. There is a hint of self-centeredness in his portrayal. Roubillac was in equal demand for the designing and sculpting of elaborate tombs, beloved in that century. His reputation was much enhanced by the magnificent tomb that he created for the Duke of Argyll in Westminster Abbey, and new orders came in quickly. Among his outstanding achievements were the tomb of General Wade and the pathetic statuary that commemorated Lady Elizabeth Nightingale. Here again the aristocratic market shaped the output of sculpture, as it did that of painting, though Roubillac allowed himself a fair measure of unflattering realism in his busts. On the whole he was at his best with ugly men, seeking to interpret character rather than to record good looks. The tombs have less appeal to modern taste, yet insofar as they express a pride in birth or in achievement, in their sentimentality and their use of allegory they help the historian to understand the mind of the age.

One pictorial art for which the century was justly famous was that of caricature. It had a mixed ancestry. Some people would father it on Hogarth, but he always protested that his paintings were comic representations of character, which he considered the legitimate sphere of the artist, but that they did not cross the boundary of distortion and exaggeration that marked the genuine caricature. Nevertheless, his engravings were sufficiently expressive of the foibles and weaknesses of mankind to make the dividing line a thin one and to prepare public opinion for the genuine caricatures that were to follow. Caricature, as a separate art, in the first part of the eighteenth century might be described as a fashionable hobby imported from Italy by young men returning from the Grand Tour. It was amusing to draw one's friends with their most prominent features and gestures wildly exaggerated, and personal caricature of this kind became popular. Reynolds as a young man showed that he had a not inconsiderable talent for this kind of thing. It was an art that, perhaps inevitably, was soon pressed into the service of politics. The men who made spirited caricatures of their friends were drawn from the same social groups as the members of the Commons and the Lords; often they were themselves members of one or the other house. That they should turn their talents to the ridiculing of their political opponents was a natural step. The satirical print had long been a useful weapon in party warfare, but it was George Townshend who in 1756 introduced the element of caricature into contemporary political prints. In the fifties and sixties these were executed mostly in black and white, but later colour was used to heighten their popular appeal. The printsellers seized on the new market with avidity and, when political tension was high, poured out a never-ending stream for the amusement of their clients. Caricature was not confined to politics, however. The absurdities of costume, of which the century produced a plentiful crop, and the ways of the fashionable world lent themselves to this form of art. From the sixties on, therefore, the product of the printshop became very much a part of the life of the town.

Like the writer and the actor, the painter improved his public image in the eighteenth century. Apart from Sir John Thornhill, whose daughter Hogarth married, artists were craftsmen who ministered to the needs of their wellborn patrons or pandered to the crude taste of the populace with equally crude prints. They had no place in the polite society of the day and no organized means of making a contact with it. The pattern of training was still the old one of apprenticeship in the studio of a man whose reputation was measured by the prices he received for his pictures. Well-known artists might run a school, known as an academy. Hogarth, who had been apprenticed to a silver-plate engraver, obtained further training at one such academy kept by Sir John Thornhill. Reynolds was apprenticed to Thomas Hudson, Gainsborough studied with the French illustrator and engraver Hubert Gravelot, who, like Thornhill, also ran an academy. When a young painter considered himself sufficiently skilled or when financial necessity drove him to seek independence, he set up for himself. Commissions depended on verbal recommendations: there was no place where an artist could exhibit his pictures and so become known. Once painted, they became the property of his patron on whose walls they hung. For a clever painter the system had some advantages. The new picture was likely to be a source of pride and a talking point for visiting friends. If it was attractive and had hit the prevailing taste, commissions flowed in, as they did for Reynolds as soon as he set up for himself in London. Gainsborough in his early London days was less successful in attracting favourable notice; after a struggling year in a studio in Hatton Gardens he returned to Sudbury in Suffolk. His next base was Bath, and it was only when he had made a reputation there that he returned in triumph to London in 1774. Hogarth, as we have seen, never did succeed in obtaining wide recognition as a portrait painter.

The common need of painters, critics, and possible patrons to have a central point was first met, in a tentative way, by the Foundling Hospital. Hogarth, who was a governor, painted for it his well known portrait of Captain Coram, its founder, and presented it with several other paintings. Highmore and Hayman made similar gifts. These provided, in the cause of charity, a nucleus of an exhibition to which the public was admitted and which proved popular. Its success showed that there was a demand for such exhibitions, and out of the disorganized painters of London grew first the Committee of Artists and later the Royal Academy. The climate of opinion was favourable to the growth of professional institutions. An English academy was being founded in Rome just as Reynolds left it in 1752, and he was anxious to see some similar enterprise set on foot in London. The first society founded along these lines met his wishes only in a limited and incidental way. In 1754 a group of scientists, noblemen, and clergy, whose gathering place was Rawhmell's Coffee House in the Strand, decided to found a society for the "Encouragement of Arts, Manufactures and Commerce." Though its interests lay largely with the more practical aspects of manufactures and commerce, it had a committee of artists of which Hayman was chairman. Both Reynolds and Johnson joined the society in the September of 1756, and in 1760 it held an exhibition of paintings to which Reynolds contributed. To be a mere adjunct to a body whose interests were largely scientific was plainly unsatisfactory from the artists' point of view, and some of the more distinguished of them ceded from the parent body and formed the Incorporated Society of Artists. It was perhaps only to be expected that feuds and rifts should appear in an experimental society composed of such men and, though it received a charter of incorporation in 1765, all was far from well in it. Indeed Reynolds, with the prudence that always distinguished him, refused to become a director, though he exhibited regularly on its premises in Spring Gardens. The feuds within the society continued as James Paine and William Chambers, the architect, struggled in bitter rivalry to control its policy. The latter's high-handed methods had antagonized many members, and the victory went to Paine. It proved a Pyrrhic victory, for Chambers, who had designed the famous pagoda at Kew for the Dowager Princess of Wales and who had had the honour of teaching drawing to the future George III, stood high in the royal favour. Followed by some of the most distinguished members of the Society of Artists he ceded and obtained from the King a charter for a Royal Academy. Chambers would doubtless have liked to be its first president, but there was a feeling that this office should be held by a painter, and Reynolds was the obvious choice. Reynolds was not entirely easy in his mind about accepting the position, but after an anxious consultation with Johnson and Burke he did so. Chambers contented himself with the very powerful office of treasurer. So, on December 10, 1768, the Royal Academy came into being, and a new landmark was created in the artistic life of Johnson's London. Though today it is often incorrectly thought of as a group of painters, its full title was The Royal Academy of Arts. In the following year Johnson was appointed its Professor in Ancient Literature, and Goldsmith was fitted in as Professor of Ancient History. That the three friends should have been so honoured was a sign of the growing social esteem given to men of letters and to artists. Reynolds had done much to bring this about. Well dressed, if at times somewhat liberally besprinkled with his beloved snuff, and a most successful host, he had the poise to mingle easily with the great. George III never did him the honour of being painted by him, possibly because of his friendship with men like Wilkes, Burke, and Sheridan, though this had not deterred the King from granting Johnson a pension, but as president of the Royal Academy he was knighted in 1769 and received an honorary D.C.L. at Oxford in 1773. In his person the artist had arrived. As Sir Joshua he did for the painter what Garrick did for the actor. The historian of Johnson's London owes him a further debt. As a very great portrait painter, living on intimate terms with some of the cleverest men of his time, he has left a pictorial record of the men who made it memorable. His brush has completed the work of Boswell's pen.

Though life could be frustrating, as it must always be, for the man who depended on his pen or his brush for his livelihood, eighteenth-century London provided a stimulating and congenial background for both. It was still small enough, when we exclude those of its inhabitants who fall into the category of hewers of wood and drawers of water, for like-minded people to meet easily and often. Though a Lord remained a Lord—indeed Johnson explicitly said that he was perfectly willing to pay that outward deference to rank that he in turn would expect to receive if he possessed it—no daunting barrier existed between the man of letters and the man of birth. Boswell's *London Journal* bears ample testimony to the width of his acquaintances, both noble and literary or artistic. Men like Lord Burlington, whom Lord Chesterfield thought almost more technically competent than befitted his rank, or Lord Lyttleton moved easily in both worlds. It was a contact that benefitted and enriched every kind of literary and artistic achievement and gave to them that touch of urbanity which was so characteristic of the age. Dr. Johnson, one feels, could have made his particular mark and created his particular circle in no other age.

SEVEN

The Poverty and Crime of London

Above everything Dr. Johnson's London was a city of contrasts. The world of fashion and of politics was one of extravagance and of wealth ostentatiously flaunted. The way of life of the solid citizen was comfortable and decent. But at the other end of the social scale was bitter poverty, degradation, and brutality. If London was a city of pleasure, it was also a city of crime, crime that was the child of violence, ignorance, and destitution. Some of the reasons for this are obvious. The metropolis was a great employer of casual, untrained labour that depended only on physical strength. Fielding wrote of the infinite number of chairmen, porters, and labourers, all leading a hand-to-mouth existence, whose means were quite insufficient to maintain their families and who, only too often, drank away whatever little sums they earned. The ordinary routine of the city's life could absorb large numbers of such men. There were also many opportunities for poor women to pick up a precarious living selling the various wares of the street trader. Today the cries of old London, such as "Lavender, sweet lavender, who'll buy my lavender," may strike a nostalgic note; the reality was less picturesque. Dirty, bedraggled women, eking out a pitiable existence by crying their wares, added to the mass of poverty. So did washerwomen, who worked incredibly long hours for a pittance. Sifting ashes and cinders was another ill-paid employment that absorbed much female labour of the lowest kind. Bad weather, a poor harvest, and consequent rise in the price of bread could soon reduce even the hardworking ones among them to a state of semistarvation. Saunders Welch, who as High Constable of Holborn and later assistant to Sir John Fielding at Bow Street had plenty of opportunity to know about such things, told Johnson that more than twenty people a week died not "absolutely of immediate hunger but of the wasting and other diseases which are the consequence of hunger."[1]

Such poverty was self-perpetuating. Casual employment, low wages, inadequate food, and appalling housing for the parents produced children stunted in body and mind alike. Contemporaries accepted as axiomatic the fact that paupers would breed more paupers, who would at best be idle and at worst criminal. These people made up the substratum of London society. Most had neither the intelligence nor the will to face the struggle to rear their children decently, many of whom were abandoned at birth. Even if they survived infancy, family ties were very slight. Fielding wrote with loathing that he had "sometimes seen mothers, but indeed they ill deserved that name, who have trepanned their children into bawdy houses and shared with the bawd the gain of their own children's prostitutions."[2] When both employment and food were so precarious, it is not surprising that families broke up easily or that the streets were full of deserted children. Fielding had much compassion for the "Shoals of Shoplifters, Pilferers, and Pickpockets, who, being deserted Children of Porters, Chairmen, and low Mechanics, were obliged to steal for Subsistence." According to him, there were "no less than 300 of these wretched Boys, ragged as Colts, abandoned, Strangers to Beds, and who lay about under Bulks and in ruinous empty houses."[3] Their sisters, whom similar circumstances forced into prostitution, he described as "that completely wretched, distempered, deserted, pitiable Body . . . whose Sufferings have so often made my Heart ache."[4] Not all these children were necessarily the offspring of habitual paupers. More respectable parents too were easily sucked into the

[1] J. Boswell, *Life of Samuel Johnson*, Vol. 3, p. 401.

[2] Sir John Fielding, Introduction to a Plan for Preserving Deserted Girls (1758), p. 46.

[3] Sir John Fielding, *An Account of the Origin and Effects of a Police, etc.* (1758), p. 17.

[4] Sir John Fielding, *Introduction, op. cit.*, p. 43.

maelstrom. Disease was rife and life for the labouring poor often short. If the countryman who came to London to practice his trade and improve his lot picked up the fevers that were almost endemic in its crowded and insanitary alleys and died, the widow might find it beyond her powers to maintain her family. Often she, too, might be removed by death, leaving a family of orphans to shift for themselves. Even if newcomers survived physically, London was full of traps and temptations for the unwary. One of the grimmest hazards was the danger of being imprisoned for debt, not in theory as a punishment but to prevent the debtor from absconding. It was only too easy to run up a large score at a tavern or alehouse, and some tavern keepers made a regular business of providing the East Indiamen with crews by getting sturdy men into their power in this way and then giving them the alternatives of gaol or a long and hazardous voyage from which they might never return. With debt an ever-present menace to freedom, it is hardly surprising that men absconded rather than face their creditors. If he stayed and was imprisoned, though he could practice his trade in a debtors' prison if that was physically possible, he was unlikely to be able to make enough to keep his family. So, whether he disappeared or not, the result as far as his wife and children were concerned was the same. Children deserted in this way had very little chance of growing into useful members of society. The odds were too heavily against them.

Another ingredient in this swirling mass of poverty was the people who were mentally subnormal or who suffered from some physical defect. Heavy though the mortality was among the labouring poor, it was not only the fittest who survived; many lingered on half-incapacitated. With so much heavy work to be done, porters often developed hernia, a complaint that made it difficult for them to continue at their work. Fever and malnutrition would likewise reduce earning capacity of both men and women. Accidents were common and surgical skill limited and often unavailable, so that the maimed, the halt, and the blind were a common sight in London's streets. What indeed could a hopelessly deformed man or woman do except exhibit the deformity and beg charity from the passersby? Though many were frauds, contemporaries could never be sure that they might not be genuine. Venereal disease was another great disabler. Jonas Hanway suggested that in 1784 as many as one of every 250 inhabitants of London died from it and that many more had their physique permanently ruined. Such guesses are not based on reliable statistics, but they do bear witness to contemporary opinion about the widespread nature of what they called "the foul disease." In addition to those maimed or diseased the dregs of London's population must have contained many people of retarded development who, in an adverse environment, were quite incapable of making a living or bringing up a family, who were probably as feebleminded as they themselves. That a feebleminded woman turned to prostitution, as often must have been the case, was a result that could hardly have been otherwise.

The problems posed by London's poor were not new. The City fathers had been struggling to find some solution to them since the mid-sixteenth century, when changing economic circumstances had first forced them to realize that the relief of poverty was not an exercise in personal charity but something that called for methodical treatment. The machinery that they had devised then was still largely operative in the eighteenth century. Tudor reformers had seen the poor as composed of three elements: people incapable of supporting themselves because of sickness, accident, or old age; deserted children, who abounded even then; and idle, semicriminal folk who could work but who preferred to scrounge a living. For the first two they designed help. The sick were to be cared for in the hospitals of St. Thomas and St. Bartholomew, refounded after the Reformation for this purpose, and poor children were to be educated and trained in habits of industry in Christ's Hospital. The idle and vicious, however, were to be disciplined in Bridewell, where work was also to be provided for those willing to work but currently out of work. To finance this programme, because voluntary contributions proved insufficient, the Common Council in 1547 decided to levy a Poor's Rate on Householders. This was the first levy of a poor rate in Britain. By the eighteenth century a national system for the relief of the poor had been imposed on top of the London experiment. This had originally been the result of piecemeal legislation to meet the needs of what was still largely a rural community, though it owed much to the experiments of London and other towns such as Norwich. By the eighteenth century this legislation, codified in

1601 and further modified by still more piecemeal enactments as economic and social circumstances changed, was clearly quite incapable of dealing with anything as complex as the problem of London's poverty.

This was largely because the national unit of organization was too small. London's earlier schemes had been designed for the City as a whole, though local administration had been entrusted to the wards. But the sheer growth of the metropolis had made this inadequate now that so much of the population lay outside the City boundaries. The result was that even though London was a social and economic unit, except for the City it lacked the administrative unity that was so essential if any comprehensive policy of dealing with destitution were to be devised and implemented. This meant that the relief of the poor for much of London had to be provided with machinery that had been intended to meet the needs of a rural community. As a result the parish became the normal unit for the administration, and its execution was left to the unpaid, annual overseers of the poor, assisted by the churchwardens and supervised by the local justices of the peace. In 1601 this was not a very onerous task: generally the number of persons needing relief was small. In a small community it was also easy to make a rough distinction between the deserving and the undeserving. There could be little imposture in a parish where everybody knew his neighbour. Moreover, the tradition of private almsgiving persisted, and the simplest organization sufficed to relieve the residue of destitution.

Such a system was clearly inadequate for the needs of London's poor. Its parishes had no unity of size or population. As London grew and as outlying villages were absorbed and transformed into urban areas, what had once been a reasonable administrative unit became unwieldy and often socially unbalanced. In a rural parish there were always enough landowners and substantial householders to pay the poor's rate, but parishes such as Spitalfields, where the silk weavers congregated, might not be able to supply the necessary funds during a trade depression. Parishes along the river to the east of the City tended to have considerable concentration of poorer labourers who depended on the loading of ships or the porterage of goods for their livelihood. In such parishes housing conditions intensified the problem of

dealing with destitution. Families lived in one room in ramshack-
le dwellings, which were grouped in back courts or in a labyrinth of narrow, filthy alleys, where the population was always
shifting and where respectable people would be reluctant to go.
In such circumstances, how could an untrained, probably unwilling, overseer of the poor decide on the genuine needs of those
who applied for relief? In any case the overseer was forced to
serve the office for only one year, and, because he was unpaid and
had his own business to attend to, he had no inducement, other
than public spirit, to spend more than a minimum of time dealing
with his unwelcome obligations. Such conditions favoured the
plausible rogue at the expense of the honest but diffident person
whose pressing necessity was apt to be overlooked.

The ratepayers had little reason to be satisfied with the
system. Where applicants for relief were numerous, considerable
funds, which came out of the ratepayers' pockets, were involved,
which the current overseers might be quite incapable of handling.
Accounts were kept in a very haphazard manner, so that it was
impossible to know whether the sums recorded had been properly
spent, or indeed whether they had been spent on the poor at all.
A dishonest overseer had many opportunities for shady dealings.
In many parishes tradesmen and shopkeepers served as overseers,
which tempted them to give allowances on the implied understanding that much of the money so given would be spent at the
overseer's shop. With so many possibilities of mismanagement, it
is hardly surprising that many ratepayers found the system unsatisfactory and looked for some remedy. One expedient was to
promote a local act of Parliament that provided the parish with a
better organization and additional facilities, often in the form of a
workhouse, half-constructive, half-deterrent in its purpose. Eighteenth-century Englishmen disliked seeing good labour go to
waste. Genuine poverty of the infant poor, the aged, and the sick
they were prepared to relieve at least in theory. But they felt that
many of those seeking relief could quite well help themselves,
either by making a more determined effort to find work or by
saving something toward hard times instead of squandering it all
at the alehouse or the ginshop. A workhouse seemed to offer a
solution to both these problems. It was to be a place where the
poor could be employed, not merely relieved, and it was hoped

that even if the inmates were not completely self-supporting, they would nevertheless be able to contribute something toward their maintenance and toward England's wealth. For the well-intentioned unemployed labourer the workhouse would be an opportunity and for the lazy and vicious a test. If a man or woman refused to accept a place in the workhouse, they argued, their need could not be desperate.

However high the hopes and sound of the theory, by 1734 the practice was proving disappointing. To provide profitable and suitable work that could be done by the odd assortment of persons and trades that applied for relief proved impossible in the long run. Though a little work was done in some of the London workhouses, except for brief spurts when some energetic man or group controlled the parish business, they became more and more a dumping ground and doss house for both the genuine poor and the shiftless unemployables. They afforded no help to those who were anxious to work but were unemployed, and they were no deterrent to those whom they were intended to discipline because, however repulsive the conditions within them might be to the decent poor, the diet and accommodation were better than the starving, shelterless life of the streets for the vagrant, the petty thief, and the prostitute and would continue to be so while the inmates were under no discipline but could come and go as they pleased, get drunk, and be disorderly.

Perhaps the most tragic aspect of their failure was in dealing with the infant poor. Where the parish possessed a workhouse, it is understandable that the overseers should provide for the deserted children left on their hands by sending them there where the services of pauper women could be utilized to nurse them. In addition many children were born in the workhouse, even though their parents were not habitual paupers. Until the establishment of lying-in hospitals, the crowded living conditions of the very poor and the extreme difficulty that a deserted wife experienced in the last days of her pregnancy drove such women to the workhouse at the time of their confinement. Indeed for the unmarried mother and the streetwalker there was frequently no alternative. Few children born in the workhouse, or admitted in the early weeks of their lives, survived unless they were discharged with their mother soon after birth. Deserted children or parish bastards had very little chance. This was partly because of the very bad sanitary state of the workhouse and partly because of the abominable treatment they received. This was true also of children who were put out to nurse with so-called parish nurses, many of whom were gin-sodden and none of whom had any standards of child care or hygiene. Moreover, it was general knowledge that no questions would be asked if death relieved a parish from providing for an unwanted child. Indeed one parish officer is reported to have said that "in the hands of our nurses after five or six weeks we hear no more of them."[5] The man who brought this terrible mortality to public notice was Jonas Hanway. *In An Ernest Appeal for Mercy to the Children of the Poor*, published in 1766, he collected facts and figures to demonstrate the urgent need for action. Describing the workhouse of the parish of St. George, Middlesex, he wrote: "There are now in this workhouse 100 men and about 20 women; here are 200 Poor sometimes crowded together. This renders such places inevitable death to infants; and it is confessed without reserve to be a rare thing for a child to be taken out alive, except it be in the hands of the mother."[6] This was no mere rhetoric: of nineteen children, whose ages ranged from three years to two months, twelve survived from a minimum of seven days to a maximum of forty seven. Hanway described the parish workhouse of St. Giles in the Fields and St. George Bloomsbury as "the greatest sink of mortality in these kingdoms, if not on the face of the whole earth."[7] As a result of his exertions a parliamentary committee of inquiry was appointed, which, when it reported in 1767, produced the grim statement that of the children under twelve months of age taken into the workhouses whose records they examined only seven in a hundred appeared to have survived for more than three years.

Even when allowance is made for the high rate of infant mortality at the time, these are horrifying figures. They even shocked contemporary complaisance to the extent that Parliament bestirred itself to provide some remedy. In 1767 an act forbade

[5]J. Hanway, *An Earnest Appeal for Mercy to the Children of the Poor*, (1766), p. 39.

[6]*Ibid.*, p. 43.

[7]*Ibid.*, p. 45.

any children under the age of six years to be kept in a workhouse for more than three weeks, at the end of which they were to be put out to nurse in the country, and to provide some guarantee for their good treatment records were to be kept until they were old enough to be bound out as apprentices. Other sections of the same act were aimed at improving their conditions in this second phase of their pauper childhood. The Poor Law of 1601 had contained well-intentioned provisions by which every child whose parents were too poor to do so was to be bound out by the parish as an apprentice to some trade and so be fitted to take his place as a useful member of the community. Unfortunately, subsequent legislation had made a mockery of these excellent aims. In an attempt to define with legal exactness who were the so-called "settled inhabitants" for which a parish would have to assume responsibility, a series of statutes from 1662 had enumerated the ways in which such a settlement could be obtained. One of these was by serving an apprenticeship in a parish. This was reasonable in that only a child who had served an apprenticeship in a parish should have the right to practice the trade so learned there. Unfortunately, this put a serious temptation in the way of the parish officers, because a child apprenticed in another parish would gain a settlement there, with the pleasing result that after forty days' residence the original parish would have no further responsibility for the child. The result was that in crowded London parishes, where the pauper child was an anonymous burden rather than the offspring of a known neighbour, it became common practice to bind out children not to secure for them a worthwhile training but merely to get rid of them. For this purpose it was immaterial that the master or mistress should be good, the trade suitable, and the little apprentice well treated. Once the parish had paid the premium and the qualifying forty days were over, it had no further interest in the welfare of the child. Nor had it any control over the master, who if he pleased might take a child solely for the sake of the premium and, once this had been paid, could neglect or actively ill-treat the apprentice until he either died or ran away to swell the number of homeless children roaming London streets. The 1767 act tried to introduce two safeguards. To ensure the choice of a reasonable training and to prevent the child's being apprenticed to what was in fact a blind-alley employment, no parish apprentice was to be bound out with a premium of less than £4-2-0. This was to be paid in two installments—the first at the end of seven weeks and the second at the end of three years. Also, the time that a pauper apprentice had to serve was shortened. Previously a girl had to serve until she was twenty-one, but a boy was not free of his indentures until he was twenty-four. This was now shortened to twenty-one. After this act the children of London's poor had a little more hope of survival.

It is impossible to estimate how much impact the system of public relief had on the London pauper; it is difficult even to hazard a guess. Considerable sums were in fact raised through the poor rates. Some of the money, it is known, was spent on parish feasts, for unpaid officers felt entitled to the perquisites of office. Some went in less acknowledged ways into their private purses. Some was expended in fighting settlement cases at Quarter Sessions, in moving paupers back to their original parishes, and in paying apprenticeship fees for children bound out in other parishes. But even after all these deductions something remained to relieve the sick and the aged of the parish. Many of them were placed in the workhouse, but many more received a trifling allowance or occasional gifts in kind—clothing, shoes, firing in winter. Whatever was given in this way rarely amounted to full maintenance; the completely destitute were taken into the workhouse. In the face of the misery of starving wretches in garrets and outhouses, which occasionally came to light, it is impossible to believe that all who genuinely needed assistance received it. Confronted with the lists of names in parish account books, all of whom are recorded as receiving some petty sum, the historian can rarely know what lay behind them, or indeed whether even the names may not be fictitious, covering some clever fraud. The probability is that only too often the scrounger, the plausible and the threatening, may have received more than his fair share of the parish funds. Certainly, whatever was given seems to have made very little impression on the mass of near destitutes that formed the lowest stratum of London society. Ordinary citizens, going about their daily business, were well aware of its existence. Boswell recorded that Johnson frequently gave all the silver in his pocket to the poor wretches who lay in wait for him as he walked between his house and the tavern where he dined.

Some no doubt were the victims of circumstance: luck had been against them; but idleness, viciousness, and drink had brought many to this state. Gin, particularly in Johnson's early London days, was the great social menace of the age. It was a fiery and lethal drink, capable of robbing people of whatever decency and self-control bad social conditions and casual underpaid work had left them. It was terrifyingly easy to obtain. Gin-shops abounded, small shopkeepers stocked it. Proprietors of cheap lodging houses found a ready market among their inmates, "gin being sold to all of them at a penny a quartern: so that the smallest sum of money serves for intoxication." When Sir Robert Walpole tried to curb the evil, which was becoming recognized as a direct threat to society, by a fierce act that aimed at stamping out its easy and unlicensed sale, London broke into gin riots. The 1736 act was a failure: the law was defied and the sale of gin either driven partially underground or defended by violent means. London's poor remained as gin-sodden and inflamed as before. It was not until the act of 1751 that some genuine control and reduction of this dangerous trade was achieved. Hogarth's terrifying and vile portrait of Gin Lane remains an unexaggerated picture of the alleys and lanes of the city with which the Doctor must have been familiar when he first came to live there in 1734. The February 1753 issue of the *Gentleman's Magazine* told its readers: "If we were to make a progress thro' the outskirts of the town & look into the habitations of the poor, we should then behold such pictures of human misery as must move the compassion of every heart that deserves the name of human; whole families in want of every necessity of life, oppressed with hunger, cold, nakedness and filth and with the diseases, the certain consequences of all this."[8] It is against this background that the historian must see their avid appetite for the temporary oblivion that gin could bring. In the haphazard arrangement of lanes, courts, and alleys that lay behind the main streets, the dregs of the population drank and slept and fought, returning at night like animals

[8]*Gentleman's Magazine,* February 1753, p. 61.

to their lairs or like nocturnal beasts of prey slinking out from them after dark to steal and pilfer and terrorize their betters in London's gloomy thoroughfares. It was not surprising that eighteenth-century London was a city of crime.

Henry Fielding, whose experiences as the Bow Street magistrate had acquainted him with most aspects of its sordid details, was inclined to attribute it less to the desperation of poverty than to the unsettlement of changing standards. In *An Enquiry into the Causes of the Late Increase of Robbers, etc.* he wrote: "I think that the vast Torrent of Luxury which of late Years hath poured itself into this Nation, hath greatly contributed to produce among many others, the Mischief I here complain of. I aim not here to satirize the Great, among whom Luxury is probably rather a moral than a political Evil. But Vices, no more than Diseases will stop with them . . . in free Countries, at least, it is a Brand of Liberty claimed by the People to be as wicked and as profligate as their Superiors. . . . It reaches the very Dregs of the People, who aspiring still to a Degree beyond that which belongs to them, and not being able by the Fruits of honest Labour to support the State which they affect, they disdain the Wages to which their Industry would entitle them; and abandoning themselves to Idleness, the more simple and poor spirited betake themselves to a State of Starving and Beggary, while those of more Art and Courage become Thieves, Sharpers and Robbers."[9] Though written more than 200 years ago, his analysis is not without relevance to modern affluent society. Few, however, would dare to advocate his remedies, which would cause a storm of protest in any country where the poorest citizen has a vote. He suggested closing public places of amusement to "the lower Order of People." His views were shared by his half brother, Sir John Fielding, the blind magistrate whose experience was also gained at Bow Street. "Time," he declared, "is the Labourer's Stock in Trade; and he that makes the Most of it by Industry and Application is a valuable subject. A Journeyman can no more afford to give or throw away his Time than a Tradesman can his Commodity; and the best Way of preventing this useful Body of Men from this species

[9]Henry Fielding, *An Enquiry into the Causes of the Late Increase of Robbers, etc.* (1751), p. 3.

of Extravagance is to remove from their Sight all Temptation to idleness: and however Diversions may be necessary to fill up the dismal Chasms of burdensome Time among People of Fortune, too frequent Relaxations of this Kind among the Populace enervate Industry."[10] Alien though such views may appear today, they were typical of the social thinking of Fielding's age.

Whatever the causes, crimes of every kind flourished in London, whose size and the confusion of streets, alleys, and courts gave an opportunity and anonymity to the criminal that could be found nowhere else. On the outskirts of the town there was a constant danger from highwaymen. Romantic literature has given these "gentlemen of the road" a glamour that is quite fictitious. Around a few of them, such as Dick Turpin, legends have accumulated that celebrate their prowess and daring. James Maclean's career, suitably embellished with a love interest, would make an excellent novel. Posing as a clergyman's son with an independent income, he took lodging in the fashionable quarter of St. James, where his credentials were accepted without question until fate caught up with him. After a successful holdup of the Salisbury coach, he came under suspicion when he tried to sell the coat of one of his victims, which was recognized as stolen property. His rooms were searched and further identifiable property, including some belonging to Lord Eglington, was found. Maclean was then arrested, tried, condemned, and hanged. Many of his fashionable friends found it hard to believe in his guilt and out of pity or curiosity flocked to visit him in Newgate.[11] But most highwaymen were shabby fellows with little romantic allure. Some were professionals, working a regular beat in league with shady landlords. More were probably the victims of idleness, extravagance, gambling, or bad luck who hoped to mend their fortunes in this way and, having done so, to return to more respectable ways.

The fear of a holdup is amusingly illustrated by Kielmansegge who describes how one evening he and a party of friends on their way to a ball near Gray's Inn Road took the long way around to avoid the traffic jams, but "provided ourselves with an armed servant on horseback, because my lady Huntingdon had

[10]Sir John Fielding, *Account, op. cit.,* p. 8.

[11]*The Gentleman's Magazine,* 1750, p. 391.

been robbed a few days previously of her watch and money by a highwayman in those parts. We remained close together in our three carriages and divided our party so that we drove in pairs, Lady Cecilia West with my brother in front, Miss Speed who had most jewelry and was most frightened with Baron de la Perriere, in the middle, whilst Lady Diana Clavering and myself closed the procession as rearguard."[12] Though the party arrived without incident at the ball, that such precautions were considered necessary is in itself sufficient commentary on the hazards of visiting after dark. It was to protect themselves against similar dangers that the residents of Knightsbridge village subscribed to provide a patrol for the lonely road between them and St. George's hospital at Hyde Park Corner. Even town streets were not exempt from these risks. At ten o'clock on September 18, 1750, to give but one illustration, a chaise was stopped at the end of Clarges Street and its occupant threatened with a pistol, which luckily did not go off.

Even the most densely built-up areas were far from safe at night, though open violence on any considerable scale seems to have come in waves rather than being a constant peril. Early in the century the so-called Mohawks, wild and raffish youths, often apparently of gentle birth, had terrorized the streets, amusing themselves by rolling old women in barrels downhill or beating up the decrepit Watch. In *London* Johnson wrote with some poetic exaggeration:

> Prepare for death if here at night you roam,
> And sign your will before you sup from home.
> Some fiery fop, with new commission vain,
> Who sleeps on brambles till he kills his man,
> Some frolic drunkard, reeling from a feast,
> Provokes a broil, and stabs you for a jest.
> Yet, ev'n these heroes, mischieviously gay,
> Lords of the street, and terrors of the way,
> Flushed as they are with folly, youth and wine
> Their prudent insults to the poor confine:
> Afar they mark the flambeau's bright approach
> And shun the shinning train and golden coach.

[12]Kielmansegge, *op. cit.*, p. 243.

Organized bands of robbers made the streets equally unsafe for richer wayfarers. Ruffians like the Wreathorchs and the Black Boy Alley Gang terrorized the town until the tough magistrate De Veil finally succeeded in breaking them up. A new crime wave occurred in 1753 when "a most notorious Gang of Street Robbers in Number about fourteen, who divided themselves into Parties, committed such daring Robberies, and at the same Time such Barbarities, by cutting and wounding those they robbed, in every part of the Metropolis, as spread a general Alarm through the Town, and deterred his Majesty's Subjects from passing and repassing on their lawful occasions after Night."[13] Less dangerous but more ubiquitious were the shoplifters, pilferers, and pickpockets who were always on the lookout for an easy victim. Some were extremely youthful. Fielding recorded the case of "four infant thieves, the oldest of which was but five years of Age," who were brought before him, "which appeared to be the Children of different Persons, collected together by one Woman to beg and steal to furnish that Beast with Gin."[14]

Closely entangled with this world of poverty and crime was woman's oldest profession, prostitution. No picture of eighteenth-century London would be complete which ignored its prevalence. Like every other profession it had its gradations. A fashionable courtesan like Kitty Fisher, whose portrait even Reynolds was happy to paint, was far above the level of poverty and crime. Less reputable, if this word can ever be applied to even the most reputable of the sisterhood, were the women who had sufficient charm and air of fashion to attract a wealthy protector but who, passing from one man to another, gradually lost their attraction and were forced to rely on a more casual trade. Such a one was Boswell's unlucky choice, Louisa, from whom he caught Signor Ghonnehea. The procuress and the pimp were well-known figures in London's underworld. For better-class patrons they often operated under the cover of running a bagnio, the eighteenth-century variant of a Turkish bath. Betty Careless kept a well-known bagnio in Covent Garden, which in 1739 was taken over by the notorious Mother Douglas, the reputed original of both

[13]Sir John Fielding, *Account, op. cit.,* p. 15.

[14]*Ibid.,* p. 19.

Mrs. Cole in Foote's play *The Mirror* and Mrs. Snarewell in Reid's *The Register Office*. Mother Needham catered to the fashionable youth in St. James's; other high-class disorderly houses were situated in Pall Mall. Less exalted clients frequented the bawdy houses in the streets around the Temple and the Thames, among which was the Star Tavern. This had been a respectable house until 1748, but the next year it was the scene of a sizable brawl. Its situation made it the haunt of sailors, some of whom were robbed of their money and their watches while enjoying the favours of the women of the house. When they were refused redress by the propriator, the aggrieved patrons promptly collected a band of fellow sailors from Wapping and with their help proceeded to break the place up. To the east were the bawdy houses of the Goodman's Fields district, and lower in the social scale many squalid houses of ill repute were located in Wapping and Rotherhithe.

In addition to brothels, the less reputable taverns and coffee-houses were always at hand to provide refreshments and accommodation for casual encounters. Boswell resorted to the Rose in Drury Lane for this purpose. Streetwalkers abounded in the Strand and its purlieus, and for those too nice to use a dark alley such taverns offered a convenient and inexpensive solution. Foreigners rarely fail to comment on the large number of prostitutes in these areas. Archenholtz computed their number at 50,-000 for London as a whole. Such a figure is an obvious exaggeration, but it is an eloquent testimony to the impression that their ubiquity made on him. He describes how "At every season of the year at the approach of night they sally from their homes well dressed, and every street and square is crowded with them."[15] Grosley corroborates his description. "About night-fall," he wrote, "they range themselves in a file in the foot-paths of all the great streets, in companies of five or six, most of them dressed very genteely. The low taverns serve them as a retreat to receive their gallants in: in those houses there is always a room set apart for this purpose."[16] Streetwalkers were recruited from many sources. The country maid, seduced by her master or her master's son, was

[15]Archenholz, *op. cit.*, p. 307.

[16]Grosley, *op. cit.*, Vol. 2, p. 55.

a stock figure in contemporary plays and novels. So were the young gentlewomen who, in Goldsmith's lines, "stoop to folly and find too late that men betray." Some were the victims of Fleet marriages. Others had no other resource to which to turn. Probably most, in spite of the romantic pen of the novelist and the dramatist, were poor men's daughters whose early background had been coarse and even criminal. Many of them were very young. Fielding writes of girls aged twelve to sixteen, "half eaten up with the Foul Distemper."[17] In what was admittedly a propaganda pamphlet Hanway declared that every year some 3000 Londoners died of some form of venereal disease. Though it was an offence to keep a disorderly house and periodically attempts were made to clean up the town, the forces of law were totally inadequate to act as a vice squad. The lowest type of brothel and gambling den, for often the two functions were united, were, as the authorities well knew, hatcheries for crime and were responsible for much of the squalor and violence that disfigured so much of the darker corners of London life. Nevertheless, they continued to flourish with something like impunity for most of the time, except when some energetic magistrate launched a new campaign against them, imposing fines on those found guilty and occasionally sentencing a procuress to the dreadful penalty of the pillory, a fate that overtook Mother Needham.

One element that contributed to the disorderliness, though not necessarily to the crime of the metropolis, was "the mob". It is not easy to be precise about either its composition or its inspiration. These varied from incident to incident. It can best be defined as a concourse of people, ranging from a few dozen to some hundreds or even thousands, who were determined to express their united feelings and to further their aims by violence if necessary. That they were an endemic feature of eighteenth-century London was probably due to the bad social and economic conditions that denied to so many of its citizens decent housing, education, or even adequate food and yet gave to others an overabundance of these things. When life was drab, conditions hard, and gin the great alleviator, it is not surprising that the outlet of violence was frequently used. The spark that lit the fire came from different

[17]Sir John Fielding, *Introduction, op. cit.,* p. 45.

sources—political, economic, and psychological. Political discontent, at a time when the Parliament was a very inadequate vehicle for popular or antigovernment views, could be most effectively expressed by demonstrations and the public presentation of petitions to Parliament. The men behind such demonstrations were most likely to be the politicians themselves, men who had a definite political end in view. But by a judicious use of oratory, the grapevine of the town, and inflammatory pamphlets men of less intelligence might be aroused to violent support. Any encouragement to surge through the streets, breaking windows, spreading destruction and manhandling suspected passersby, was welcome to the semicriminal, semivagrant inhabitants of slumlike alleys and courts. These were the terrifying and violent fringe that collected around any more orderly demonstration and gave the mob its special character, but historical investigation has shown that they were not its core. After the incident had been contained and arrests made, the trials of the rioters again and again established the fact that many of them were respectable members of the wage-earning population—apprentices, journeymen, even small shopkeepers. Their ostensible motive was frequently political, as when they attacked Walpole's excise bill in 1733, shouting "No Popery, No Wooden Shoes" or broke windows for Wilkes and Liberty or joined the ranks of the fanatical Lord George Gordon in the No Popery Riots that shook London in 1780; basically, however, it was economic and psychological. These men were making their protest against the terms on which society was forcing them to sell their labour, however little they realized the force that drove them on. Today when international finance and transport cushions the effect of a bad harvest on the cost of living, at least in the countries of the industrialized, capitalistic world, it is difficult to realize the importance of the harvest in a preindustrial community. Wages remained traditional, but the price of bread varied to an alarming extent according to the success or failure of the harvest. After 1715 for the first half of the century, with the exception of a few years such as 1727, 1729, and 1740, harvests were good and bread cost from a penny farthing to 3 halfpence a pound. After the middle of the century the position became more difficult, and prices fluctuated sharply between 1756 and 1773. They were high again in 1775 and 1776, with bread costing 2 pence a pound. Bread was the staple food of the labouring poor, and with an average wage of 9 to 12 shillings a week, much casual labour, and rents between 2 to 3 and 6 a week, this price was catastrophic. Even in good times there was little enough left over for meat or cheese, for clothes or firing, for the solace of beer and gin; when the price of bread soared, it meant a grim struggle for those who had such a little margin.

So it is not surprising that from 1768 industrial unrest was constant. Trade after trade began to demonstrate, to petition, and to break into rioting when they could get no satisfaction. In that year the coal heavers, an essential London trade, the sailors who manned its port, the watermen, an integral part of its transport, and a mass of industrial crafts, such as hatters, coopers, glass grinders, sawyers, tailors, and weavers all put forward demands for a rise in wages. When these were refused, strikes followed. In May 1768 practically every ship on the Thames seems to have been immobilized by the concerted action of a well-organized strike committee. The coal heavers, too, resorted to violence in support of their claims, attacking their enemies with cutlasses and bludgeons and raising a lusty cry, which combined their own grievances with antigovernment resentment, of "Wilkes and coal heavers for ever." Some of the most violent of these demonstrations were associated with the silk weavers of Spitalfields who, as we have seen, had been hit by the postwar importation of French silks. By May of 1763, driven on by distress, they appealed to Parliament for legislative action, marching with their banners and accompanied by their wives and children from Spitalfields to Westminster. Their action, though the weavers themselves were an orderly and respectable body of men, gave an opportunity for violent and criminal elements to get out of hand, and by the May 17 London was in the hands of the mob. Prudent citizens put up their shutters and stayed indoors; imprudent ones ran the risk of being chased, beaten up, and robbed. Though the weavers were told that their petition would receive consideration, mob hysteria prevailed and considerable damage was done before the troops were called in to restore order. On such occasions window breaking and looting were common occurances; the residences of unpopular ministers in particular being favorite targets.

Violence was not always far below the surface. At times the

savagery of the mob was directed against individuals when it literally thirsted for blood. When the notorious Mrs. Brownrigg, who had beaten and starved her workhouse apprentices until they died, was finally brought to justice and condemned, the crowd danced around her in frenzied glee as she was driven to Tyburn for execution. They called on the clergyman who had the duty of accompanying her to pray not for her soul but for her damnation, and as the cart moved away, leaving her dangling, a roar went up that, it was said, could be heard at Charing Cross. Similarly, when a journeyman shoemaker named Williamson, who had married a half-witted girl for her money and then maltreated her until she died, was arrested and taken to Newgate, the prison was surrounded all day by a crowd shouting for his blood. Sometimes a savage crowd dealt with its victim itself. When bad harvest pushed up the price of bread in 1767 causing rioting and strikes, weavers who refused to take part were apt to have their looms broken by fellow weavers. To stop this kind of intimidation, breaking looms was made a hanging offence. One Clark, an informer whose information had led to the hanging of two weavers, was recognized in Whitechapel, seized by the mob, and stoned to death in broad daylight. Unpopular criminals, or those who had no friends to protect them, who were condemned to the pillory might receive terrible injuries at the hands of a sadistic mob. Mother Needham died as a result of such injuries. Violence, then, whether that of the mass or that of the individual, ran like a red thread through the social fabric of London.

Eighteenth-century society was singularly ill-equipped to defend itself against the criminal and the vicious elements in its midst. Its major policy, if anything so *ad hoc* can be dignified by such a description, was to decree the death penalty for any crime that threatened serious social inconvenience and to offer a reward for the detection and apprehension of the criminal. The result was an indiscriminate penal code which punished more than a hundred offences by hanging. The majority of these were against property. To cut down a tree, to destroy a fishpond, to consort with gypsies, was to commit a felony, and all felonies were punishable by death. This meant that anyone who engaged in a life of even minor crimes risked death on the gibbet. At the Old Bailey in 1753 one woman was condemned to death for stealing a pair of stays. Such indiscriminatory severity defeated the intentions of the legislators: it hindered rather than helped society in its fight against the criminal. First, it could not help encouraging brutality and violence. As Johnson wrote, "to equate robbery with murder, is to reduce murder to robbery, to confound in common minds the graduations of iniquity, and to incite the commission of the greater crime to prevent the detection of the lesser. Why indeed if the Law rate human life so cheap should the criminal rate it more dearly?" Second, such severity made many jurors unwilling to convict persons charged with petty thefts. Similarly, owners of stolen property hesitated to prosecute and witnesses to give evidence. It is a maxim of the law that it is the certainty of punishment that deters. In London the chances of not being caught, or if caught of not being convicted, were such that crime flourished.

It could hardly have been otherwise while the forces of law and order remained disorganized and ineffective. The main responsibility rested in the hands of the magistrates, who were at once police officers, insofar as they had the power of arrest and controlled the parish constables, and judges with power to convict and sentence when they sat on the bench. In rural areas, where the justice of the peace was a substantial landowner, a sense of public duty or personal pride made men eager to perform these tasks. The work of a justice in the built-up areas in London, except in the City where, as we have seen, control was exercised by the Lord Mayor and the aldermen, was less attractive. It involved constant contact with unpleasant and frequently extremely unclean persons. It was sordid and disagreeable. Middle-class men of good standing, shopkeepers and lawyers, were too busy with their own affairs to have time for public service, the foundation for which in eighteenth-century conditions was the leisure that came from the possession of a private income. The justice who had none was forced to become a "trading justice", that is, he dealt in justice as a mercer might deal in silk. The office could be profitable, for although he received no salary, his fees could be considerable. But to obtain good fees, business had to be brisk, with the result that his office, which at this time was situated not in a public building but in his own residence, was more like a commercial enterprise than a public institution. To say that such a magistrate dealt in justice does not necessarily imply that such a man was either dishonest or corrupt, and indeed much of the business that came to him was legitimate. But there was always a temptation to outstep the limits of probity, to create business by "inflaming the quarrels of porters and beggars" for the fees they brought. Still worse was the temptation to abuse his power by using it to direct a flow of bribes into the magisterial pocket. Streetwalkers were arrested not to clean up the streets but to collect bail, and once that had been paid, prosecution rarely followed. Genuinely law-abiding persons were arrested on trumped-up charges for the same purpose. On the other hand, persons who should have been committed to prison were granted bail if they were in a position to pay for it, particularly if they could accompany it with a bribe. Keepers of disorderly houses who came to an agreement with the local magistrate might feel secure from the interference of the constable. Protection money is no new twentieth-century racket! From such evidence as there is it would appear that the City Marshall, who was entrusted with the suppression of vice within the City's boundaries, on occasion ran similar rackets. As a result only the unorganized criminal or the vice operator who refused to pay was in serious danger of gaol and the gibbet from magisterial activity. Henry Fielding called it some of the "dirtiest money on earth."

Apart from the magistrates and parish constables, who for the most part were equally venial or careful never to be found when trouble threatened, the only other official guardians of law and order were the Watch. The City, as we have seen, made some effort to secure a more reliable force, but outside its boundaries the generality of Watchmen, as described by Fielding, were "poor old decrepit people who are from want of bodily strength incapable of getting a living by work." By appointing a pauper a watchman, the parish avoided having to provide for him out of the poor rate, but this policy was hardly conducive to the nocturnal security of the parishioners. Wealthy parishes, such as St. George's Hanover Square, organized and paid for a more efficient set of watchmen, but the average standard of strength and courage was low enough not to deter even the most nervous and inefficient of criminals. This lack of public protection left the responsibility of guarding both property and person with the individual. The owner of stolen property was supposed to apply himself for a warrant for the arrest of the thief if, as seldom happened, he could identify him. It was a troublesome business, and even though the thief might hang, the stolen goods were not necessarily recovered. If the goods were valuable, it was more effective to advertise a reward for their return with no questions asked. This practice became so usual that the notorious Jonathan Wild set up in business as a recoverer of stolen goods on what practically amounted to a commission basis, which was extremely convenient for the thieves who now had a safe, well-organized market for their booty. To maintain a profitable flow of business Wild gradually built up a widespread organization among the thieves of London, helping to organize the defence or escape of those he found satisfactory and informing against those who in any way failed him. In an attempt to stifle this trade, a statute in 1718 decreed the death penalty for restoring goods, known to be stolen, in return for a reward, unless at the same time the thief was prosecuted. Because most private people were either unable or unwilling to enforce the law, their failure forced society to fall back on the thief taker. The old adage "set a thief to catch a thief" had some relevancy to the seething underworld of London's crime. Only persons familiar with its denizens possessed the necessary knowledge to act as informers, and they were encouraged to do so by substantial rewards. Anyone whose information led to the arrest and conviction of a highwayman or housebreaker, for instance, could receive a reward of £40, no inconsiderable sum in terms of the purchasing value of the pound at that time. Because an accomplice who turned king's evidence and betrayed his partner could both claim the reward and receive a free pardon for his share in the crime, treachery was added to the prevailing vice of violence.

This appeal to greed and treachery did little to improve the effectiveness of the law. Informing was added to London's disreputable careers, but against well-organized criminal gangs it could do little. Anyone who informed against one of their members would not be left long to enjoy the reward and could be reasonably sure of an unpleasant death. So the semiprofessional informer concentrated on the petty criminal, as often as not inciting his prospective victim to commit the felony for which he afterwards intended to betray him. With so little in the way of effective checks it is hardly surprising that robbery, housebreaking, pilfering, pickpocketing, running brothels and gaming houses, pimping and bullying, as well as private, and often drunken, unpremeditated violence and murder, built up into an antisocial force that at times constituted a serious threat to the property and persons of respectable Londoners.

When public disturbances such as riots not only got completely out of hand but also had some political connotation, as did those connected with John Wilkes, the government could use the military to restore order. This they were reluctant to do without serious provocation; the dislike of a standing army was deeply ingrained in Englishmen, and nothing was more likely to bring ministers into opprobrium and to strengthen the hand of the politicians in opposition than to use soldiers to restore order when civilians rioted. It is understandable, therefore, that ministers liked to be able to call on the services of a dependable magistrate who would deal with incipient trouble, collect information, and make arrests of a semipolitical character. Such a magistrate unofficially became the Court Justice. Because of his success, previously mentioned, in breaking up the gangs that were terrorizing London's streets, the Westminster magistrate De Veil had attracted the favourable notice of the administration and from 1729 seems to have been acting in this capacity. It is probable that he also received a small pension for his services. He was capable though corrupt. Keepers of bawdy houses and gaming establishment found it wise to buy his protection, and if he was successful in clearing the streets of the most obvious crimes of violence, which he did, the methods that he used, as a trading justice, are reputed to have brought him in a steady income of some £2000 a year. In his later years he moved to Bow Street, so beginning the long association between it and the forces of the law.

The man who first began to make an honest as well as an effective onslaught on London's crime was Henry Fielding. The onetime manager of the little theatre in the Haymarket and the satirical playwright, who helped to goad Walpole into securing the licensing act at first sight seems an unlikely candidate for this role. His appointment was characteristic of the times. George

Lyttleton, who had been a school friend of his at Eton, was anxious to do him a favour: funds were low and Fielding was not a wealthy man. He therefore procured the appointment for him, supposing that, like his predecessor De Veil who had died in 1744 and had been followed by a weaker man, Fielding would make a good thing out of it. On this he miscalculated, to the enormous benefit of law-abiding Londoners. Fielding's health was already precarious when in 1748 at the age of forty-one he became the Bow Street magistrate, and the very heavy task to which he now felt called undoubtedly helped to shorten his life. In 1751 he was joined by his blind half brother John who, after Henry's death in 1754, became the principal magistrate for Westminster and continued his struggle for the suppression of crime until his death in 1780. Between them the two men evolved an imaginative and constructive programme. Legally the magistrates could call on the services of the constables for the apprehension of criminals, but these officers, as we saw, were local, unpaid, and generally unwilling, anxious merely to get through their year of office with as little trouble to themselves as possible. Most of them were small tradesmen. However, among them Henry Fielding found a few reliable and public-spirited men whom he organized to act as a body under Saunders Welch, the efficient High Constable of Holborn. When their year of office was over, six of them agreed to continue the fight against crime, though the only renumeration they could hope to receive were the rewards offered for the apprehending and convicting of malefactors. They received scant gratitude for their exertions. The public despised them as thief takers and therefore venial and corrupt, and they were often cheated out of the rewards that they had fairly earned. Discouraged by such shabby treatment, the first little band of Bow Street men disintegrated. Yet even so short an experiment had demonstrated that a small body of resolute men, prepared to pursue and track down the thieves and bullies of the town, could be surprisingly effective.

The result of their disappearance seems to have been a fresh crime wave, so that by 1753 the streets had become so unsafe that the government was driven to issuing a proclamation that offered a reward of £100 per head for the capture and conviction of the members of a particularly dangerous and well-organized gang. At

the same time the Duke of Newcastle asked the Fieldings to
devise some plan for a more effective policing of the town and
showed his appreciation of the serious nature of the new outbreak
by actually managing to provide a small sum of money to be used
for this purpose. At last the fight against the criminal could be
organized on at least a semiofficial basis. Fielding arranged that
one officer should always be on duty at Bow Street, and he impressed on the public, by a series of advertisements in the *Public
Advertiser*, the importance of reporting immediately, together
with the relevant details, robberies, housebreakings, woundings,
murders, in short, any kind of crime. This type of information had
a twofold importance. It enabled his little force of thief takers,
which had now been reconstituted from reliable sources, to set
out in immediate pursuit before the stolen property could be
disposed of, and it also enabled him to build up a register of very
valuable criminal records. Lists of stolen property were made,
reputable pawnbrokers notified, suspected persons recorded, and
houses of ill repute, where thieves might congregate, enumerated.
By 1754 John Fielding was in sole control, and in 1755 he was
joined at Bow Street by Saunders Welch who became his assistant. Between them the information for a successful counterattack
was accumulated. Though petty crime abounded, London's underworld was not so extensive that a rather full dossier of the
haunts and habits of its more serious criminal population could
not be obtained. Bow Street paid for useful information, and the
public were encouraged to cooperate and to use its services. To
claim that John Fielding, who for his efforts was knighted in 1761,
stamped out major crime would be absurd and untrue, but there
seem to have been fewer holdups in the more populated parts of
the town, though they did of course, as we have seen, occur. A
new device seems to have contributed to this improvement. In
1763, in response to the political tension and rioting that marked
this year, ten mounted men, supplied with arms, were paid 4
shillings a night to act as horse patrol. The first experiment was
short-lived, because the government refused to find the necessary
money, but some sort of a flying squad was so clearly needed to
pursue highwaymen and the ordinary Watch was so plainly
inadequate to police the built-up areas that in 1782 patrols were
organized to cover the areas four miles beyond the stones' end,

that is, the paved streets. There were to be sixty-eight, fifty-five men, who received 2 and 6 a night, and thirteen captains who were paid 5 shillings. Gradually, therefore, during the years of Dr. Johnson's residence in London considerable improvement in the protection of the private citizen seems to have taken place. When he first came there, law-abiding people were almost defenceless against the threat to property and to life and limb except for the protection that they could provide for themselves. By the time he died the streets were better lit and better patrolled, and the Bow Street men—they were not called Bow Street runners, the title by which they are better known, until the nineteenth century—had made it safer for Londoners to go on their lawful occasions. No longer was it necessary "To prepare for death, if here at night you roam."

If no longer so applicable to the streets, this warning might well have been given to anyone committed to one of London's prisons, unless he or she came there with a well-filled purse. Prisons were regarded primarily as places of detention, a halfway house between freedom or the gibbet or transportation. They were not meant either to punish or reform, merely to keep the arrested person safe until the trial. To some extent this explains the strange anomalies and appalling hardships suffered within them. Public control over their running was very slight, and until the eighteenth century the gaolers, like modern headwaiters, bought their positions and recouped themselves from their clients. There were many ways of doing this—some legal, some customary, others made possible by a savage use of unrestrained power. The legal charges were chiefly a matter of fees to be paid on entering and on discharge, and until these were forthcoming even an innocent person, cleared by the courts, could be detained indefinitely. The customary payments included every sort of charge for even the smallest amelioration of intolerable conditions. In London serious offenders were usually committed to Newgate, the oldest and one of the most notorious prisons of London. The building was an imposing one, adorned with statues of Peace, Liberty, Security, Plenty, Justice, and Fortitude. Only the latter applied to the inmates. Justice there was none, not even in the allotting of quarters. Rich prisoners were accommodated in the part of the prison called the Castle, where at least they had

some light, air, and a modicum of privacy. Prisoners who could
afford 2 shillings a week could at least hire a bed in some less
unpleasant part of the prison, but those unable to meet this
charge were housed in a common ward, stone-floored, often
underground, stinking and filthy, where the air was so foul that
their whole persons were impregnated with its indescribable
odour. Here they lay without covering or bedding. If the poor
prisoner did not die of hardship and exposure, he might well die
of starvation, because the only food provided was a scant ration
of stale bread and contaminated water. Additional food had to be
bought at the gaoler's price. So had candles and firing. The profits
from these sales were large, but greatest of all were those from
the prison Tap. Far from being forbidden, the sale of strong
drink was encouraged, and the prisoner who could afford it could
pass the time in riotous drunkenness or in the stupor of oblivion.

It is not surprising that Newgate was a place of concentrated
misery, drunkenness, and debauchery. There was no attempt,
other than for financial considerations, to segregate the prisoners,
and those who could "oblige" the turnkeys could wander where
they wished. On the debtors' side in the common wards bankrupt
tradesmen still tried to carry on their trade, hoping to make
enough to secure release. People from the outside world, friends
of the prisoners or mere sightseers, came and went with the
compliance of bribed turnkeys. Prisoners in the condemned cells,
waiting for execution, could talk freely with their friends and
visitors, separated from them only by a high wooden barrier
topped with fierce iron spikes. The whole gaol was one vast
bawdy house. Prisoners struck up liaisons with one another, and
for a fee the gaoler would arrange to have them locked up together in a private cell overnight. Most prisons had an evil reputation
in this respect. At Clerkenwell[18] it was reported that visitors to the
prison, seeing a likely looking girl, could arrange, for an appropriate fee, to be left alone with her in a more secluded part. Keepers
of houses of ill repute found poor female prisoners a source of
supply and, having paid their fees, took them back to their ba-
gnios. A female prisoner who was penniless had to sell herself or

[18]*Reasons Offered for the Reformation of the House of Correction in
Clerkenwell* (1757), especially p. 13, 14, and 26, gives a vivid account of
the state of this gaol.

starve. To this dismal picture must be added the torment of heavy fetters for those prisoners who could not pay for "easement", and the constant danger of gaol fever for all prisoners, which was a particularly virulent form of typhoid. To a twentieth-century reader the condition of such places is almost incredible. Moreover, there was no safeguard against such horrors being endured by the technically innocent, for people were committed to these places for safekeeping before they stood their trial.

The penalty for most criminal offences was hanging, but there was many a slip between Newgate and Tyburn. If the innocent sometimes were convicted, the guilty frequently escaped. Perjury was common, and so-called "men of straw" were willing for a consideration to provide a false alibi. Legal technicalities, such as a slip in the wording of an indictment, helped many a prisoner, with the aid of a clever lawyer, to escape the gallows. Juries, too, were often unwilling to convict and deliberately undervalued property in order to prevent its theft becoming a hanging matter. Also, a lengthy trial, necessary for the thorough sifting of complicated evidence, was unpopular with judges. Moreover, since juries were shut up without either food or drink until they had reached their unanimous verdict, they too were reluctant to spend much time in arriving at a verdict. As Pope wrote bitterly in *The Rape of the Lock*,

> The hungry judges soon the sentence sign
> And wretches hang that jurymen may dine.

When the wiles of the professional informer and thief taker are added to the hazards of rushed justice, it seems probable that innocent people did at times fall victims to the system. Mercifully not all those who were convicted of felony were hanged. Many received a conditional pardon on agreeing to be transported, a sentence that could only be substituted for the death penalty with the prisoner's consent! In the crowded, ill-ventilated courts of the Old Bailey death was a threat to judge and jury as well as to the prisoner at the bar, for the germs of the gaol fever that they brought with them from their stinking cells made no distinction between the innocent and the guilty, the criminal and the judge. In spite of the contemporary precaution of a huge bunch of sweet-smelling herbs on the judge's bench, whose presence was believed to give protection, time and again judge and jury alike fell victims to the dreaded gaol fever.

Except in a purely formal way, in that a clergyman accompanied the condemned prisoners on their last journey to Tyburn, the established church as an institution appears to have concerned itself very little with either crime or the criminal, but the opposite holds true for the sect of the Methodists. The followers of both John Wesley and George Whitefield were inspired with an intense desire "to call sinners to repentence." Though neither man was a Londoner and much of their work was done elsewhere, both had close links with London society. Wesley was friendly with Johnson, who complained that he never would relax long enough for the pair of them to have the kind of leisurely conversation that the Doctor loved. Another friend was Dr. Pepusch, with whom Wesley occasionally spent an hour or two discussing music. Johnson had affection and respect for Wesley, but was less favourably impressed by Whitefield, whose flamboyant, emotional style of preaching he disliked. The glimpses of London that are revealed in so many of the extracts in Wesley's *Journal* bring out still another aspect of the capital. Again and again there is a record of preaching to large congregations at the Foundry, his London headquarters, or in St. Bartholomew's where "deep attention sat on every face." Here was the underlying seriousness and concern with religion that was as much a mark of the eighteenth century as its licentiousness and that characterized so much of Johnson's own thought. It was to the poor and the social outcast that Wesley made an appeal with often dramatic consequences. There was, for instance, the case of Mary Cheesebrook who was "without God in the world," being a kept mistress. An acquaintance brought her one evening to the chapel in West Street, "where God gave her a new heart . . . and from that time she procured for herself by hard labour what was needful for life and godliness."[19] Other Methodists did spectacular work with the prisoners in Newgate. Here the name of Sarah Peters deserves to be remembered. On October 9, 1748, she and a friend went to visit a young man named James Lancaster, who had once been a Methodist

[19]John Wesley, *The Journal,* November, 22, 1747.

convert and who had subsequently lapsed into evil ways. "He asked them to go into his cell, which they willingly did, although some dissuaded them from it because," as Wesley recorded, "the gaol-distemper (a kind of pestilential fever) ranged much among the prisoners." There they were joined by six or seven other prisoners, all under sentence of death, and soon the little congregation, exhorted by Sarah Peters to repentence, were all in tears. Until the morning of their execution Sarah and her friends visited them constantly "and had the comfort of finding them every time more athirst for God then before." Against the grim despair of Newgate one can imagine faintly just how much those visits must have meant to the men in the condemned cell. When faced with the last journey to Tyburn, the little band of converts mounted the cart joyfully, declaring that "It is but a short time, and we shall be where all sorrow and sighing shall flee away."[20] The execution was on October 28; on November 3 Sarah developed gaol fever; on the 13th she was dead.

Tyburn days were very much a part of London life. Eighteenth-century people believed in the deterrent effect of public punishment, though in view of the evidence it is sometimes difficult to know on what grounds. They did more than believe in it; many of them enjoyed the spectacle of its being inflicted. The streak of cruelty that found satisfaction in cockfighting and dogfighting, in bear baiting and prizefighting, found the same sadistic pleasure in hurling things at some helpless creature in the pillory or watching some petty thief being flogged at the cart's tail. Women were not exempt. Elizabeth Boyes was whipped for stealing pewter pots, another woman for taking a barrel of oysters. In March 1752 a confidence man was sentenced to be committed to Bridewell for six months of hard labour and to be whipped six times in six different London streets. Minor punishment of this kind was an everyday sight, but hangings were a different matter; they were staged with pomp and ceremony. People of every class—the nobleman, the gentleman, the apprentice, the riffraff of the town—all flocked to them. If a notable criminal or a well-known highwayman was to be hanged, special stands were erected and houses with a view of the gibbet com-

[20]*Ibid.*, November 13, 1748.

manded a high price for window seats, while among the crowd piemen sold their wares and ballad singers their sheets. It was a cheerful, merry occasion celebrated as a public holiday. Not every one, even then, regarded it in this lighthearted way. Boswell confessed that "My curiosity to see the melancholy spectacle of the executions was so strong that I could not resist it though I was sensible I should suffer much from it. In my younger years I had read in the Lives of the Convicts so much about Tyburn that I had a sort of horrid eagerness to be there. . . . Accordingly I took Captain Temple with me, and he and I got upon a scaffold very near the fatal tree, so that we could clearly see all the dismal scene. There was a most prodigious crowd of spectators. I was most terribly shocked and thrown into a deep melancholy."[21] Doubtless, other spectators were drawn there by a similar horrid eagerness, but many went as connoisseurs, as men today might go to watch a popular sport, commenting on the behaviour of the condemned men in their last moments and giving their admiration to those who made a gallant end. Though the crowd could be dangerous and abusive to prisoners whose crimes had outraged public opinion, to the man who had captured its imagination it was prepared to accord an almost triumphal farewell.

It was a long journey from Newgate to Tyburn. The first stop was by St. Sepulchre's Church where Robert Daw, a merchant tailor, had left an endowment of £1-6-8, in the year 1612, so that the bellman might toll the great bell as the procession of the condemned went past and deliver the traditional exhortation to them to repent in their last hour. To provide religious consolation on this final journey a chaplain sat with the condemned man in the cart, which also, a grim touch, carried the hangman and the coffin. In front rode the City Marshall and in the rear marched a company of redcoats. Pelted with flowers if he were popular and with filth if an object of hatred, the prisoner and the procession came at length to Tyburn where the biggest crowds were waiting. There was an interval for the prisoner to make his final peace with God and his farewell speeches to the crowd. Kielmansegge, intent on missing no side of London life, went to "see a man

[21]J. Boswell, *London Journal*, p. 252.

hanged a l'anglaise, a young man named Lee, who had been engaged as a clerk or book keeper at a tradesman's and had been tempted to issue false bills upon his former employer, in order to get sufficient money for his amusements. This was found out before much damage had been done, and as the consequences of such forgeries are very disastrous, especially in this commercial country, the penalty is death. He was not insolent but had courage enough to read to the public, sufficiently loud, a speech in which he acknowledged the wrong he had committed, and representing himself as an example and a warning to his hearers. As he was a Methodist one of the clergymen of that denomination got onto the cart after the chaplain had left it, and prayed with him for some time. During the whole time, whilst he stood on the cart underneath the gallows, a rope was kept round his neck. When he had finished his devotions, and had taken leave of his friends, who had come upon the cart to see him, the cart, with all the people standing on it drove off and he remained hanging. His best friends at once held him down by the feet so that from the first moment nobody noticed the slightest movement."[22] Death by hanging was in fact slow strangulation because the drop was not sufficient to break the victim's neck, and to pull down the feet in this way was an act of mercy frequently performed.

Public executions had been intended to strike terror into the spectators, rather than provide them with macabre entertainment, and even by the middle of the century wise men like Henry Fielding were arguing that the publicity of the occasion did more harm than good, that it had the effect of turning the criminal into a public hero, that the cold terror of the occasion was lost in its flamboyant drama, so that a gallant death seemed a fitting end to a daring career. The final scene of *The Beggar's Opera*, showing MacHeath in the cart Tyburn-bound, was faithful to the canons of the time. In protest against them Fielding wrote: "If Executions therefore were so contrived, that few could be present at them, they would be much more shocking and terrible to the Crowd without Doors, as well as much more dreadful to the criminals themselves, who would thus die in the Presence only of their Enemies, and where the boldest of them would find no

[22]Kielmansegge, *op. cit.*, p. 159.

Cordial to keep up his Spirits, nor any Breathe to flatter his Ambition."[23] By the seventies some men were seriously beginning to reevaluate the deterrent effect of both public executions and the almost indiscriminate use of the death penalty. As early as 1770 a committee of the House of Commons was appointed to consider the question of capital punishment, and though nothing tangible resulted from it, its very appointment was a straw in the wind. In the seventies also John Howard started his investigations into the appalling state of the prisons that were to do so much to bring about reform. By 1779, with the support of the great legal commentator Blackstone, who had written of the melancholy truth, that among the variety of actions which men are liable to commit no less than a hundred and six have been declared by Act of Parliament to be felonies without benefit of clergy, or in other words to be worthy of instant death, an act looking to reformation, rather than to deterrence, through the establishment of penitentiaries with their regime of hard labour, solitude, and religious instruction, had been placed on the statute book. If there was as much poverty, there was probably less crime in London when Johnson died than when, as a young man, he first roamed its streets. Yet when the executions outside Tyburn were abolished, he declared, though whether out of sheer cussedness who can say, that "Executions are intended to draw spectators. If they do not draw spectators, they don't answer their purpose. The old method was most satisfactory to all parties: the publick was gratified by a procession, the criminel was supported by it."[24] By the end of the century reformers were more and more feeling that neither of these consequences was of benefit to society.

[23]Henry Fielding, *Enquiry, op. cit.*, p. 121.

[24]Boswell, *Life of Samuel Johnson*, Vol. 4, p. 188.

EIGHT

The Philanthropy of London

If London was a city of poverty and crime, it was also shot
through with philanthropy. It is an old saying that charity is the
child of poverty and abundance, and in London both were to be
found in close juxtaposition. Dr. Johnson was no believer in the
virtues of poverty, saying frankly that "When I was running about
this town a very poor fellow, I was a great arguer for the advantages of poverty; but I was, at the same time, very sorry to be
poor. Sir, all the arguments which are brought to represent poverty as no evil, show it to be evidently a great evil. You will never
find people labouring to convince you that you may live happily
on a plentiful fortune."[1] On one occasion he wrote to Boswell:
"Resolve not to be poor: whatever you have spend less. Poverty is
a great enemy to human happiness; it certainly destroys liberty,
and makes some virtue impractical and others extremely
difficult."[2] A little later he wrote: "Frugality is not only the basis
of quiet but of beneficence. No man can help others that wants
help himself; we must have enough before we have to spare."[3]
Many a successful merchant and prosperous citizen felt the same.
For the immoral, for the shiftless, for the idle there was little
sympathy, but for the sick, for the orphaned child, and the homeless street waif who had never had a chance there was much.

[1] J. Boswell, *Life of Samuel Johnson.*

[2] *Ibid.*, Vol. 4, p. 159.

[3] *Ibid.*, Vol. 4, p. 163.

Eighteenth-century benevolence was essentially social; it aimed to make the objects of its charity useful members of the community and to prevent the human wastage caused by premature death, by disease, and by lack of training and self-discipline. This at once dictated the object of charity and presented the charitable with some difficulties, and between these two poles its performance oscillated throughout the century. It was almost impossible to help the deserving without the risk of encouraging some anti-social vice. Would the help given to deserted children encourage immorality and bastardy? Would a home for repentent prostitutes encourage women to go on the streets? Was it not just that people who had embraced an evil way of life should be made to pay the full price of their misdoings?

This somewhat practical benevolence was by no means a London monopoly; charity schools and energetically supervised workhouses, particularly in the early part of the century, operated in many provincial towns. But though not unique, London, as the capital city, had the wealth, the enterprise, and the need to engage in large-scale philanthropy. This was no new activity for her citizens. Since the sixteenth century, when the emergence of a new type of poverty had faced the City with new problems, the corporation had accepted the organization of civic charity as one of its functions, building in many cases on medieval foundations. In the sixteenth century St. Thomas's and St. Bartholomew's hospitals were refounded for the care of the sick. Bethlem Hospital, long known as Bedlam, provided treatment and shelter for the lunatic poor, and deserted children were housed and educated in Christ's Church Hospital. All these institutions were active in Johnson's day, but they were no longer adequate to meet the needs of a rapidly growing London, and the eighteenth-century saw numerous new foundations financed not by the City in its corporate capacity but by private individuals. Little new was attempted for the mentally deranged, whose treatment by modern standards remained shockingly unenlightened, but for deserted children, for the sick poor, and for child bearing women much was done.

In the earlier part of the century this charitable impulse expressed itself chiefly in providing better and more ample facilities for dealing with the sick poor. Without some such help the situation of the poor man or woman who had an accident or fell sick was one of great difficulty. The services of a surgeon or physician were completely beyond their financial resources, and in the overcrowded dwellings that were the common lot of most of them a serious illness was little short of a disaster. The new hospitals, which were intended to meet this need, were a combination of an old tradition and the beginning of a new approach. Hospitals in the Middle Ages had been places of refuge rather than of healing. Often they were primarily for the old, though age and sickness frequently went together, and were almshouses rather than hospitals as the twentieth century understands these terms. To make this kind of provision for the poor brethren of one's craft was a normal charitable activity, and London had many such "hospitals." Some catered for less than a dozen people. But by the beginning of the eighteenth century the whole approach to the treatment of disease had been altered by the scientific revolution in late seventeenth century. There was more knowledge of the cause of disease, of the human anatomy, and of new treatments. Hospitals were no longer places of refuge where the sick or the leper could be nursed until death intervened; they were places whose aim, however imperfectly implemented, was to cure. Quite apart from the scientific aspects of this approach, these aims were in harmony with the materialistic charity of the age. The sick poor were a burden on society: they could contribute nothing to its productive power. But the cured sick man once again becomes the labourer. The London Hospital claimed that its patients had been "re-instated in their honest and industrious Capacities of working, and, so far as our Observation reaches, their Morals much amended, whereby the Publick again enjoy the Benefit of their Labour, and they and their poor Families are preserved from perishing, and prevented from being an Incumbrance to the Community."[4] The eighteenth-century point of view could hardly have been better summarized.

Such hopes, together with the growing interest in medicine, combined to produce a spate of new hospitals in London. Archenholtz considered their foundation a further proof of how ardently the spirit of charity "glows in the bosom of the English" and

[4]Maitland, *op. cit.*, Vol. 2, p. 1312.

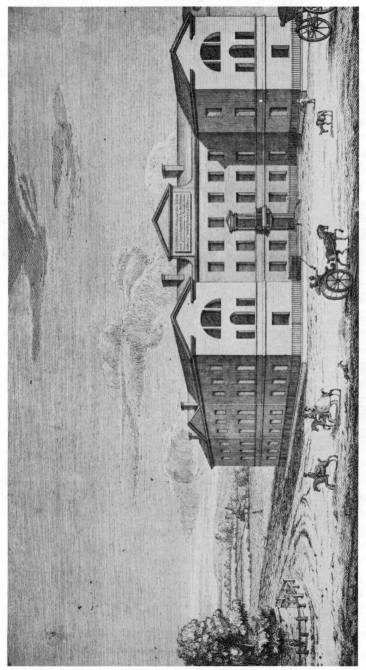

St. George's Hospital, surrounded by open country.

257

wrote enthusiastically of the "prodigious number which are regulated with the greatest order, i.e. kept with astonishing cleanliness and neatness."[5] Like many foreign visitors, he was prone to exaggeration. The number of hospitals was not prodigious, and their internal economy left much to be desired. Nevertheless, the new foundations were impressive. The earliest of these, Guy's Hospital near St. Thomas's in Southwark, was already functioning when Johnson came to London. This was true also of the Westminster, which had started in a single house in Petty France in 1720, though four years later the trustees were able to take bigger premises in Chapel Street. There was a certain divergence of opinion between them on the management of charity, and in 1733 some of them decided to organize a subscription list for a separate venture, which led to the foundation of St. George's Hospital in 1734. The site was chosen "on account of its Air, situation and Nearness to Town."[6] Today the hospital still occupies its old site amid all the swirling traffic of Hyde Park Corner. The London Hospital was very much the child of John Harrison, a young surgeon of only twenty-two, who was the moving spirit behind its foundation. It was intended chiefly to serve "Manufacturers, seamen in the Merchant Service and their Wives and Children" and was situated on Prescott Street, in Goodman's Fields. The original building consisted of four houses in not very good condition, and the pressure on beds soon made it necessary for the governors to look for new premises elsewhere. There was much heartburning and anxious deliberation over this, and finally, because the hospital was intended to be used by the districts developing to the east of the City, it was decided to buy some land in Whitechapel Road. Some of the governors thought this a most unwise step, because this road was one of the main thoroughfares out of London and was in consequence one of the haunts of footpads and highwayman. Today its dangers lie in the busy traffic, not in the risk of the lonely traveller being robbed and perhaps murdered after dark. By 1757 the central block with 161 beds was ready for use. Meanwhile a group of philanthropists had started a similar venture in 1745 for "the sick and lame of Soho,"

[5]Archenholtz, *op. cit.,* p. 187.

[6]Maitland, *op. cit.,* Vol. 2, p. 1312.

known as the Middlesex Infirmary, later to become the Middlesex
Hospital. Their first premises were very modest—a couple of
houses in Windmill Street. Off Tottenham Court Road there was
an, as yet, undeveloped area of marshes and ponds where Londoners used to go snipe shooting. Here they acquired land. In
1757 their new building was described as "a neat, plain and not
inelegant red brick building having all the decent appearance and
all the accommodation one could wish in a house devoted to
charity, without that ostentatious magnificence which too often in
a great measure defeats the humane and noble ends of such pious
and charitable institutions where those sums are squandered in
useless decoration that ought to be employed in administering
health to the sick and giving feet to the lame."[7] A contemporary
print depicts the building as consisting of a central block with
two wings that enclose a small courtyard, separated from the
street by tall iron railings on either side of a handsome gateway
surmounted by a pediment. This was very much the pattern of
the eighteenth-century hospital. Count Kielmansegge described a
similar arrangement at St. Thomas's: "In front it has a large iron
gateway, which forms the street side of the square, the other sides
of which are taken up by the main building and two wings, in
front of which a covered stone colonnade runs, with benches
under it. On each side of the entrance gate is a stone statue representing an invalid. There is a clock over the main building, and
under it, in a niche, a statue of King Edward VI, with a gilt septre
in one hand, and the charter of foundation in the other."[8] Like
the new hospitals, it too had been forced to expand, and four new
courts had been added in an extensive building programme. Built
in red brick with white facing, it was a pleasant and dignified
building.

Raising the money to finance this ring of new hospitals called
for much energy, enterprise, and organization. Except for Mr.
Guy's hospital, which was amply supplied with funds from the
beginning, the hospitals for the most part started in a modest way
in houses that they adapted, as best they could, to the business of
nursing the sick. Yet even this called for the tying up of some

[7]John Noorthouck, *A New History of London* (1772), p. 732.

[8]Kielmansegge, *op. cit.*, p. 188.

capital in order to rent, or buy, premises and to equip them, and required some regular income to meet day-to-day expenses. Once the decision had been taken to expand, to acquire land, and to engage in substantial building operations, the need for greatly increased revenues became urgent. The method used both to raise the initial capital and to increase the subsequent revenue was that already used so effectively by the charity schools. The promoters formed a small committee and campaigned to interest the wider public for the purpose of soliciting donations and subscriptions. The net they cast was a wide one; the subscription charity was an important socially integrating force in the life of the metropolis. The support of the nobility was essential for success, but this was not difficult to obtain. Many of the peers took their responsibilities as leaders of society seriously and did in fact play an active part in the world of philanthropy. The Duke of Northumberland became the president of the Middlesex in 1750, the Duke of Richmond held the same office in the London, St. George's was favoured by the royal family and boasted as its second president the Prince of Wales. Sir Robert Walpole, Lord Burlington, and Lord Chesterfield were among its aristocratic subscribers. Bankers and City men were equally prominent, and many of them were founding fathers for London's hospitals. Henry Hoare helped to establish the Westminster, the Barclays were interested in the London. Below the well-known names came those of the gentry, and still further down the social ladder came the solid Londoners and middling folk. The constitution of each hospital varied in its details, but the general pattern was to attract as large a body of subscribers as possible by allowing everyone who subscribed 4 or 5 guineas a year to attend the board of governors so long as the payment was kept up, while a more substantial donation entitled the donor to be a governor for life. It was a high-sounding title, and some hospitals had as many as 300 governors, which, had they all taken an active part in the administration, would have led to chaos. But for the majority the position was purely honourary, the usual procedure being to elect a working committee at the annual court. To maintain the flow of subscriptions and to attract legacies and endowments once the initial enthusiasm had died down required adroit publicity. The London Hospital kept its needs before the public through the medium of the charity sermon, a favourite eighteenth-century device for raising money for charity. The annual sermon was given by some distinguished churchman at one of the City churches, usually Bow Church in Cheapside. From there the whole congregation marched in procession, headed by a band and to the accompaniment of church bells, to wherever the dinner, which followed the service, was to be held. This was a lavish affair that lasted from five in the afternoon to after midnight and was catered by the two festival stewards for the year, the diners' contributions going directly into the hospital's funds. Softened with wine, food, and good company, the guests were in a mood to respond generously to the appeal for funds. In 1748 the Bishop of Worcester, for example, launched the fund for the hospital's new building programme. Then as now charitable activities bridged social ravines; royalty often attended, and the nobility, members of Parliament, the gentry, and substantial City men were all there in force.

During the fifties and sixties these drives for funds were generally successful, but in the second part of the century there was a marked falling off as new charitable experiments caught the public imagination; by then, however, the voluntary hospitals had acquired permanent homes. The majority of these buildings had solidity and some dignity, but their internal economy was less satisfactory. To say that sanitation was imperfectly understood would be a gross understatement. Windows were usually kept closed; they were always closed in the "foul wards," where patients suffering from venereal diseases were treated. Hospital beds were made of wood, often with testers that harboured dust. The bedsteads themselves harboured vermin. At Guy's in 1739 the hospital court was informed that "the Patients in this Hospital were annoyed in a very grevious manner with Buggs," and it was resolved "that it be referred to Mr. Troar to take such steps as he shall think most effectual for clearing the men's wards thereof."[9] Some hospitals had a regular bug catcher; others were forced constantly to spend sums on what seems to have been a losing fight with these vermin. This is understandable when it is remembered that many of the patients taken in must have been filthy

[9]H. C. Cameron, *Mr. Guy's Hospital* (Longmans, 1954), p. 66.

both in their persons and in their clothing; St. George's even provided "some of the Miserable with Cloathes." St. Thomas's had a society that supplied patients with clean body linen once a week, and Guy's required any patron recommending a patient to provide him or her with clean body linen every week. From the hospital accounts it would appear that the sisters frequently undertook the washing of such linen for 3d per week per patient. One cannot imagine the ward sister of any modern hospital doing such menial tasks, but the sisters and nurses, even at Guy's which paid higher salaries than most of the London hospitals, were very humble members of society. Nursing had not yet become a profession, and little was required of them beyond the keeping of order in the wards, at times no mean task, feeding the bedridden patients, and occasionally washing them. At night these duties were entrusted to an even less desirable type of female, the watchers, who for a pittance took over the duties of night nurse.

So it is not surprising that the wards were not overclean by modern standards. Sometimes they were deficient even by contemporary standards. At the London Hospital the visiting committee was informed by the nurses in New George ward that "they have had no water for several days past, pump being as they say out of repair. Ashes has not been cleaned away these 2 months which the Cooks says blows in at the windows the top of the dust hill being raised above the level of the windows." No wonder that one visitor reported "the house very offensive, so much so that I could not Bare the Smell."[10] In view of such conditions it seems astonishing that so many patients were cured and that the hospital beds available were always full until we remember that such living conditions were the normal lot of the London poor, who, because the hospitals were charitable institutions, were the ones treated in them. It was, for instance, a provision of the London Hospital that "No Persons of known Ability to pay for their Cure, are allowed to partake of the Charity."[11] Another reason for the number of cures effected was that hospitals only admitted those persons whom they thought they could

[10]E. W. Morris, *A History of The London Hospital* (Edward Arnold, 1926), p. 92.

[11]Maitland, *op. cit.*, Vol. 2, p. 1313.

treat successfully. The London refused to take in "any with infectious Distempers, or deemed incurable by the Physicians and
Surgeons, or any consumptive or asthmatick Condition." St.
Thomas's had similar regulations. It was partly because of his
compassion for such people that Mr. Guy founded his hospital for
those "who, by reason of the small hopes there may be of their
cure, or the length of time for which for that purpose may be
required or thought necessary, are or may be adjudged or called
incurable and as such not proper objects to be received into or
continued in the present hospital of St. Thomas's or other hospitals, in or by which no provision has been made for distempers
deemed or called incurable."[12] At a time when hospital beds
were limited in number, there was some justification for taking in
only those most likely to benefit—a practical attitude very characteristic of the philanthropy of the average citizen. It has also
been suggested that many of the patients admitted were merely
suffering from deficiency diseases and that the provisions of more
spacious and less overcrowded living quarters where each inmate
had the luxury of a separate bed, which was generally the case,
combined with a more generous diet, might well account for
many of the cures. St. Thomas's in 1752 provided 14 ounces of
bread a day together with a quart of beer in winter or three pints
in summer as basic rations. In addition milk porridge was served
for breakfast four mornings a week and water gruel on the other
three days. The allowance for dinner was half a pound of meat
for five days a week, with either four ounces of butter or six
ounces of cheese on the other two. For supper patients had a pint
of broth. Then as now patients grumbled. The same visiting
committee that had reported on the deficiency of water and
superabundance of ashes at the London Hospital also reported on
February 26, 1770: "Visited the House & had Greate Complaintes
in ould Jno' Ward met being bad & the Lounces very smoll." One
of the patients accused the nurse of giving "Better Vituals to her
dog."[13] Many of the cases admitted were accidents; broken limbs
were common. Not all patients were cured. One unfortunate man
taken into the London with a fractured leg developed bad ab-

[12]Cameron, *op. cit.,* p. 47.

[13]Morris, *op. cit.,* p. 91.

scesses that had to be opened and though he was provided with "large nosegays to prevent his being affected by the stench of his leg,"[14] he died! This treatment was probably inspired by the contemporary belief that unpleasant smells were themselves a medium for the spread of disease, as witness the practice of placing a large nosegay before the judges at the Old Bailey. Despite the hazards of the eighteenth-century hospital, the number of patients discharged as presumably cured was larger than might have been expected in such conditions. In 1734, for instance, Guy's discharged 1524 patients and buried only 277; the Westminster cured 705 and buried 48 in 1747.

Except in the case of an accident, the usual method of admission to one of London's hospitals was to obtain a letter of recommendation from a governor or subscriber. When this could not be obtained and when the hospital demanded the payment of certain charges before it would admit a patient, the parish seems to have undertaken this responsibility in the case of paupers. Both St. Thomas's and Guy's required an entrance fee of 3 and 6 pence from every patient accepted into a "clean ward" and one of 10 and 6 from those admitted in the "foul ward." In addition the sponsoring subscriber or parish had to be "security for the Payment of Four Pence per Day" for maintenance and was required to promise, if the patient died, to "take away his Body or pay the Fees for his Burial to the Steward,"[15] a somewhat discouraging liability! Not all the hospitals charged fees. St. George's provided their patients with "Advice, Medicine, Diet, Washing, Lodging" without expecting to be reimbursed.

The majority of the patients were a rough lot. The rules drawn up for the various London hospitals illustrate vividly both the character of their expected inmates and the attitude of the subscribers to the objects of their charity. Many of the patients seem to have been walking cases and sadly in need of discipline. Most hospitals required them to attend promptly when the surgeons and physicians made their rounds, and to be present at meals and chapel services, but otherwise they seem to have had considerable freedom to come and go. St. George's ordered,

[14]*Ibid.*, p. 58.

[15]Cameron, *op. cit.*, p. 66.

though, "That no Patient is to be suffered to go out of the Hospital without Leave in Writing, and that, to avoid Offence, no Leave is to be given to any Patient to go into St. James' Park, or the Green Park, called Constitution-hill, upon any Pretence what so ever."[16] The fashionable world, whose generosity supported the hospital, was not to be discommoded by the sight of its unsavoury inmates! Guy's threatened any patient "found strolling about the Streets, or frequenting Publick Houses, or Brandy Shops"[17] with the loss of the next day's food. This, a slightly odd penalty for a hospital to impose on its sick patients, was common practice. If guilty of more serious offenses, such as smoking in bed or bringing spirituous liquor into the hospital, patients were discharged forthwith whether they were cured or not. Among the rules that regulated the behaviour of patients within St. Thomas's were the following revealing provisions: "That Patients shall not Swear or take God's name in vain, nor revile, or miscall one another, nor strike nor beat one another, nor steal Meat or Drink, Apparel, or other thing, one from the other; nor abuse themselves by inordinate Drinking, nor incontinent Living, nor talk, nor act immodestly upon pain of Expulsion."[18] Such provisions were not merely academic: at the London Hospital, for example, on one occasion "One George Nesbitt in old George's Ward Got Drunk on Sunday and abused the Nurse and swear, Cursed, and used much abuseful Language."[19] Similar incidents were not uncommon.

Eighteenth-century philanthropists were firmly convinced of the social value of the Christian religion. Every hospital, therefore, included among its regulations careful provisions for the moral regeneration of its patients, who were to be made conscious of the debt they owed to God and their social betters for the restoration of their health. Good principles made dependable, hardworking people; it was little use restoring their bodies if their health was to be frittered away in debauchery and their time in

[16]Maitland, *op. cit.*, Vol. 2, p. 1304.

[17]Cameron, *op. cit.*, p. 66.

[18]*An Abstract of the Orders of St. Thomas's Hospital in Southwark* (1752).

[19]Morris, *op. cit.*, p. 91.

idleness. Patients at St. Thomas's were constantly to "attend the Worship of God in the Chapel on Sabbath and other Days, on pain of forfeiting of one Day's Allowance for the first Offense, without reasonable excuse; and upon after Offending, to be punished at discretion of the Treasurer or Steward." In addition it was ordered that "When they go to or return from their Meals and Beds, they crave God's Blessing, and return Thanks to God."[20] The London Hospital required patients who were discharged as cured to give thanks in the chapel and to attend "at the weekly Committee after their Cure and only those who attend their Cure and return Thanks will receive a Certificate thereof, which will entitle them to further Relief."[21] This feeling of obligation was something on which contemporary opinion laid great stress. When Count Kielmansegge visited the Foundlings, he noted with approval that the children "must attend Divine Service regularly, and that their masters must remind them of their lowly circumstances and inculcate humility, so that they shall not disdain the meanest work. The object of this is to mark a certain difference between the Children, although innocent and forsaken by their parents, and such as are reared by their parents in virtue and humanity, although they may have been just as poor."[22] That people of sensibility, compassion, and charity could consider such an attitude right and proper is an illumination of the social thinking of the eighteenth century.

However well intentioned, the usefulness of these hospitals was limited by the fact that all, except Guy's, excluded incurables and none were prepared to take infectious diseases. Scattered attempts, less well endowed and organized, were made to meet these needs. Some attempt was made to combat the ravages of smallpox, which before Lady Mary Montagu had introduced the practice of inoculation as a result of her travels in the East, had been considered one of the inescapable hazards of life. By the early forties there was something of a vogue for inoculation, which from a simple process had been elaborated by the medical profession into something that only the well-to-do could afford.

[20]Abstract, op. cit.

[21]Maitland, op. cit., Vol. 2, p. 1313.

[22]Kielmansegge, op. cit., p. 88.

Charitable men tried to fill this gap by providing the necessary facilities for the poor. For this purpose a Dr. Poole in the early forties managed to collect sufficient funds to enable him to have two houses for the rites of inoculation: one where people could be subjected to a preinoculation course of treatment and the other where the operation itself took place. Some provision was also made for persons who contracted the disease, who understandably became very unpopular with people living in the neighbourhood. Indeed the house at Cold Bath Fields, Clerkenwell, had to discharge its patients after dusk to avoid their being maltreated by the local inhabitants.

There were fewer experiments in the field of mental illness. Eighteenth-century London had two institutions for the treatment of insanity, St. Luke's in Moorfields and the better-known and older foundation of Bethlem, currently and popularly known as Bedlam. This had been rebuilt in 1675, and two more wings were added in 1734, the result being a handsome and dignified building. It was one of the sights of the town; that the eighteenth-century tourist should consider watching the lions in the Tower or the lunatics in Bedlam for an hour or two equally entertaining is eloquent evidence of the contemporary attitude to the deranged. Grosley, that most conscientious sightseer, described how "In one of the visits which I paid Bedlam hospital, I happened to enter a hall filled with women of different ages, who were dressed very neat and clean and drinking tea together. The president of the assembly, who was the daughter of a French refugee spoke French: she immediately took me by the hand, and presented me to the society, forced me to drink a dish of tea, and, with great humour, gave me the history of the madness of her companions: it was occasioned either by love or religious enthusiasm. . . . Before I entered the hall I enquired whether I could be there in safety; and was assured, that I could. This was the gayest and most noisy of all the coteries I had seen in London. From the bottom of the gallery joining the room where the women were seated there issued piercing and continuous cries. These were uttered by a handsome young woman, whose head was turned by one of the leaders of the new sect, called Methodist."[23] Not all

23Grosley, *op. cit.*, Vol. 1, p. 243.

the inmates were so harmless. Grosley continued his description by writing that "One entire ward of Bedlam contains a row of large cells, in each of which was a poor unfortunate wretch, chained down in bed. Whilst I was going round, one of the madmen, having disengaged himself from his chains, leapt stark naked, upon the back of the person that accompanied me, who was the keeper of the ward. The keeper seized him by the arms and carried him back to the cell, without giving him time to change his attitude."

Though the list of new foundations and of old foundations that were reorganized and enlarged bears witness to the philanthropy of the age, they were never sufficient to meet the needs of all those who required medical attention. To some extent this gap was filled by another medical charity, which provided dispensaries for the sick poor who could not afford the services of a doctor however badly they might be needed. In 1769 Dr. George Armstrong opened a dispensary in Red Lion Square for the relief of the "Infant Poor;" next year the General Dispensary in Aldersgate provided treatment for adults as well. The work of these dispensaries was in some ways similar to that of an outpatient department in a modern hospital in that they provided the poor with both advice and medicine. It was a charity that benefitted both those who gave and those who took: the doctors who worked in them came in close contact with the disease and squalor of London's population, and men began to see the connection between dirt and disease. To them the subsequent movement for public health owed a substantial debt. But perhaps no section of the community needed assistance against preventable death more than the pregnant women of London. As the promoters of the London Lying-in Hospital for Married Women declared, "It cannot but greatly move our Compassion as Men, and deserve our attention as Members of the Community, to reflect how many unhappy Women, together with their tender Infants, have for want of a timely Assistance of a Man-midwife, in difficult and uncommon Causes, and even after a safe delivery, for Want of proper Diet, Medicines and Attendance, either perished or been deprived of the Use of their Limbs, or otherwise impaired in their Constitutions, as to have become useless to their Families and burthensome to the Publick . . . in that perilous Time of their Lying-in, is too well known."[24]

The serious study of gynecology was still in its early stages, and the man midwife, as the practitioners of the new art were called, was still something of a novelty. Because the importance of sterilizing instruments was not realized, it is hardly surprising that puerperal fever was a common hazard of childbirth and that difficult confinements frequently ended in death. The need for lying-in facilities was twofold: pregnant women were in desperate need of skilled attention, and doctors who specialized in gynecology were in equal need of opportunities to improve their skill. The importance of the voluntary hospital in providing this kind of training had already been demonstrated as early as 1739. Largely owing to the initiative of Sir Richard Manningham, one of London's pioneer man midwives, the parish of St. James's Westminster had set aside one ward of its parochial infirmary for maternity cases. In 1747 the Middlesex extended its activities to include some provision for lying-in, and by the middle of the century it was coming to be felt that "to establish a proper Provision for the wives of poor Tradesmen or others labouring under the Terror, Pains and Hazards of Childbirth" was "the only kind of Charity that appears to be wanting in this populous and opulent City."[25] The next few years saw a marked increase in this kind of charity, though the first foundations were strictly for the use of the virtuous poor. Applicants for admission to the City of London Lying-in Hospital had to produce their marriage certificates before being admitted. The Westminster Lying-in Hospital took a more humane attitude. Its governors "unanimously resolved to admit such as are Deserted and in Deep Distress to save them from Dispair, and the lamentable Crimes of Suicide and Child Murder." Even here, however, the main recipients were intended to be "the Wives of distressed Householders and also common soldiers and sailors." In addition to hospital facilities, a Lying-in Charity was founded in 1759 to train midwives to attend poor women in their own homes. There was much to be said for this

[24]Maitland, *op. cit.*, Vol. 2, p. 764.

[25]*Ibid.*, Vol. 2, p. 764.

practice where deliveries were expected to be normal, for by avoiding the heavy overheads of institution nursing more women could be helped for the same financial outlay. In the absence of reliable statistics it is impossible to know how effective these charities were in saving the lives of both mothers and children, but at least they bear witness to the contemporary awareness of the need to do so. They signposted the way to the future development of gynecology, and even in their early stages they cannot have been negligible.

Many of the most characteristic of London's eighteenth-century charities originated in, or were closely connected with, the need to save infant lives and train boys and girls to be useful members of the society. The most famous was the Foundling Hospital. Later it was to become a well-known institution, but when Johnson first came to the capital it was still in its embryonic stages. The need for some such institution was great. The depth of poverty to be found in London is something that the modern Western world finds hard to visualize. Both employment and health were precarious, and the man threatened with imprisonment for debt had only two alternatives—the loss of liberty or flight. Often this meant abandoning a wife, sometimes pregnant, often burdened with a family of small children. Because the standard of sexual morality was low, single women, if young, attractive, and unprotected, were by many men considered fair game. Some of them were maidservants up from the country and unused to the temptations of the Town. Others were employed at starvation wages. Still others were professional prostitutes. For all these women a child was a disaster. Few women could earn enough to support an extra mouth, and the parish was a harsh refuge; indeed, overseers were often tempted to give the women a trifling bribe to leave the parish rather than to provide relief for them. The consequence was that many women were forced to abandon their newly born infants, depositing them secretly in streets and alleys, doubtless in the hope that either parish officials or some tenderhearted passerby would take pity on them. Many of the infants, filthy, unfed, and wrapped only in rags, died of exposure.

The credit for the establishment of a Foundling Hospital to care for deserted children belongs to Captain Coram. Neither the

A contemporary print of the Foundling Hospital, showing the pride of Londoners in this charity.

idea nor the institution was original. Such hospitals were already in existence on the Continent and had been advocated earlier in the century for England. But the task of first convincing the London public that the scheme was socially desirable and then raising the necessary funds was formidable. Many people thought that such a hospital would be an incentive to vice, arguing that if a woman could dispose of her bastards so easily, one of the major curbs on immorality would be removed. In the face of the widespread prevalence of such views money was hard to raise. Thomas Coram was a retired sea captain. Earlier in life he had been engaged in a shipbuilding venture, first at Boston and then at Taunton, Massachusetts. He had other connections with colonial America in that he had been one of the trustees for Georgia. About 1720 he came to live in Rotherhithe and, so the story goes, as he made his daily journey between his house there and the City, he was repeatedly distressed by the number of deserted infants that he saw lying helpless in the roadway. For over seventeen years he struggled with public apathy and active disapproval —lobbying, badgering influential men, and women, getting up memorials, and collecting signatures. In the end his persistence was rewarded. On October 17, 1739, a charter was granted to the governor and guardians of the Hospital for the Maintenance and Education of Exposed and Deserted Children. It is sad to have to record that after so devoted service to so good a cause Coram soon found himself in disagreement with the governing board and ceased to be a member.

As a temporary measure a house was rented in Hatton Gardens, but it was the intention of the governors to find a permanent home in a healthier area. Accordingly by the end of the year some fifty-six acres were bought from the Earl of Salisbury in the then-open country northeast of Bloomsbury Square, which then represented the farthest frontier of bricks and mortar. The west wing was finished and occupied first, then the chapel. When completed, it was an imposing building, described as "built of brick on regular lines, without much external decoration, and is comfortably arranged with two wings; an appropriate plan for a hospital. The chapel is in the centre of the building, and communicates with the wings by arched passages. Before the house is a large open courtyard. In the court are small stone pillars, with a

good many lanterns, right up to the great gateway; between them
are paths for the benefit of the children, and on each side are two
large gardens. A high wall encloses the whole."[26] When the
Foundlings was built, it had no facilities for exhibiting works of
art, which, once they had left the artist's studio, disappeared into
oblivion in some great house. But as part of a publicity campaign,
if one may use so modern a term, the hospital encouraged artists
to present pictures to be hung in the great hall as a lure to visitors. Handel, who was a governor, was a prominent benefactor:
he not only presented the organ for the chapel but once a year
gave a performance of the *Messiah* there, the proceeds of which
went to the hospital.

The early management of the charity was prudent and
efficient. To begin with, twenty children were admitted on Lady
Day 1741, all of whom were required to be under two months old
and free from any infectious disease. The desperate need of
some such institution was emphasized by the scenes of disorder
that took place on admission days; sometimes as many as a
hundred women, all clutching their infants, struggled and kicked
and pushed to be among the first twenty. As a result it was decided to institute a ballot system. The fortunate mothers who drew a
white ball were allowed to submit their offspring for inspection; if
any of these children was found to be unsuitable, the babies of
those whose mothers had drawn a red ball were similarly inspected. For the unfortunate women who drew a black ball there was
no second chance. Although the intake of babies was thus limited,
the record of the hospital, by contemporary standards, was remarkably good. Of the 1384 children admitted between 1741 and
1756, only 724 died. Today a death rate of some 52 per cent
would hardly be considered satisfactory; nothing brings home
more vividly the hazards facing the eighteenth-century infant
poor than these appalling figures. Nevertheless, their chances of
survival in a parish workhouse were so much slighter that the
governors of the Foundlings could take a legitimate pride in their
achievement. But the record soon turned worse.

This was due, at least in part, to the early success of the
scheme. Balloting was clearly an unsatisfactory method of selec-

[26]Kielmansegge, *op. cit.*, p. 86.

tion, because it gave no certainty that the children taken would be those most in need. Yet while its funds were dependent on voluntary subscriptions, numbers had to be severely limited. Accordingly the governors decided to apply to Parliament for a grant to enable it to continue and extend its work. In 1756, faced with the outbreak of hostilities with France, politicians were very conscious of the problem of manpower, and saving the lives of young children was felt to be not only humane but politically wise. The hospital therefore was given an annual subsidy of £10,000 on condition that it took all the children left with it. This put a burden on it, under the weight of which its administration and standards collapsed. Instead of the previous careful selection, a basket was hung outside the gate, and no questions were asked. On the first day no fewer than 117 babies were placed in it. In the next four years an avalanche of unwanted infants descended on the hospital, particularly when the age of admission was raised first from two months to six and then to a year, while at the same time the parliamentary grant was increased to £30,000. The Foundlings became a dumping ground for unwanted children of England. Many, instead of being brought by their mothers, were handed over to any tinker or carrier who, for a small fee, would bring the poor unfortunate babies from the provinces and put them in the basket. Many no doubt died on the journey, some were stripped of whatever clothes they wore and left naked. Many were diseased or enfeebled by hardship. Even with all the resources of modern child care infants subjected to such treatment would present a serious problem, and in the state of medical knowledge of that time it is not surprising that the death rate soared. Out of 14,934 babies admitted in less than four years, 10,389 died. Understandably, criticism mounted both from those who blamed the hospital and those who felt that their earlier forebodings had been more than justified—that the number of babies brought to the hospital was proof that this wholesale provision for unwanted children was encouraging immorality. The Foundlings was once again forced to limit its activities, and the parliamentary grant was withdrawn.

The aim of the Foundlings was not merely to save infant lives; it was to turn its children into useful members of society. From their third to their sixth year they were taught to read, to learn the catechism, "to be quick and agile, and are made fit for work, as far as their health and strength permit. Later on they are given harder tasks, and are made to dig, hoe, plough, plant, cut wood and carry loads, so as to accustom them especially for farm work and service at sea. Some help in the garden, others in the kitchen, do washing, and be useful in the household, so as to be able to go out to service as maids."[27] Jonas Hanway in *Letters on the Importance of the Rising Generation* indulged in some elaborate calculations designed to prove that, since it cost £86-5-0 to raise and train a boy at the Foundlings until the age of fifteen and since in a working life of twenty-three years he might expect to earn £412-7-5, the gain to the economy would be £326-2-5.[28] It was this mixture of philanthropy and what Hanway called "political prudence" that was responsible for another successful eighteenth-century charity, the Marine Society. This aimed at rescuing the young ragamuffins who, without a training, a home, or a family, half-naked and half-starved, scrounged and stole for a living in London's streets. No one was likely to employ them, nor had they any wish for steady work. An early death from malnutrition, from disease, or on the gallows seemed their inevitable destiny. It was this kind of human wastage that the promoters of the Marine Society hoped to eliminate to their own benefit and to that of England. In 1756 the need to enlist men for the navy was pressing, but practical difficulties stood in the way. Today we take for granted a disciplined, trained, and uniformed force; one of the first things a new recruit does is to be "kitted up." In the eighteenth century sailors were expected to provide their own equipment; because wages were always in arrears, this required a modest outlay on clothes if the young sailor were not to suffer extreme hardship from the cold. This difficulty faced both boys and adult men who volunteered for the sea service, and to meet it a small group of men formed a society to provide equipment. However, when in January 1757 the King announced a bounty of 30 shillings and an advance of two months' pay for this purpose, the Marine Society turned its attention more specifically to reha-

[27]*Ibid.*, p. 89.

[28]J. Hanway, *Letters on the Importance of the Rising Generation* (1767), Vol. 2, p. 95.

bilitating London's homeless boys for whom conditions on His Majesty's ships, though grim by modern standards, were less demoralizing than the apprenticeship that such youths had served to violence and crime in London's underworld. The clothes provided were practical and of good quality, and in addition, with that nice attention to sound moral instruction so characteristic of the century, each boy received a copy of *Christian Knowledge made Easy*. With the coming of the peace the Society had to adapt its aims to the new conditions. When naval crews were paid off, it made strenuous efforts to find masters in the merchant navy. Such men usually objected to taking on as members of the crew the riffraff of jails, workhouses, and the streets, and in consequence the Marine Society concentrated more on helping poor but still respectable boys who might otherwise been forced by distress to embark on a life of crime. Philanthropy is not the less laudable because it comes to the help of the deserving rather than the debased, and the Marine Society remained one of the most successful of London's charities.

One section of London's helpless children, though desperately in need of help and protection, failed to get it despite strenuous efforts on the part of Jonas Hanway, who throughout his career showed a wonderful sympathy with the suffering of the young. These were the little climbing boys, the drudges of the chimney sweeps. By the eighteenth century London was a coal-burning town, and the pall of smoke, on which so many foreigners commented, was a visible testimony to the multitude of its chimneys. As housing grew more elaborate, the wide straight flues of an earlier date gave way to narrower and more complicated ones. The architects of eighteenth-century London seem to have had little regard to the difficulties that their sweeping would entail. This was done by small boys, the smaller the better, who were forced up into their suffocating blackness to remove the accumulations of soot. Parents whose desperate poverty could induce them to murder newborn children or to abandon them to death by exposure had little compunction in selling for a pound or two to the chimney sweeps such of their offspring as had survived the hardships of their lives and reached the age of five, six, or seven. The trade was a poorly paid one, in which men of any sensibility were hardly likely to engaged; aside from the horror of his occupation, the climbing boy was also ill-clothed and ill-housed. Many suffered from twisted and distorted limbs or from skin diseases and running sores. Yet so familiar was the citizen of London with the pitiable little objects that kept his chimneys clean that it was not until the seventies that any movement was started to improve, insofar as any improvement was possible, their miserable existence. In 1773 Hanway became interested in their lot. Always ready to take up his pen in support of any worthy cause, he wrote a tract entitled *State of Chimney Sweepers' Young Apprentices* to stir public sympathy and succeeded in getting together a small committee to discuss further action. Though it drew up a letter addressed to the master sweepers, following it up with another in the same year, its protest made no impact on the generality of Londoners. People who viewed young lads hanged for theft were not likely to risk the discomfort of smoky chimneys for the sake of the raw knees and elbows of the climbing boys. Yet the campaign was not utterly barren of results. In 1788 a mild measure did reach the statute book. There, however, it remained a dead letter, and London's chimneys continued to be swept as they had been in Johnson's day.

Although they refused to do anything to make life more bearable for the miserable climbing boys, many Londoners were alive to the need to tackle what today would be called juvenile delinquency at its source, namely the ignorance and lack of religious training that characterized so many of the children of the poor. The movement for charity schools, where poor children could be taught to read, and in some cases to write and cast accounts, was in no sense peculiar to London, and its roots stretched into the seventeenth century. The purpose of the movement was social discipline achieved through an elementary education and a religious training. On the practical side there was the added inducement for citizens to subscribe to such charities in that an expanding commerce and industry needed ever greater numbers of workpeople capable at least of reading simple instructions or checking consignments of goods. Because of the size of her population and the wealth of her inhabitants, London's contribution to the charity school movement was substantial. Even before the end of the first decade of the century Westminster and the City could jointly boast of some fifty-four charity schools.

These schools had an important bearing on the financing of later charitable activities, insofar as their promoters relied on the subscriptions of the many rather than on the massive donations of the few for their funds. In particular they used the charity sermon, preached by some popular and eminent divine, to stire up people's benevolence. Every year one Sunday was devoted to this purpose, on which the charity school children marched in procession to St. Sepulchre's, Snow Hill, or Christ Church, Newgate.

Charity schools, it was hoped, would do something to prevent young boys from drifting into a life of crime and young girls into one of prostitution. To men like Sir John Fielding it was clear that just as homeless and destitute boys "became thieves from necessity so their sisters are whores from the same cause."[29] Could nothing be done for these women? The existence of large numbers of them was clearly a social nuisance and even danger. They spread infection, in spite of the somewhat clumsy precautions that Boswell and his like attempted to observe; they were a source of moral degradation, ready to contaminate the youth of the town. In addition, as the associates of pimps, thieves, and bullies, they swelled the mass of disorder and crime that seethed in London's underworld. Furthermore, they offended against the canons of the age in that they added nothing to the economic wealth of the country and indeed detracted from it. Yet once a woman had become a prostitute, no other way of life remained open to her. Contemporary society drew its lines with harsh and final severity. Because sexual morality was lax, the virtue of a respectable woman had to be carefully guarded; it was her vital passport to marriage and security. For the woman who had lost it, however tricked and innocent she might have been, there was no way back. The man who took up their cause was Robert Dingley, who by 1750 was trying to interest other men of philanthropic outlook in the possibility of reclaiming those prostitutes who had not yet become hardened to a life of vice. He received some support—Dr. Johnson, for instance, contributed a letter in *The Rambler* in March 1751, stressing the need for charity for these pitiable outcasts from society—but campaigning for such a cause

[29]Sir John Fielding, *Introduction to a Plan for Preserving Deserted Girls* (*1758*), p. 44.

was uphill work. Even Hanway—Charles Dingley had been a partner of his in the Russian trade—when asked to write in support of a plan for a house for repentent prostitutes, had declined, saying that for a man of under forty to do so would be to call forth the comments of the unkind. It was not until 1758 that he finally associated himself with Charles and Robert Dingley in the project. In spite of protests that such an institution would weaken the barriers against unchastity if women no longer felt that they were taking an irrevocable step, enough subscriptions were collected to open a hospital in Prescott Street, Goodman's Fields, for this purpose.

From the beginning the Magdalen House never lacked applicants. Its management was strict but imaginative. It was to be a place of refuge to which unfortunate or weak-willed girls would come voluntarily, not a place of punishment. Though meals were frugal and discipline firm, there was no attempt to humiliate the inmates. Individuality disappeared in anonymity. Each woman wore the dress of the House, a neat, grey dress covered by a white stomacher, apron, and kerchief, long black mittens, and, when attending chapel, a shallow, broad-brimmed straw hat. Since the purpose of the charity was to enable the women to return to respectable ways of life, considerable pains were taken to teach them a trade, most of those chosen involving little more expenditure than a supply of materials and needles. Weaving, silk winding, and knitting were also practiced. The day started and ended with prayers in the chapel. Into this regular life no recriminations and no echoes of the past were allowed to enter. Each woman was known only by her Christian name; the staff were forbidden to reveal to any one the surname to prevent any possibility of an inmate's identity being discovered; visitors from the outside world were allowed only with the consent of both the governor or committee member and of the former prostitute they wanted to see. No one, once having entered, was to be subjected to the temptation to return to her former ways. The regime appears to have been remarkably successful. Hanway reported that out of 291 women received, twenty-seven had been reconciled to their parents, eighty-two were placed out as servants in respectable families, four had died, ten were distempered in mind and had to be sent to St. Luke's, some seemed prepared to amend their ways but left because they could not endure the confinement that residence in the Magdalen entailed. Only forty apparently proved beyond the power of the Society to reform.

This creditable record was a tribute to the sober and realistic way in which the affairs of the Magdalen had been handled. Most of those taken in were young, many in their teens. As a matter of policy women over thirty were not eligible, being thought by then past any help that the hospital could give them. Anyone who had contracted a venereal disease was also excluded. New entrants were for a time segregated from the rest of the women, until the officers were sure that their desire to repent would not evaporate after a few days of disciplined living, thus unsettling the rest. The permanent residents were organized in groups or wards of twelve, and new entrants were assigned to the ward whose members came most nearly from the same social background. Status was important in the eighteenth century, and from a practical point of view a girl brought up in decent surroundings who had been seduced and betrayed would have been pulled down, not reclaimed, by having to endure the constant company of a product of London's slums. Even a degree of personal privacy was planned for, because each woman had not only a bed to herself but a curtain that she could pull around it in order that at night she might pray undisturbed. Because the Magdalen depended on voluntary subscriptions and donations, constant efforts had to be made to excite and sustain public interest and support. Unlike the Foundling Hospital, it could not be thrown open to the public, for to allow people to gaze on the penitent whore, as they were permitted to gape at the lunatics at Bedlam, was directly opposed to the policy of the governors. Though Hanway devoted time amidst all his charitable enterprises to writing pamphlets in support of the Magdalen, something more permanent and personal was needed. Very cleverly they managed to make the Sunday services in their chapel a fashionable occasion. Part of the attraction was the first chaplain, William Dodd, a young cleric of only twenty-one with a considerable gift of eloquence. Hanway called him "the ingenious Mr. Dodd" and quoted approvingly from his sermons, which were intended to open his congregations' pockets by an appeal to their emotions, as when he asked them to imagine the dying prostitute's last words of reproach to her seducer. "Oh look upon me and see what cause thou hast to exult. Behold these wretched tatters, which scarce cover my diseased limbs, where are the remains of their former lovliness? See my tongue cleaves to the roof of my mouth with hunger, and with anguish. But worst of all my soul . . . my soul in horrible danger of eternal death."[30] In his first sermon parents were exhorted to consider their own daughters "like lovely flowers, blooming round you." They are warned that "very often that beauty hath proved a fatal snare" and that if Londoners really mean to "preserve our children, our servants, our dependants of every kind in innocence and virtue" from the pollution of the streets, they should support the Magdalen charity with "hand and heart."[31] Overdramatic as his sermons undoubtedly were, with their mixture of pathos and self-interest, they appealed to the popular taste. The hospital prospered; even Queen Charlotte became a patron.

For the young preacher the results were disastrous. He became one of George III's chaplains in 1763 and, overwhelmed by success and popularity, took a house in Southampton Row in the fashionable Bloomsbury area, where he set up as a fashionable tutor. His next extravagance was a country house at Ealing and a grand coach. By 1774 William Dodd was heavily in debt and in desperation forged a bond in the name of Lord Chesterfield, possibly hoping that because Chesterfield formerly had been one of his pupils, he would escape prosecution. This hope proved vain: he was tried, convicted, and sentenced to death. At the end he lost faith in his own eloquence and appealed to Dr. Johnson to help him to frame a petition for mercy. Though the Doctor was more an acquaintance than a friend, he did his best, concocting both a *Speech to the Recorder of London* and a personal appeal addressed to the king. His efforts were unavailing, and Dodd was duly hanged, in spite of the recommendation of the jury to mercy and petitions from various quarters. It was about Dodd that Johnson made his famous remark: "Depend upon it, Sir, when a man knows he is to be hanged in a fortnight, it concentrates his mind wonderfully."[32] The sanctity of credit

[30]J. Hanway, *Reflections, Essays and Meditations* (1761), Letter VIII.

[31]*Ibid.*, Letter IX.

[32]Boswell, *Life of Samuel Johnson*, Vol. 3, p. 167.

and commercial paper ranked high with London's citizens. Dodd's services to charity were not allowed to tip the scales in his favour as against his disservice to commerce; credit was thought to be of more importance than charity.

Nevertheless, it is clear that Londoners were proud of their charitable achievements. They boasted of "the truly Christian Spirit of Benevolence, which at this time so generally prevails amongst us, to the great Honour of this Age and Nation."[33] In the brief space of a single chapter it is not possible to do more than select a few of the many examples of eighteenth-century philanthropy in London, but these have been chosen, as far as possible, because they are representative of the kind of charitable enterprise on which Londoners thought it right and proper to spend time and effort, as well as money. One contemporary summarized them as "many noble Institutions for training up Orphans, and other indigent Children, in the Knowledge and Practice of their Duty to God and their Country, for relieving the Industrious Poor under the accidental Calamities of Sickness, Lameness or Lunacy; and for restraining, and, if possible, reclaiming the Dissolute and Debauched."[34] Such aims illustrate vividly the nature of eighteenth-century philanthropy. Its undisguised materialistic approach, undisguised because contemporaries felt no need to hide it, today appears harsh, unsympathetic, and almost unchristian. The poor were to be cared for because their labour was the basis of the wealth of the community. Christianity was not so much to be directed toward the saving of souls as toward securing social discipline. Here the contrast between the generally accepted view and that of John Wesley is striking. To the Methodists the redemption of the individual was the first and overriding object; helping the poor with medicine and advice and finding employment for the workless and clothing for the naked came next. For them philanthropy was only the handmaiden of religion. But for the majority of solid and sober folk the emphasis was rightly placed on the value of morality to society as a whole. As we have seen, Fielding would have closed most public places of amusement to "the Lower Order of People" on the ground that they

[33]Maitland, *op. cit.*, Vol. 2, p. 764.

[34]*Ibid.*, Vol. 2, p. 764.

were a constant temptation to those who should have been more profitably employed to waste both time and money. At the same time he was content that "Persons of Fashion and Fortune" should make pleasure their main "Business," because he was not immediately concerned with private morality in this sense. His problem was to find some cure for the crime and debauchery of London, which threatened alike the safety of its streets, the sanctity of property, and even life itself. Yet before twentieth-century critics condemn much of the philanthropy of Dr. Johnson's London as a mixture of insulting condescension and downright hypocrisy, it must be seen against its background. The poor of London, for whom these charities were intended, were only too often ignorant, drunken, and brutal. The gulf between the very poor and the substantial citizen was so wide that they might almost have been members of another race and another civilization. If help and charity were needed, so were discipline and the inculcation of a few simple standards of responsible behaviour. The benevolence of eighteenth-century London was not the less genuine because it expressed itself in language that strikes a discordant note to modern ears.

Tailpiece

Such was the London that Samuel Johnson knew and loved. It is a platitude that New York or San Francisco is no more the United States than London is England, yet in so far as a great city can mirror a country, eighteenth-century London reflected Georgian England. Both economic and social factors made London not only the capital but also a microcosm of England. Because of the Parliament, toward which the nobility and gentry gravitated, London was a great concourse of the "Agricultural Interest," which represented not only much of the wealth of the country but a way of life. It could speak for the broad acres, the arable and the pasture, that stretched all around and embraced the capital. Moreover, the landed classes were not the only ones that came to London. The drover brought his cattle, the countryman sought his fortune there and, though now a Londoner, kept his country loyalties. At every opportunity the city was deserted for the countryside. Those who could afford it had their country villas, the equivalent of the modern weekend cottage, or took lodgings during the summer in the ring of pleasant villages that surrounded the town. Poorer Londoners sported on Greenwich Hill or flocked to rural tea gardens on Sundays, happy once more to breathe the country air, to indulge in country sports, and for a few hours to get away from the smoke and filth of the town. Even the town still retained some rural aspects. Milkmaids drove their cows through the streets and celebrated May Day with garlands of flowers and songs. There was, as we have seen, a brisk demand for the wares of the street flower sellers. London was full of stables and cowsheds, and pigs were still kept in backyards. Metropolitan London was not yet divorced from rural England.

Nor was it divorced from the sea. The English like to think of themselves as a seafaring people; the sea was the lifeline of their trade, and London was the greatest of their ports. It was no accident that the leading institution for marine insurance in the world, Lloyd's of London, should have had its beginnings in the eighteenth-century City. Along the Thames ships were not only loaded and unloaded; they were built and fitted out and manned. In all the riverside parishes sailors abounded, adding their own distinctive flavour to the life of the town. Not all of them sailed to distant ports. Fishermen brought their catches to Billingsgate; you could buy as fresh fish in London as anywhere on the coast. Nor did provincials and Londoners in other ways react very differently to contemporary situations. When times were hard and bread dear, the London coal heavers fell back on mob violence and on strike action. So did the miners of northeast England, filling the solid citizens of Newcastle with panic and dismay. If a London craftsman read his newspaper and discussed politics with his cronies in a coffeehouse, in country towns the local newssheet, or the latest intelligence from London, was equally eagerly devoured, particularly in time of war. If the countryman delighted in the thrills of the cockpit, in the metropolis the spectacle was equally popular and so were bruising matches. Not even literature and the drama were the preserves of the capital. County towns had their assemblies, sometimes their theatre, their circulating libraries, and even their philosophical societies and coteries of learned men.

Nevertheless, the argument cannot be pushed too far. Even though the nobility and gentry straddled both worlds, creating an illusion of unity, a Londoner in the heart of rural England would have been as bewildered and dismayed as a countryman when he first experienced the delights and terrors of the city. Although it drew on the country for so much both economically and to replenish its population, which was continually eroded by the unhealthiness of urban life, London, by its very size, was a place apart. Nowhere else could be found the concentrations that marked its life—concentrations of wealth, political power, culture and poverty, crime and violence. Did its uniqueness give it a character of its own? Such a question is almost impossible to answer. London's people were proud and turbulent. Grosley thought the porters, labourers, sailors, and chairmen "as insolent a rabble as can be met with in countries without law or police," prepared to jeer at foreigners and the well-dressed English alike. Yet in other passages he describes Londoners, though haughty and ungovernable, as "good natured and humane," citing as evidence the way in which during public festivities children and persons of low stature were pushed to the front so that their view should not be obscured. In spite of the deference normally paid to persons of rank, little was shown when feeling ran high. An earl's windows were as likely to be broken as anybody else's when the mob got out of hand. Though comparatively few Londoners were entitled to vote in elections, they had no inhibitions in expressing their political prejudices when these were aroused by the actions of their superiors at Westminster. Lord North's coach was mobbed on occasion, Sir Robert Walpole was hustled in the Parliament yard itself. Their refusal to be excluded by social position from the amusements of their betters has already been commented upon. Vauxhall, Ranelagh, the Cockpit, the theatre, were open to all who could pay their footing, and their behaviour in these places was that of a people conscious of their rights. Occupants of the second gallery at the theatre banged with their cudgels and threw their orange peel, and no one dared to say them nay. Londoners considered themselves as good as anybody and better than any foreigner. "No Popery! No wooden shoes!" was typical of their sentiments; so was "Wilkes and Liberty." Yet in spite of its pride and its violence, London was a curiously tolerant, curiously universal place. Boswell noted that one of its characteristics was that "nobody was heeded by his neighbour." A man could lead his own life there and go his own way. The man of letters, the rake, the financier, the artist, the great lord or lady, the woman of the town, the small shopkeeper and the craftsman, were part of its common life, sharing its festivities, endangered by its riots, involved in its politics, taking the air in St. James's Park. Here was no Paris as opposed to Versailles. Londoners were proud of London, and of them all none loved it more than Samuel Johnson.

Index